ZAGATSURVEY®

1999/2000

SEATTLE PORTLAND RESTAURANTS

Edited and coordinated by
Nancy Leson, Providence Cicero
and Carrie Floyd

Published and distributed by
ZAGAT SURVEY, LLC
4 Columbus Circle
New York, New York 10019
Tel: 212 977 6000
E-mail: zagat@zagatsurvey.com
Web site: www.zagat.com

Acknowledgments

In Seattle, thanks to Rosemary Cicero, who opened a lot of mail and helped us get organized; Caroline Cummins, Emma Waverman, Stephanie Wolfe and Deb LaMontagne, whose cheerfulness never wavered in the face of much fact checking; Kristy Hoffman, Janet Swett and Ginny Lee, who tend our children with such loving care; David Bronleewe and Mac McCarthy, our patient husbands, for knowing when to listen and when to give advice, and for their calm in the throes of our deadline fevers; and special thanks to our children, Adriana Providenza Bronleewe and Nathaniel Wilgen McCarthy, who remind us every day that life is precious and ought to be enjoyed.

In Portland, thanks go to Joan Menefee and Carrie Birrer for their part in disseminating and collecting *Surveys,* and Steve Lapp, the ultimate support staff.

© 1999 Zagat Survey, LLC
ISBN 1-57006-154-8

Contents

Starters	5	
What's New	6	
Key to Ratings and Symbols	8	
	SE	**PO**
Map	10	132
Most Popular Restaurants	11	133
Top Ratings		
• Food and by Cuisine	12	134
• Decor, Outdoor, Romantic, Rooms, Views	15	137
• Service	16	138
Best Buys	17	139
ALPHABETICAL DIRECTORY, RATINGS AND REVIEWS	19	141
INDEXES		
• Cuisines	96	178
• Locations	103	182
• Brunch	109	185
• Buffet Served	109	185
• Business Dining	109	185
• Caters	110	185
• Cigar Friendly	110	186
• Dancing/Entertainment	111	186
• Delivers/Takeout	111	186
• Dessert/Ice Cream	112	187
• Dining Alone	112	187
• Fireplaces	113	188
• Game in Season	113	188
• Historic Interest	114	188
• Hotel Dining	114	188
• "In" Places	114	188
• Late Late – After 12:30	115	188
• Meet for a Drink	115	189
• Noteworthy Newcomers/Closings	115	189
• Offbeat	116	189
• Outdoor Dining	116	189
• Oyster Bars	117	–
• Parking/Valet	117	190
• Parties & Private Rooms	120	191
• People-Watching & Power Scenes	121	192
• Pubs/Bars/Microbreweries	121	193
• Quiet Conversation	121	193
• Romantic Spots	122	193
• Saturday/Sunday Dining	123	193

- Senior Appeal 124 195
- Singles Scenes 125 195
- Sleepers/Teflons 125 195
- Teenagers & Other Youthful Spirits 125 196
- Theme Restaurants.............. 126 196
- Visitors on Expense Accounts 126 196
- Wheelchair Access 126 196
- Wine/Beer Only 126 196
- Winning Wine Lists.............. 128 197
- Worth a Trip.................... 128 197
- Young Children 128 197

Notes............................ 199
Wine Chart...................... 204

Starters

Here are the results of our *1999 Seattle/Portland Restaurant Survey* covering some 822 restaurants in the Seattle and Portland area.

By regularly surveying large numbers of local restaurant-goers, we think we have achieved a uniquely current and reliable guide. We hope you agree. More than 1,430 people participated. Since the participants dined out an average of 3.5 times per week, this *Survey* is based on about 260,260 meals per year.

We want to thank each of our participants. They are a widely diverse group in all respects but one – they are food lovers all. This book is really "theirs."

Of the surveyors, 58% are women, 42% are men; the breakdown by age is 15% in their 20s, 26% in their 30s, 28% in their 40s, 23% in their 50s and 8% in their 60s or above.

To help guide our readers to Seattle and Portland's best meals and best buys, we have prepared a number of lists. See, for example, Seattle's Most Popular Restaurants (page 11), Top Ratings (pages 12–16) and Best Buys (pages 17–18) and Portland's Most Popular Restaurants (page 133), Top Ratings (pages 134–138) and Best Buys (pages 139–140). On the assumption that most people want a quick fix on the places at which they are considering eating, we have tried to be concise and to provide handy indexes.

We are particularly grateful to our editors and coordinators: Nancy Leson, the *Seattle Times* restaurant critic; Providence Cicero, a food columnist for *Seattle Magazine* and a restaurant critic for the *Seattle Post-Intelligencer*; Carrie Floyd, a food writer and associate editor for *Portland Best Places*.

We invite you to be a reviewer in our next *Survey*. To do so, simply send a stamped, self-addressed, business-size envelope to ZAGAT SURVEY, 4 Columbus Circle, New York, NY 10019, so that we will be able to contact you. Each participant will receive a free copy of the next *Seattle/Portland Restaurant Survey* when it is published.

Your comments, suggestions and even criticisms of this *Survey* are also solicited. There is always room for improvement with your help.

New York, New York Nina and Tim Zagat
May 12, 1999

What's New

Don't put down that fork! Just take a deep breath, loosen your belt and ask "Where shall we eat next?" The restaurant boom that began a few years ago was only a ground swell with no end in sight. October '98 saw the dazzling debut of Downtown's Pacific Place, a four-story, atrium-domed, upscale retail extravaganza housing five restaurants: Cafe Starbucks, Desert Fire, Gordon Biersch and Il Fornaio – with Jeremiah Towers' Stars Bar & Dining as its splashy showpiece.

Beautiful Brasa kicked off '99 in equally high style. Developed by star chef Tamara Murphy and general manager Bryan Hill (ex Campagne), its robust Mediterranean menu and sophisticated setting underscore the new energy apparent in Downtown Seattle. Other Downtowners new to this edition of the *Survey* include icon Grill (where American classics like meat loaf and mac 'n' cheese go upscale), as well as El Niño and Yakima Grill, both specializing in contemporary Latin American fare.

This summer, New York–based impresario Drew Nieporent is set to open his first Northwest venture, Earth & Ocean, in the new W Hotel. And Rick Yoder's wildly popular Wild Ginger is expected to move to new, expanded quarters at Third and Union (near the Seattle Symphony's new home, Benaroya Hall) late next fall.

Belltown, needless to say, is not laying dormant. Chef Kerry Sear left his exec chef's post at the Four Seasons Olympic Hotel to concentrate on Pacific Northwest cuisine at the as-yet-unopened Cascadia (ETA summer '99).

Elsewhere around town, affordable French food at Figaro Bistro on Lower Queen Anne has fans sighing *mais oui*, while nearby, Duke's goes Italiano at La Palina. On Capitol Hill, the soigné Capitol Club holds sway, tiny, romantic Bistro Lautrec holds its own, and lovely Cassis adds *joie* to local Francophiles' *vivre*. Circa brings internationally inspired pub grub to West Seattle, while the menu at Bis on Main – a stylish cafe in Bellevue's Old Town – pays homage to Italy, France and New Orleans.

Increased competition has led to several closures, retoolings and reincarnations. Peter Cipra closed his beloved Labuznik after more than 20 years, while Laura Dewell, chef-owner of the late, great Pirosmani, is now at Credenzia's Oven. In Bothell, Relais has morphed into the Hillside Bar & Grill, where chef-owner Eric Eisenberg's menu now stretches from burgers to bouillabaisse. Asia Grille's former location in University Village will soon be the site for a new venture by Jeremy Hardy and Peter Levy, the dynamic duo behind Jitterbug Café, 5 Spot and Coastal Kitchen.

Meanwhile, Portland's Pearl District, the city's SoHo-esque enclave of art galleries and institutions, continues its rapid growth, adding restaurants and cafes at a pace that rivals that of the rising condominiums. Former warehouses are now home to some of the city's more colorful places to dine – Cafe Azul, Fratelli and Le Bouchon. The Downtown scene, though more sedate at night compared to the Northwest District and the Pearl, still cooks after dark with high-caliber hotel dining rooms like the Portland Steak and Chophouse and Typhoon! on Broadway.

A few new neighborhood cafes – most notably, Bernie's Southern Bistro and John Street Cafe – seem like they've always been here. And, in addition to neophyte NW bistros like Laslow's, Lucy's Table and Southpark Seafood Grill, Portland will always make room for a good value (La Buca, Noho's Hawaiian Cafe, Pasta Veloce), as well as for those who veer off the beaten path (The Tao of Tea).

Luckily, every restaurant that has opened does not mean another has closed, though we've had to say good-bye to longtime favorite Ron Paul Charcuterie. Shakers, one of the original Pearl District cafes and a breakfast institution, recently changed its ownership and name to Cindy's Helvetia Cafe.

Given all this action, covering the local restaurant scene is a daunting task, but always an exciting one. To add incentive, tabs remain reasonable by West Coast standards, with the average cost of a meal $21.65 in Seattle and $19.82 in Portland, as compared to $28.49 in SF and $24.32 in LA.

Our thanks go to you for sharing your knowledge, along with the candor and wit that makes this *Survey* so much fun to edit. For that, we raise a glass – and a fork – in a toast to your collective contributions.

Seattle, WA	Nancy Leson
Portland, OR	Providence Cicero
May 12, 1999	Carrie Floyd

Key to Ratings/Symbols

This sample entry identifies the various types of information contained in your Zagat Survey.

(1) Restaurant Name, Address & Phone Number

(2) Hours & Credit Cards

(3) ZAGAT Ratings

F	D	S	C
23	5	9	$19

Tim & Nina's ◐ S ⌀

4 Columbus Circle (8th Ave.), 212-977-6000

▨ "What a dump!" – open 7 days a week, 24 hours a day, this successful "deep dive" started the "deli-tapas craze" (i.e., tidbits of pastrami, corned beef, etc. on cracker-size pieces of stale rye); though the place looks like a "none-too-clean garage" and T & N "never heard of credit cards or reservations", "dirt cheap" prices for "great eats" draw demented crowds.

(4) Surveyors' Commentary

The names of restaurants with the highest overall ratings, greatest popularity and importance are printed in **CAPITAL LETTERS**. Address and phone numbers are printed in *italics*.

(2) Hours & Credit Cards

After each restaurant name you will find the following courtesy information:

◐ .... *serving after 11 PM*

S .... *open on Sunday*

⌀ .... *no credit cards accepted*

(3) ZAGAT Ratings

Food, **Decor** and **Service** are each rated on a scale of **0** to **30**:

F	D	S	C

F	....	*Food*
D	....	*Decor*
S	....	*Service*
C	....	*Cost*

23	5	9	$19

0 - 9	....	*poor to fair*
10 - 15	....	*fair to good*
16 - 19	....	*good to very good*
20 - 25	....	*very good to excellent*
26 - 30	....	*extraordinary to perfection*

▽ 23	5	9	$19

▽ .... ***Low number of votes/less reliable***

The **Cost (C)** column reflects the estimated price of a dinner with one drink and tip. Lunch usually costs 25% less.

A restaurant listed without ratings is either an important **newcomer** or a popular **write-in**. The estimated cost, with one drink and tip, is indicated by the following symbols.

-	-	-	VE

I	....	*$15 and below*
M	....	*$16 to $30*
E	....	*$31 to $50*
VE	....	*$51 or more*

(4) Surveyors' Commentary

Surveyors' comments are summarized, with literal comments shown in quotation marks. The following symbols indicate whether responses were mixed or uniform.

◩ .... *mixed*
◼ .... *uniform*

Seattle's Most Popular

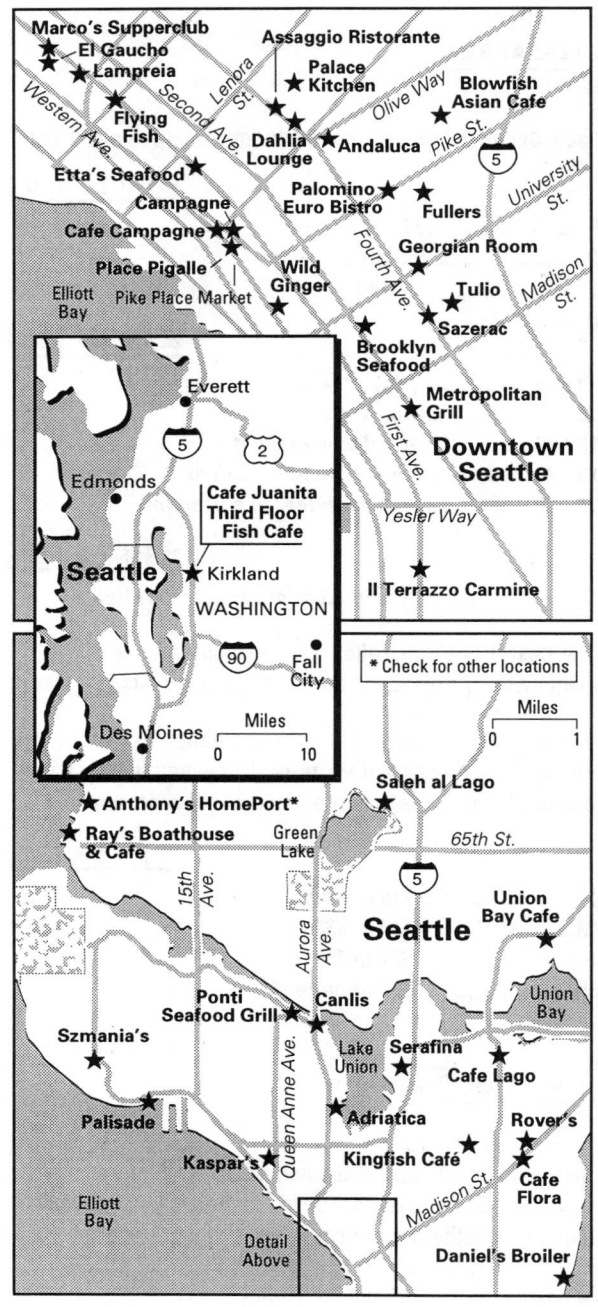

Seattle's Most Popular Restaurants

Each of our reviewers has been asked to name his or her five favorite restaurants. The 40 spots most frequently named, in order of their popularity, are:

1. Wild Ginger
2. Dahlia Lounge
3. Campagne
4. Rover's
5. Canlis
6. Flying Fish
7. Etta's Seafood
8. Saleh al Lago
9. Cafe Campagne
10. Palisade
11. Kaspar's
12. Szmania's
13. Il Terrazzo Carmine
14. Metropolitan Grill
15. Fullers
16. Ponti Seafood Grill
17. Andaluca
18. Palace Kitchen
19. Lampreia
20. Cafe Flora
21. Ray's Boathouse & Cafe
22. Georgian Room
23. Adriatica*
24. Blowfish Asian Cafe
25. Kingfish Café
26. El Gaucho
27. Marco's Supperclub
28. Anthony's HomePort
29. Cafe Juanita
30. Assaggio Ristorante
31. Place Pigalle
32. Palomino Euro Bistro
33. Daniel's Broiler*
34. Brooklyn Seafood
35. Union Bay Cafe
36. Tulio*
37. Third Floor Fish Cafe*
38. Serafina
39. Sazerac
40. Cafe Lago

It's obvious that many of the restaurants on the above list are among the most expensive, but Seattle diners also love a bargain. Were popularity calibrated to price, we suspect that a number of other restaurants would join the above ranks. Thus, we have listed over 100 Best Buys on pages 17–18.

---

* Tied with the restaurant listed directly above it.

Top Ratings*

Top 40 Food Ranking

- **28** Rover's
  Campagne
- **27** Tosoni
  Fullers
  Shiro's Sushi
  Wild Ginger
- **26** Saleh al Lago
  Cafe Campagne
  Nishino
  Dahlia Lounge
  Kingfish Café
  Inn at Langley
  Il Terrazzo Carmine
  Szmania's
  Le Gourmand
  Cafe Juanita
  Kaspar's
  Shoalwater
  Toyoda Sushi**
- **25** Cafe Lago

Canlis
Georgian Room
Union Bay Cafe
Etta's Seafood
Reiner's
Lampreia
Chez Shea
Paseo Caribbean
La Panzanella
Hunt Club
Flying Fish
Metropolitan Grill
Shanghai Garden
- **24** Third Floor Fish Cafe
  Adriatica
  Ponti Seafood Grill
  Pecos Pit BBQ
  Macrina Bakery
  Ruth's Chris
  Place Pigalle

Top Spots by Cuisine

American (Northwest)
- **27** Fullers
- **26** Dahlia Lounge
  Inn at Langley
  Szmania's
  Kaspar's

American (Traditional)
- **24** Ruth's Chris
  Daniel's Broiler
  Ark, The
- **23** Union Square Grill
  El Gaucho

Bar-B-Q/Chile
- **24** Pecos Pit BBQ
- **19** World Class Chili
  Texas Smokehouse
- **18** Armadillo Barbecue
- **16** Mac's Smokehouse

Bistro/Cafe
- **26** Cafe Campagne
- **25** Union Bay Cafe
- **24** Place Pigalle
  Shea's Lounge
- **23** Brie & Bordeaux

Breakfast†
- **26** Cafe Campagne
- **24** Macrina Bakery
- **23** Cafe Nola
- **21** Maltby Cafe
  Hi-Spot Cafe

Brunch
- **26** Kingfish Café
- **25** Etta's Seafood
- **24** Ponti Seafood Grill
- **23** Brie & Bordeaux
  Salish Lodge

---

* Excluding restaurants with low voting.
** Tied with the restaurant listed directly above it.
† Other than hotels.

Top Food

Burger/Sandwich
- **22** Red Mill Burgers
- **21** Shultzy's
- **20** Botticelli Caffè
  Three Girls Bakery
- **19** Bakeman's

Cajun/Creole/Southern
- **26** Kingfish Café
- **22** Alligator Soul
  Ezell's Fried Chicken
- **20** Sazerac
  Burk's Cafe

Chinese
- **25** Shanghai Garden
- **22** Noble Court
- **21** Hong's Garden
  Snappy Dragon
- **20** Sea Garden

Coffeehouses
- **20** Caffe Ladro
- **19** Honey Bear Bakery
  Still Life in Fremont
- **18** Brusseau's
  B&O Espresso

Dessert
- **20** Famous Pacific
  Café Dilettante
- **19** Honey Bear Bakery
  Still Life in Fremont
- **18** B&O Espresso

French
- **28** Rover's
  Campagne
- **26** Cafe Campagne
  Le Gourmand
- **23** Brie & Bordeaux

Greek
- **18** Yanni's
- **17** Bacchus Rest.
- **16** Costas Opa
- **15** Byzantion
  Costas Greek Rest.

Hotel Dining
- **27** Fullers
  Sheraton Hotel
- **26** Inn at Langley
  Inn at Langley
  Shoalwater
  Shelburne Inn
- **25** Georgian Room
  Four Seasons
  Hunt Club
  Sorrento Hotel

Indian
- **24** Shamiana
- **20** Chutneys
- **19** Raga
  Banjara
  Chutneys Grille/Hill

Italian
- **26** Saleh al Lago
  Il Terrazzo Carmine
  Cafe Juanita
- **25** Cafe Lago
- **24** Tulio

Japanese
- **27** Shiro's Sushi
- **26** Nishino
  Toyoda Sushi
- **24** Nikko
- **23** Sanmi Sushi

Latino/Southwestern
- **22** Cactus
- **21** Bandoleone
- **20** Santa Fe Cafe
  Yakima Grill
- **19** Dulces Latin Bistro

Mediterranean
- **24** Third Floor Fish Cafe
  Adriatica
  Shea's Lounge
- **23** El Greco
  Andaluca

Top Food

Mexican/Tex-Mex
- **22** Cactus
- **21** El Camino
  Burrito Loco
  Galerias
- **19** Rosita's Mexican Grill

Middle Eastern
- **22** Mediterranean Kitchen
  Phoenecia at Alki
- **21** Kabul Afghan
- **20** Zaina Food*
- **19** Capitol Club

Newcomers/Rated
- **26** Kingfish Café
- **23** Brie & Bordeaux
  Shallots Asian Bistro
  Chinoise Café
- **22** Cassis

Newcomers/Unrated
- Brasa
- Figaro Bistro
- Il Fornaio
- Matt's in the Market
- Stars Bar & Dining

Offbeat
- **26** Kingfish Café
- **22** Alligator Soul
- **21** Swingside Cafe
- **20** Luau Polynesian
- **19** Pontevecchio

Pan-Asian
- **27** Wild Ginger
- **23** Shallots Asian Bistro
  Chinoise Café
- **22** Roy's Seattle
- **21** Noodle Ranch

People-Watching
- **27** Wild Ginger
- **25** Flying Fish
- **23** Palace Kitchen
  El Gaucho
- **19** Axis

Pubs/Taverns
- **20** Hilltop Ale House
- **19** Maple Leaf Grill
  Bick's Broadview Grill
  Two Bells Tavern
- **18** Belltown Pub & Cafe

Seafood (Contemporary)
- **25** Etta's Seafood
  Flying Fish
- **24** Third Floor Fish Cafe
  Ponti Seafood Grill
- **22** Palisade

Seafood (Traditional)
- **24** Ark, The
- **23** Oyster Creek Inn
  Shuckers
- **22** Ray's Boathouse
- **21** Elliott's Oyster Hse.

Steakhouses
- **25** Canlis
  Metropolitan Grill
- **24** Ruth's Chris
  Daniel's Broiler
- **23** Union Square Grill

Thai/Vietnamese
- **23** Bai Tong
- **21** Saigon Bistro
- **20** Bahn Thai
  Noodle Studio
  Fremont Noodle Hse.

Vegetarian
- **22** Carmelita
  Cafe Flora
  Plenty Cafe
- **21** Green Cat Cafe
- **18** Gravity Bar

Wild Cards
- **27** Tosoni (Continental)
- **25** Paseo (Caribbean)
- **22** Pasta & Co. (Takeout)
- **19** Bungalow Wine (Eclectic)
- **17** Afrikando (Senegalese)

Worth a Trip
- **26** Inn at Langley
  Langley
  Shoalwater
  Seaview
- **24** Ark, The
  Nahcotta
- **23** Salish Lodge
  Snoqualmie
  Oyster Creek Inn
  Bow

---

* Low votes.

Top 40 Decor Ranking

- **28** Georgian Room
- **27** Canlis
- **26** Salish Lodge
- **25** Palisade
  - Inn at Langley
  - Andaluca
  - Campagne
  - Fullers
- **24** Hunt Club
  - Il Terrazzo Carmine
  - Ponti Seafood Grill
  - Rover's
  - Dahlia Lounge
  - Reiner's
  - Chez Shea
  - Shea's Lounge
  - Nikko
  - Spirit of Washington
  - Painted Table
- **23** Queen Mary
  - Yarrow Bay Grill
  - Ray's Boathouse & Cafe
  - Space Needle Rest.
  - Sazerac
  - Oyster Bar/Chuckanut
  - Wild Ginger
  - Kingfish Café
  - Capitol Club
  - Pescatore
  - Szmania's
  - Place Pigalle
  - El Gaucho
  - Third Floor Fish Cafe
  - Cliff House
  - Il Bistro
  - Anthony's Pier 66
  - Cafe Campagne
  - Daniel's Broiler
  - Shoalwater
- **22** Kaspar's

Outdoor

- Anthony's Pier 66
- Campagne
- Christina's
- LeoMelina Rist.
- Pescatore
- Pink Door
- Ponti
- Ray's Boathouse & Cafe
- Rover's
- Waters

Romantic

- Andaluca
- Brasa
- Campagne
- Canlis
- Chez Shea
- El Gaucho
- Il Bistro
- Lampreia
- Lush Life
- Mona's Bistro
- Rover's
- Stars Bar & Dining

Rooms

- Andaluca
- Brasa
- Canlis
- Dahlia Lounge
- El Gaucho
- Flying Fish
- Fullers
- Georgian Room
- Il Fornaio
- Kaspar's
- Painted Table
- Palisade
- Sazerac
- Szmania's

Views

- Anthony's Pier 66
- Anthony's/Point Defiance
- Canlis
- Cutters
- Elliott's Oyster House
- McCormick & Schmick's Harbor.
- Ray's Boathouse & Cafe
- Salty's
- Space Needle Rest.
- Third Floor Fish Cafe
- Waters
- Yarrow Bay Grill

Top 40 Service Ranking

- **27** Canlis
- Rover's
- **26** Georgian Room
- **25** Fullers
- Campagne
- Inn at Langley
- Szmania's
- Tosoni
- Saleh al Lago
- Reiner's
- **24** Le Gourmand
- Il Terrazzo Carmine
- Hunt Club
- Kaspar's
- El Gaucho
- Chez Shea
- Metropolitan Grill
- **23** Dahlia Lounge
- Shoalwater
- Relais
- Daniel's Broiler
- Cafe Juanita
- Adriatica
- Shea's Lounge
- Shuckers
- Cafe Campagne
- **22** Painted Table
- Palisade
- Lampreia
- Shallots Asian Bistro
- Oyster Bar/Chuckanut
- Union Square Grill
- Etta's Seafood
- Salish Lodge
- Stanley & Seafort's
- Andaluca
- Bistro Provencal
- Place Pigalle
- Wild Ginger
- Phoenecia at Alki

Best Buys

80 Top Bangs For The Buck

This list reflects the best dining values in our *Survey*. It is produced by dividing the cost of a meal into the combined ratings for food, decor and service.

1. Dick's Drive-In
2. Shultzy's
3. Caffe Ladro
4. La Panzanella
5. Honey Bear Bakery
6. Frankfurter
7. Bagel Oasis
8. Bakeman's
9. Jack's Fish Spot
10. Pecos Pit BBQ
11. Paseo Caribbean
12. Botticelli Caffè
13. Red Mill Burgers
14. Mondo Burrito
15. Three Girls Bakery
16. Ezell's Fried Chicken
17. Kidd Valley
18. My Favourite Piroshky
19. Famous Pacific
20. World Class Chili
21. El Puerco Lloron
22. B&O Espresso
23. Still Life in Fremont
24. Taco Del Mar
25. Sisters European
26. Original Pancake Hse.
27. Mad Pizza
28. Macrina Bakery
29. Pasta & Co.
30. Sit & Spin
31. Café Dilettante
32. Burrito Loco
33. Mae's Phinney Ridge
34. Saigon Bistro
35. Fremont Noodle Hse.
36. Green Cat Cafe
37. Pagliacci Pizza
38. Briazz
39. Maltby Cafe
40. Luna Park Cafe
41. Noodle Studio
42. CJ's Eatery
43. Two Bells Tavern
44. Hong's Garden
45. Catfish Corner
46. Pegasus Pizza
47. Zeek's Pizza
48. Pasta Ya Gotcha
49. Queen Mary
50. Brusseau's
51. Noodle Ranch
52. Gravity Bar
53. Hi-Spot Cafe Cafe
54. Bai Tong
55. Delcambre's Ragin' Cajun
56. Fremont Classic Pizzeria
57. Hilltop Ale House
58. Nickerson St. Saloon
59. Texas Smokehouse
60. Streamliner Diner
61. Mac's Smokehouse
62. Rosita's Mexican Grill
63. Mama's Mexican Kit.
64. Bahn Thai
65. Cool Hand Luke's
66. Racha
67. Sunlight Cafe
68. Big Time Pizzeria
69. Red Door Alehouse
70. Ayutthaya
71. Bay Cafe
72. Eggs Cetera's
73. Chile Pepper
74. Delfino's Pizzeria
75. El Greco
76. Hattie's Hat
77. Black Pearl
78. 74th St. Ale House
79. Emmett Watson's
80. Chinoise Café

Additional Good Values
(A bit more expensive, but worth every penny)

- Afrikando
- Armadillo Barbecue
- Asian Wok & Grill
- Banjara
- Belltown Pub & Cafe
- Blue Water Diner
- Coyote Creek Pizza
- 5 Spot
- Galerias
- Hale's Ales Brewpub
- Jalisco
- Jitterbug Café
- Julia's of Wallingford
- Kingfish Café
- Longshoreman's Daughter
- Maggie Bluffs
- Olympia II Pizza
- Pazzo's
- Plenty Cafe
- Pyramid Alehouse
- Salmon Bay Café
- Snappy Dragon
- Triangle Lounge

Alphabetical Directory of Seattle Restaurants

Seattle

	F	D	S	C

ADRIATICA S   24 | 21 | 23 | $36
1107 Dexter Ave. N. (3 blocks north of Mercer St.), 206-285-5000
☑ "Romance is in the air" at this "cute old home" perched high above Lake Union, a "perennial favorite" and contender for "the best Mediterranean" in town; skeptics argue it's "riding on its reputation", but most say it's still "worth the long flight of stairs" for a taste of "great seafood" ("the squid is exquisite"); unfortunately, one and all agree "it's a shame" that "development ruined the view."

Afrikando S   17 | 17 | 20 | $17
2904 First Ave. (Broad St.), 206-374-9714
☑ Touted as "Seattle's only sub-Saharan", this yearling brings a "bit of Senegal" to Belltown; the "owners make you feel very welcome", and enthusiasts find "out-of-the-ordinary food", like vegetables smothered in peanut sauce, "yummy"; but dissenters register their "disappointment."

Al Boccalino S   21 | 19 | 21 | $33
1 Yesler Way (Alaskan Way), 206-622-7688
☑ A "hole-in-the-wall with romantic atmosphere", this Pioneer Square Italian can claim loyal fans who cite the "pretty authentic" fare and say it holds its own "in a city with many" rivals; critics grumble it "has declined in both service and quality" in the wake of management turnover.

Aleko's Pizzeria S   ▽ 23 | 7 | 17 | $10
8310 Fifth Ave. NE (83rd St.), 206-525-4746
■ "Waay above average pizza!" rave devotees of the exceptional thin-crust pies tossed by pizzameister Alex Skoulis, who also fashions "good Greek-style" novelties like the spinachy 'spanakopizza'; although this Maple Leaf storefront has a handful of tables, delivery is a popular option and the carry-out trade is brisk.

Alligator Soul   22 | 14 | 19 | $19
2013½ Hewitt Ave. (bet. Broadway & Lombard Ave.), Everett, 425-259-6311
Hilbo's Alligator Soul S
7104 Woodlawn Ave. NE (bet. 71st & 72nd Sts.), 206-985-2303
■ "If you like your gumbo hot" (and many do), this coupla Cajuns in Green Lake and Everett provide "a return trip to New Orleans" courtesy of owner Hilbo Craig; the Southern cooking is "not for wimps", so expect "seasoning without compromise" spicing up "down-home food and plenty of it"; regulars kindly describe the "funky surroundings" as "warm" despite the "noisy" background.

Seattle

| F | D | S | C |

ANDALUCA ⓢ   23 | 25 | 22 | $32
Mayflower Park Hotel, 407 Olive Way (4th Ave.), 206-382-6999
■ "What a sexy place!" gush admirers of this Downtowner's "rich interior", eyeing its warm wood and secluded booths; the "varied menu" of "innovative" Mediterranean dishes is also attracting notice, and "very attentive" service complements the tony surroundings; a natural choice for business lunches, it's also a prime spot to "go with friends and order lots of different things to share", from "elegant tapas" to "molten chocolate cake."

Andy's Diner   12 | 11 | 14 | $16
2963 Fourth Ave. S. (Hanford St.), 206-624-4097
◪ A bastion of "plain American food" at "reasonable prices", this "stationary train" parked south of the Kingdome is the place for an "authentic 1940s dinner with waitress to match"; although followers commend the "reliable" "drink and a quick steak" menu, tougher customers call it "a real has-been."

Angelina's Trattoria ⓢ   14 | 14 | 16 | $18
2311 California Ave. SW (Admiral Way), 206-932-7311
■ This "typical pasta house" in West Seattle offers a "reliable", "family-friendly" setting for standards from the "run-of-the-mill" Italian kitchen; although it's nothing fancy, some consider the "warm clatter and chatter" and the "homey" "neighborhood" environment a pleasant return to the ordinary.

Angel's Thai Cuisine ⓢ   17 | 12 | 16 | $16
235 Broadway E. (Thomas St.), 206-328-0515
■ "Simple, delicious and affordable" sums up the virtues of this Capitol Hill Siamese, which boosters call a "place to introduce someone" to "solid" if "Americanized" Thai favorites; the "decor is sparse" and there's "no atmosphere", so regulars advise "get a window seat."

ANTHONY'S AT POINT DEFIANCE ⓢ   19 | 19 | 20 | $26
6135 Seaview Ave. W. (61st St.), 206-783-0780
ANTHONY'S BEACH CAFE ⓢ
5910 N. Waterfront Dr. (Vashon Ferry Dock), Tacoma, 253-752-9700
ANTHONY'S BEACH CAFE/HOMEPORT ⓢ
Edmonds Marina, 456 Admiral Way, Edmonds, 425-771-4400
ANTHONY'S HOMEPORT
Everett Marina Village, 1725 W. Marine View Dr., Everett, 425-252-3333
135 Lake St. S. (Moss Bay Marina), Kirkland, 425-822-0225
(Continues)

Seattle F | D | S | C |

ANTHONY'S HOMEPORT (Cont.)
Percival Landing, 704 Columbia St. NW (Capitol Blvd. & Olympia Farmers Mkt.), Olympia, 360-357-9700

ANTHONY'S OYSTER BAR & GRILL/HOMEPORT S
Des Moines Marina, 421 S. 227th St., Des Moines, 206-824-1947
◪ "Beautiful sunsets", "comfortable surroundings" and "reliably good fish" win support for this "corporate coastal" seafood chain, though the "fab view" tends to outshine the "unimaginative" menu; admirers praise the early-bird 'sunset dinners' for "good value", but detractors mutter that the "standard" finfare is "overpriced" and knock the surroundings as "tourist central."

Anthony's Pier 66 S   21 | 23 | 20 | $29 |
2201 Alaskan Way (Bell St./Pier 66), 206-448-6688
■ "A serious Anthony's", this is a "showcase for the bounty of Northwest seafood" set in a "stunning" nautical-inspired space with a "phenomenal" second-story view of Elliott Bay; though undeniably "touristy", it has a following that celebrates the "imaginative" fare (including a three-tier 'tower' appetizer of ahi tuna and alder-planked salmon) and deems it "a little pretentious but a treat nonetheless."

Aoki Japanese Restaurant S   20 | 14 | 18 | $19 |
621 Broadway E. (Roy St.), 206-324-3633
■ This "minimalist" Japanese offers "no ambiance", but it compensates with some of the "best sushi on Capitol Hill" and follows through with winners like "delicious udon", "buttery rice" and "soybeans in the pod"; the consensus view is "no frills, but on the money."

Ark, The S   24 | 18 | 21 | $32 |
273rd St. (Nahcotta Dock, off Sandridge Rd.), Nahcotta, 360-665-4133
◪ A "destination" overlooking Willapa Bay, this seafooder is a longstanding Long Beach "must eat" for shellfish chauvinists – it even maintains its own oyster beds; most deem the "innovative, excellently prepared" food "worth the trip", though hedgers report it "has disappointed" on occasion; N.B. goodies from the in-house bakery are added incentive.

Armadillo Barbecue S   18 | 11 | 13 | $14 |
13109 NE 175th St. (131st Ave. NE), Woodinville, 425-481-1417
◪ "Don't mind the dark and the smoke", they only enhance the flavors of the "good, sloppy BBQ" at this "funky" Woodinville "dive" where the "irreverent" staff proudly encourages a "psycho garage atmosphere"; the "hijinks" are as big a draw as the smoked bones, even if a handful of foes frown on the "seedy" surroundings.

Seattle | F | D | S | C |

Arnie's S | 17 | 18 | 19 | $24 |
Manners Sq., 1900 N. Northlake Way (34th Ave.), 206-547-3242
The Landing, 300 Admiral Way (Dayton Ave.), Edmonds, 425-771-5688
714 Second St. (Mukilteo Speedway), Mukilteo, 425-745-0601
◪ "Solid seafood" "priced fairly" wins support for this local chain, and each location boasts a "beautiful view" to complement its Pacific NW menu; they're "consistent", and regulars praise the early-bird meal as a "bargain", but detractors say the scenery can't compensate for "lackluster" eating and advise leaving these "dinosaurs" to "visitors from out of town."

Asiana S | 21 | 15 | 18 | $17 |
(fka Thai Restaurant)
101 John St. (1st Ave. N.), 206-285-9000
◪ Those who sense that this venerable Seattle Center Thai "seems to have lost its edge" might give it another whirl, since it now boasts a fresh moniker, a Pan-Asian focus and a new interior design (not reflected in the above decor score); the able kitchen team and personable staff are held over from the old days.

Asian Wok & Grill S | 18 | 16 | 17 | $16 |
3601 Fremont Ave. N. (36th St.), 206-675-8508
■ Even in funky Fremont they "love the radish roses" and the "healthy" wok work at Danny Wong's latest venture, a "Pan-Asian extravaganza" with a "massive" menu of "well-prepared", veggie-heavy items; "the strip-mall ambiance" is a weak point, but the "eclectic" eats have enough character to keep it satisfying.

ASSAGGIO RISTORANTE | 22 | 21 | 21 | $28 |
2010 Fourth Ave. (Virginia St.), 206-441-1399
■ "All of the Italian favorites" are on hand at this "festive" Downtown trattoria: "honest food", "pretty murals" and "warm service"; devotees swear by "the dipping oil" and tout the "excellent pastas" ("love the mushroom pappardelle"); affable owner Mauro Golmarvi "works the dining room" – a "beautiful setting" that's usually "busy" and "noisy."

Athenian Inn | 13 | 15 | 14 | $15 |
Pike Place Mkt., 1517 Pike Place Mkt. (bet. Pike & Pine Sts.), 206-624-7166
◪ A love-hate relationship enfolds this Pike Place Market "landmark" where the "great view" of Elliott Bay is a city treasure, but the "vast" surf 'n' turf menu rates "not too great"; still, die-hards insist it's ideal "for breakfast" and relaxing over "every beer you could possibly want", and locals go "again and again" to soak up the "feel of old Seattle."

| Seattle | F | D | S | C |

Avenue One ⓢ 20 | 21 | 20 | $32
1921 First Ave. (bet. Stuart & Virginia Sts.), 206-441-6139
◼ Seattle's first funeral parlor has morphed over the years into an "elegant", "trendy" French bistro near Pike Place Market, where a "tasty" menu includes "lots of meat" prepared with a Northwest touch; as beautiful young things pick and choose from the "good wine list", critics grumble about "attitude" overload; P.S. the tiny "back room" provides fireside seclusion and a "fabulous Sound view."

Axis ●◐ⓢ 19 | 20 | 17 | $31
2212 First Ave. (bet. Bell & Blanchard Sts.), 206-441-9600
◼ A high-energy, "oh-so-Belltown" urban space, this "happening" hunting ground for the "'it' crowd" presents a "hip" International Mix of dishes that arrive in "family-style" portions meant for sharing; the "innovative" cuisine can be "delicious", but it's the "scene" that comes first here; contrarians consider it an "overpriced" "yuppie dive" with a "pretentious staff and atmosphere."

Ayutthaya ⓢ 18 | 13 | 18 | $15
727 E. Pike St. (Harvard Ave.), 206-324-8833
■ "Fast, cheap and crowded" is the consensus on this "intimate" Capitol Hill Thai, a "long-time favorite" for "filling lunches" stirred up with "yummy veggies"; partisans praise the kitchen's skill ("each dish is a picture") and the "pleasant staff", returning for more in spite of "minimal decor."

Azteca ⓢ 12 | 13 | 15 | $15
Shilshole Marina, 6017 Seaview Ave. NW, 206-789-7373
2319 NW Market St. (24th Ave.), 206-782-7079
1823 Eastlake Ave. E. (Yale Pl. E.), 206-324-4941
Northgate Mall, 543 NE Northgate Way (5th Ave.), 206-362-0066
University Village, 2686 S. University Village Mall (25th Ave. NE), 206-524-2987
150 112th Ave. NE (bet. 4th & 8th Sts.), Bellevue, 425-453-9087
1321 SE Everett Mall Way (opp. Everett Mall), Everett, 425-353-7588
31740 23rd Ave. S. (320th St.), Federal Way, 253-839-6693
25633 102nd Pl. SE (Smith St.), Kent, 253-852-0210
17555 Southcenter Pkwy. (south of Minkler Blvd.), Tukwila, 206-575-0990
◼ There's no denying the popularity of these "roll-up-your-sleeves" Mexicans where fans fuel up on "gloppy", "chain" versions of "Americanized" "favorites"; the "reasonable" prices and "kid-friendly" outlook make them a "family staple", though adversaries argue this is "Taco Bell" territory.

Bacchus Restaurant ⓢ 17 | 17 | 15 | $18
806 E. Roy St. (bet. Broadway & Harvard Ave. E.), 206-325-2888
■ Saganaki flambées light up the interior of this Capitol Hill Greek, a "cozy" room where restored murals adorn the walls; the "reasonably priced" fare includes Attic attractions like gyros, rounded out by faves like lentil soup and squid.

Seattle

| | F | D | S | C |

Bagel Oasis S   18 | 7 | 11 | $7
462 N. 36th St. (Dayton Ave.), 206-633-2676
2112 NE 65th St. (22nd Ave.), 206-526-0525 ⊭
11606 98th Ave. NE (116th St.), Kirkland, 425-823-5404
◪ "Go early" for the "freshest", "most authentic bagels in town" at these "bare-bones" Fremont, Kirkland and Ravenna nosheries, which also supply bialys and "healthy, filling" sandwiches to the cream-cheese crowd; "noisy" patrons and "glacial service" make them uninviting "for sit-down dining", but they're "cheap and convenient" compared with "schlepping cartons of bagels back from New York."

Bahn Thai S   20 | 15 | 19 | $16
409 Roy St. (5th Ave. N.), 206-283-0444
■ This "dependable" standby on lower Queen Anne serves as a "great intro to Thai food", with a "varied" menu of "fresh", "authentic dishes" prepared "to your taste for heat" ("specify if you can't handle spiciness"); pad Thai partisans commend the kitchen's grasp of "noodle texture", and the "very organized", "friendly staff" provides "fast" "pre–Seattle Center" service.

Bai Tong S   23 | 13 | 19 | $15
15859 Pacific Hwy. S. (160th St.), Seatac, 425-431-0893
■ Bangkok expats "fresh off a plane" would be grateful for this "jewel" near Sea-Tac airport, which provides "excellent" Thai that ranks as the "best in the city"; the "revised American diner" decor strikes some as "strange", but it's a "comfortable environment" where fans can focus on the "tasty" soups and noodles.

Bakeman's ⊭   19 | 7 | 16 | $8
122 Cherry St. (2nd Ave.), 206-622-3375
■ Seattle's "sandwich Nazi" presides over this Downtowner, a "cheap lunch" "institution" where "turkey's the thing", stacked to the sky on "sandwiches served with NY deli attitude"; lawyers and jurors congregate over "hearty soups", "world-famous egg salad" and meat loaf that "can't be beat"; "lightning" service is a given, though the room ain't much – good thing they've got takeout.

Bamboo Garden Vegetarian Cuisine S   17 | 10 | 18 | $14
364 Roy St. (bet. 3rd & 4th Aves. N), 206-282-6616
◪ A "true treat" for the "vegan" vanguard, this meat-free Chinese near the Seattle Center manages to "keep kosher" for good measure; boosters applaud the "fascinating fake meat" and other "fool-the-eye food", declaring it unbeatable "when you're feeling guilty about being a carnivore"; skeptics sniff they "aren't fooling anyone" with that "weird soy stuff" and hint the plastic decor "needs work."

Seattle | F | D | S | C |

B&O Espresso 🅢 | 18 | 16 | 12 | $10 |
Broadway Mkt., 401 Broadway E. (Republican St.), 206-328-3290
204 Belmont Ave. E. (E. Olive St.), 206-322-5028 ☾

Cherry St. Espresso
103 Cherry St. (1st Ave.), 206-621-9372

■ Frequented by "people in black" flaunting "tattoos and nose rings", these local patches of "coffee and dessert" "heaven" are favored for their "atmo" and for "lingering" over delicacies like "sublime sour-cream lemon pie", "bourbon-tainted New Orleans cake" and an "espresso shake that should come with a 12-step program for addicts"; the downside is "service with an attitude."

Bandoleone 🅢 | 21 | 17 | 18 | $22 |
2241 Eastlake Ave. E. (Lynn St.), 206-329-7559

■ Spain and the New World unite in the "imaginative" Latin cuisine featured at this "low-key", intimate Eastlake taverna where "inventive" tapas lead off an "impeccably executed" menu highlighting zesty grilled meats; the mixmaster serves up "perfect margaritas" and "sangria to die for", and the weekend brunches, monthly wine tastings and Monday cigar nights all have followings of their own.

Banjara 🅢 | 19 | 14 | 17 | $16 |
2 Boston St. (Queen Anne Ave. N.), 206-282-7752

■ Aficionados applaud the "good renditions" of "classic" Northern Indian cuisine at this neighborhood spot atop Queen Anne Hill; the "fresh" lunch buffet offers "good variety", and at dinner a staff dressed in traditional garb presents "consistently good" tandoori and vindaloo favorites; pros pronounce it "a cut above the ordinary", and "modest prices" boost its popularity.

Bay Cafe 🅢 | 18 | 15 | 19 | $15 |
3 Bay Bldg. (opp. post office), Lopez Island, 360-468-3700

■ A "favorite breakfast spot" that draws "commercial fishermen" among others, this congenial island outpost is also known for its "imaginative" International cuisine and "great service"; new owners plan an expansion that will furnish open-air seating, even as locals lament "we don't want it to be too discovered"; N.B. not to be confused with the Bay Cafe at Seattle's Fisherman's Terminal.

Bella Rosa Bistro 🅢 | ▽ 19 | 17 | 18 | $24 |
3410 NE 55th St. (east of University Village), 206-527-3400

■ This U-District yearling is off to a "very promising start", proving this 'hood just can't have too many tiny, romantic bistros; the kitchen specializes in "Italian with a twist", throwing in French and Moroccan elements like the chef's signature couscous with lamb sausage.

Seattle | F | D | S | C |

Bell St. Diner S | 19 | 18 | 16 | $19 |
2201 Alaskan Way (Bell St.), 206-448-6688

⚡ "Forget about going upstairs [to upscale sibling Anthony's Pier 66]" scoff loyalists, who find the casual fish-house feel makes this docksider a "great place to lay low" and enjoy "really tasty" bites like mahi tacos and cioppino; "crowds", "noise" and "prepubescent" servers are turnoffs, but you "can't beat the view" – only "don't treat me like a tourist."

Belltown Billiards ◐ S | 14 | 15 | 12 | $18 |
90 Blanchard St. (1st Ave.), 206-448-6779

⚡ Many do claim to show up at this "hot" Belltown hangout to sample from an "adventurous" menu featuring "truly Italian pasta" and pizza; on the flip side, "the yuppie pool hall thing" is alive and well, with an attendant "meet market" scene that entices those who "don't go for the food"; N.B. chef Dino D'Aquila's departure is not reflected in the above food rating.

Belltown Pub & Cafe S | 18 | 16 | 16 | $16 |
2322 First Ave. (bet. Battery & Bell Sts.), 206-728-4311

■ "Classy pub grub" qualifies this "unpretentious" Belltown bar as being "great for a quick, casual bite to eat"; it has made its name with "surprisingly creative" Northwestern takes on burgers and steaks, and the "friendly bartenders" dispense a "great variety" of microbrews to help the "yupped-out", nonsmoking clientele wash it all down.

Benjamin's on Lake Union ◐ S | 17 | 18 | 18 | $25 |
809 Fairview Pl. N. (Valley St.), 206-621-8262

■ Most of the accolades for this Lake Union surf 'n' turf haven are reserved for the "great view" and the "amazing Sunday brunch"; otherwise, the menu "tries hard" but "could be a lot more creative", though the "late-night appetizers" appeal to after-hours and post-event groups.

Bick's Broadview Grill S | 19 | 15 | 17 | $19 |
10555 Greenwood Ave. N. (N. 107th St.), 206-367-8481

■ North-Enders gloat that there's "something good in Greenwood", pointing to the "innovative" New American menu at this "friendly" "neighborhood" eatery; given the management's "hot sauce hype" (a vast collection is on display), the grilled food leans toward "spicy", but the timid can indulge in enormous salads that "feed two – or more"; N.B. grape fans welcome the low markups on wine.

Big Time Pizzeria S | 18 | 14 | 14 | $13 |
7824 Leary Way (Cleveland St.), Redmond, 425-885-6425

■ The move to a roomier, exposed-brick setting has "greatly improved" the feel of this "high-quality pizza joint" in Redmond, and the made-from-scratch philosophy and "interesting toppings" keep the crowd calling for more; with "good beer" and a selection of budget "bar food", it's the ultimate "noisy" "grad student hangout."

Seattle

| | F | D | S | C |

Bilbo's Festivo S   – | – | – | M |
511 North Beach Rd. (A St.), Eastsound, Orcas Island, 360-376-4728
Followers of this "very special *Hobbit*-like place" on Orcas Island insist it's home to some of "the best Mexican fare in the state"; the cozy cantina-style house fills up fast, so it's wise to reserve – patio seating is the most coveted.

Billy McHale's ◐ S   11 | 13 | 13 | $16 |
Factoria Mall, 4065 128th Ave. SE (Coal Creek Pkwy.), Bellevue, 425-746-1138
1800 S. 320th St. (bet. I-5 & Pacific Hwy.), Federal Way, 253-839-4200
18430 33rd Ave. W. (184th St. SW), Lynnwood, 425-775-8500
15210 Redmond Way (152nd Ave. NE), Redmond, 425-881-0316
241 SW 7th St. (Rainier), Renton, 425-271-7427
10115 S. Tacoma Way (Hwy. 512), Tacoma, 253-582-6330
■ These "no-surprises" suburban steakhouses offer a "cookie-cutter" experience that multitudes rely on for "family" dining; "big burgers", "cheap steaks" and fried-onion loaf headline a menu that is "not for the gourmet", causing foes to plead "hold the grease"; while "overhead trains" divert the rugrats, an "amazing margarita selection" attracts adults to the "loud and very busy bar."

Bis on Main   – | – | – | M |
(fka Fortnum's Cafe)
10213 Main St. (102nd Ave. NE), Bellevue, 425-455-2033
New owners have transformed this once-cutesy cafe into a stylish little bistro in Bellevue's Old Town that attracts a natty Eastside clientele with a French-meets-Italian-meets-Cajun menu featuring meat, seafood, soups and housemade desserts; the Louisiana influence is its strongest suit, so think duck gumbo, shrimp étoufée and pecan pie.

Bistro Lautrec   21 | 19 | 20 | $26 |
315 E. Pine St. (bet. Bellevue & Melrose Aves.), 206-748-0627
■ Providing "a Parisian experience" (minus the "jet lag") on the fringe of Capitol Hill, this "warm", "very romantic" French offers a "fine menu" of "delectable" aliment, "served professionally"; recently spruced up, the Left Bank decor adds to the charm of the "comfortable", "crowded" room.

Bistro Pleasant Beach S   ▽ 19 | 18 | 19 | $27 |
(fka Pleasant Beach Grill)
241 Winslow Way W. (bet. Finch Pl. & Wood Ave. SW), Bainbridge Island, 206-842-4347
■ The former Pleasant Beach Grill has come down from a Bainbridge hilltop to a "more convenient" location near the Winslow ferry landing; the ambiance remains "classy" (if casual), and chef Hussein Ramadan still blends Med flair and Northwest ingredients; some hold that "dropping cocktails was a real mistake", but there's a spacious new patio to compensate.

Seattle | F | D | S | C |

Bistro Provençal S | 23 | 19 | 22 | $33 |
212 Central Way (Lake Washington Blvd.), Kirkland, 425-827-3300
◪ Gallic charm has warmed patrons to this Downtown Kirkland mainstay where chef-owner Philippe Gayte's Traditional French cuisine is "pretty authentic" and the "unpretentious", "romantic" country ambiance is "safe for business or pleasure"; the "nice prix fixe" deal can keep the tab low, but some suggest "a spring cleaning" is overdue.

Bizzarro Italian Cafe S | 19 | 20 | 18 | $21 |
1307 N. 46th St. (Stone Way), 206-545-7327
■ "*Abbondanza* with attitude" (and "garlic breath") is in style at this "funky garage" in Wallingford, where the menu runs to "solid" Italian delivered by a "friendly" if "irreverent" staff, and the "quirky decor" includes a surreal ceiling hung with a slew of "fantastic" found objects; in short, "the name says it all."

Black Pearl S | 20 | 12 | 17 | $15 |
7347 35th Ave. NE (NE 75th St.), 206-526-5115
■ One of Ravenna's "favorite Chinese" spots makes its mark with "simple" food, including potstickers ("the sixth food group"), "delicious noodles" and "succulent orange beef"; "name changes" have rocked supporter confidence, but the consensus is this stalwart is "better than ever."

BLOWFISH ASIAN CAFE ●S | 21 | 21 | 18 | $23 |
Paramount Hotel, 722 Pine St. (8th Ave.), 206-467-7777
◪ "Definitely not your grandmother's Chinese" joint, this "trendy" Downtown Pan-Asian maintains an "electric atmosphere" complete with robata bar and a rocking wok station; loyalists laud the "fresh, innovative" chow, and both the "happy-hour dim sum" and "the best late dinner in town" have found followers, though the unimpressed dismiss this as a "wildly overrated" "Wild Ginger wanna-be."

Blue Water Diner S | 17 | 18 | 16 | $16 |
305 Madison Ave. N. (bet. Winslow & Wyatt Ways), Bainbridge Island, 206-842-1151
◪ Classic Americana defines the eats and the atmo at this "ultimate diner", restored and transplanted from Philly to Bainbridge Island; "quick and easy" comfort food like homemade biscuits and gravy, chicken and dumplings, and cheese steaks fulfills the faithful, even if cynics shrug "without the nostalgia it's just a corner restaurant."

BluWater Bistro ●S | 19 | 18 | 17 | $22 |
Yale St. Landing, 1001 Fairview Ave. N. (Yale St.), 206-447-0769
■ The "new spot to be seen" on Lake Union is this Regional American where chef Peter Levine's Northwestern menu matches beef, pork, chicken and a fresh sheet of seafood specials to the "laid-back" "Southern California ambiance"; in "pretty weather", the youngish clientele heads deckside to sip Blu margaritas while window-shopping for yachts.

Seattle	F	D	S	C

Boat Street Cafe 🅂⊘ — | — | — | M
909 NE Boat St. (Brooklyn Ave.), 206-632-4602
"Simplicity is everything" at this "cozy" U-District favorite where "fresh, fresh, fresh" fixings produce "wonderful sandwiches", "the best eggs Benedict" around and an ambitious dinner menu; "slate tabletop" decor and "sweet service" enhance the "quaint" feel.

Botticelli Caffè — 20 | 14 | 15 | $10
101 Stewart St. (bet. 1st & 2nd Aves.), 206-441-9235
■ Seattle's panini pandemonium originated at this tiny cafe near Pike Place Market before going city-wide, and aficionados still converge here to relish "the perfect panino", along with "real Italian espresso" and "great international people-watching"; fans find it "fresh, simple, fast and inexpensive."

Brasa ◐ — | — | — | M
2107 Third Ave. (Lenora St.), 206-728-4220
This bold Belltown beauty marks the long-awaited return of ex Campagne chef Tamara Murphy and her contemporary rendition of Mediterranean cuisine, much of it cooked over open fire; the sensuous dining room is designed for lingering, and the bar is a prime site for a pre- or post-event bite.

Briazz ◐ — 14 | 12 | 12 | $10
1400 Fifth Ave. (Union St.), 206-343-3099 🅂
The Bon Marché, 300 Pine St., main fl. (3rd St.), 206-447-7599 🅂
The Bon Marché, 300 Pine St., 6th fl. (4th St.), 206-341-9009
1000 Second Ave. (bet. Seneca & Spring Sts.), 206-224-3100 🅂
Metropolitan Towers W., 1100 Olive Way (Minor Ave.), 206-587-2557
Westin Bldg., 2001 Sixth Ave. (Virginia St.), 206-256-4595
2590 University Village (25th Ave. NE), 206-523-8646 🅂
Newport Corp. Ctr., 3626 132nd Ave. SE (Newport Way), Bellevue, 425-373-3177
One Bellevue Ctr., 411 108th Ave. NE (NE 4th St.), Bellevue, 425-635-0353
◪ The "Starbucks of sandwiches", this chain of Euro-stylish, self-service cafes "fills a niche" by offering "upscale fast food" in the form of "pre-packaged" light bites (the University Village branch expands the concept to include ready-to-heat entrees); although the "low-fat options" and "huge variety" are a hit, detractors rant about "plastic food" and "the most expensive soggy sandwiches in town."

Bridges Bar & Grill ◐🅂 — 13 | 13 | 13 | $18
2947 Eastlake Ave. E. (Allison St.), 206-320-0785
■ Boasting an Eastlake site that commands the "cheapest view of Lake Union", this Regional American is more popular for its "great location" than its "ho-hum food", though the Sunday breakfast draws devotees of fresh scones and French toast; all agree it's a "nice place for a beer and a snack", especially when the 200-seat deck is open.

Seattle | F | D | S | C |

Brie & Bordeaux S | 23 | 18 | 20 | $26 |
2227 N. 56th St. (Kirkwood Ave.), 206-633-3538
■ Attached to a Greenlake wine and cheese shop, this "charming neighborhood cafe" simulates "a quick trip to Provence" courtesy of chef Scott Samuel and his "imaginative" French-inspired cuisine; a "mouthwatering" "cheese display" and "excellent vino" complement the "splendid" cooking; P.S. the "exquisite brunches" are a weekend treat, but lunch is no longer served.

Broadway New American Grill ●S | 12 | 13 | 14 | $17 |
314 Broadway E. (bet. E. Harrison & E. Thomas Sts.), 206-328-7000
◪ A "handy" Broadway locale on Capitol Hill makes this "cool, trendy hangout" a crossroads for "a very mixed crowd" joined by the odd "voyeur", but the "good old Americana" on the menu is "not memorable" and service is apt to be "temperamental"; "a great place to meet" but a "poor place to eat", it's preferred for the "lively" happy hour and "late-night" scene.

Brooklyn Seafood, Steak & Oyster House S | 21 | 20 | 19 | $28 |
1212 Second Ave. (University St.), 206-224-7000
◪ The "oyster samplers and beer samplers" are the draws at this "classic" surf 'n' turf house, a "crowded" but "comfortable" Downtown junction for lawyers who lunch; the "knowledgeable staff" may seem "surly at times", but "the crowds pour in" and though some "don't know why" those who do sigh "ah, the oysters."

Brusseau's S | 18 | 13 | 13 | $12 |
117 Fifth Ave. (Dayton St.), Edmonds, 425-774-4166
◪ The sunny patio makes this "small, quaint" bakery-cum-luncheonette a downtown Edmonds fixture for dawdling over fruit pies, sticky buns or soup/salad/sandwich combos; owners come and go but the formula remains popular, even if critics complain it's a bit "overrated."

Buca di Beppo S | 14 | 19 | 18 | $19 |
701 Ninth Ave. N. (Roy St.), 206-244-2288
4301 200th St. SW (44th Ave.), Lynnwood, 425-744-7272
◪ Some "love it", some argue it "reeks of excess", but all cry "mamma mia, what corn!"; these Little Italy theme parks (one near Seattle Center, the other in suburban Lynnwood) come complete with a "shrine to Sinatra" and a Pope's Table for patrons to admire as they tuck into "king-size portions" of "common-denominator" pizza and pasta; this is the place for "big, loud gatherings" or "to take kids", though the "crowds" and no-reservations policy discourage those who "hate the wait."

Seattle F | D | S | C |

Bungalow Wine Bar & Café S   19 | 20 | 20 | $20 |
2412 N. 45th St. (bet. Eastern & Sunnyside Aves.), 206-632-0254
■ "Move me in" say denizens of this "charming", "rehabbed old house" in Wallingford, where a "limited menu" of Eclectic eats is designed to "perfectly complement" 60-plus wines by the glass; a "knowledgeable staff" is on hand, and the "informal fun" is enhanced by live classical guitar music, patio dining and monthly wine tastings.

Burk's Cafe   20 | 16 | 18 | $20 |
5411 Ballard Ave. NW (22nd St.), 206-782-0091
■ Supplying "New Orleans comfort food" from pickled okra to pecan pie, this "local Ballard hangout" wins the hearts of the area yat contingent; the "full-flavored", "homestyle" Cajun-Creole specialties "may be a bit too hot for some", but loyalists "love the jambalaya" and declare "no other gumbo will do", saving their censure for the "intriguing but not terribly efficient" servers.

Burrito Loco S   21 | 12 | 19 | $13 |
9211 Holman Rd. NW (Greenwood Ave.), 206-783-0719
■ Boosters are crazy about "the real thing" at this Greenwood "neighborhood joint", a strip mall Mexican that prides itself on "authentic", "cheap and healthy" fare, including "the best burritos this side of LA", tongue tacos, a "must-have" mole, and *horchatas* and *churros* for the sweet tooth; eat in or take out, the portions are "enough for two meals."

Bush Garden S   18 | 16 | 17 | $24 |
614 Maynard Ave. S. (Lane St.), 206-682-6830
◪ "If you liked Trader Vic's in the '60s", this I.D. Japanese "is your place"; now "a Seattle institution", it covers all the bases with a sushi bar, tatami rooms and a karaoke lounge, though the disenchanted dis the "shabby" surroundings and gripe "the sushi dinner might satisfy a canary."

Byzantion, The S   15 | 15 | 15 | $17 |
601 Broadway E. (E. Mercer St.), 206-325-7580
◪ This "small and cozy" storefront Hellene on Capitol Hill offers a "good breakfast", and partisans praise the "fab" phyllo wraps; tougher customers deem the "Greek grub" "decent" but "predictable" and knock the "slow service."

Cactus S   22 | 19 | 17 | $21 |
4220 E. Madison St. (42nd Ave. E.), 206-324-4140
■ "The secret's out" so "the wait is long", but diners are willing to sacrifice for a taste of the "incredible" Southwestern cuisine, "superb tapas" and "fine" Mexican fare at this Madison Park powerhouse where the festivities spill out to the sidewalk tables; advocates advise the "fajitas equal two meals" and the "bananas in rum sauce rock", and award special mention to the "best margaritas ever"; the only quibble: "prickly" service.

Seattle

| F | D | S | C |

CAFE CAMPAGNE 🆂 | 26 | 23 | 23 | $25 |
Pike Place Mkt., 1600 Post Alley (Pine St.), 206-728-2233
■ "Ooh la la!", this "first-class bistro" is Post Alley's own "slice of Paris", serving French comfort fare that "rivals its big sister [Campagne] upstairs" for "consistency and quality", amounting to "champagne food at beer prices"; the Gallic setting is ideal for a "rainy-day breakfast", "terrific Sunday brunch" or romantic dinner – this is a "treat" at a cost that "can't be beat."

Café Dilettante ●🆂 | 20 | 16 | 12 | $12 |
416 Broadway E. (bet. Harrison & Republican Sts.), 206-329-6463

Dilettante Chocolates 🆂
Pike Place Mkt., 1603 First Ave. (Pine St.), 206-728-9144
■ "Awesome desserts" are the draw at this Capitol Hill "chocolate heaven", which is "unbelievably crowded on weekend nights" with chocoholics looking for a "fix"; the goods range from "decadent" cakes and truffles to "amazing ice cream desserts", and "people-watching" from the Broadway vantage point compensates for weak service; N.B. the Pike Place offshoot is a sweetshop only.

CAFE FLORA 🆂 | 22 | 21 | 19 | $21 |
2901 E. Madison St. (29th Ave. E.), 206-325-9100
☑ Even fauna fanciers won't "miss meat" at this "light, airy" Madison Park Vegetarian; the "inspired" menu features such wonders as "mashed potato tacos", "portobello Wellington" and "organic wines", and the glass-enclosed "greenhouse room" is a "restful" retreat; the "laid-back", sometimes "snooty" service is a minus, though, and hard-core herbivores gripe about "not enough vegan choices" on the "very cheesy menu."

Café Huê 🆂 | ∇ 18 | 15 | 18 | $16 |
312 Second Ave. S. (bet. Jackson & Main Sts.), 206-625-9833
☑ This large, rather formal Vietnamese near Pioneer Square has "all the right things on the menu" but fails to elicit much enthusiasm; the fixed-price lunch and dinner deals are a steal, but skeptics suspect the food is "watered down" to please the American palate.

CAFE JUANITA 🆂 | 26 | 20 | 23 | $34 |
9702 NE 120th Pl. (97th Ave.), Kirkland, 425-823-1505
■ "Sometimes forgotten", this "creekside" Kirkland Northern Italian is a "warm and inviting" "class act" that's "worth the money" and "the drive" to experience chef John Neumark's evolving menu; standouts include "fantastic lamb shanks", rabbit, housemade bread and "wonderful desserts", matched with "personal service" and "perhaps the best vino list for the money in town" (the Cavatappi winery is annexed to the cafe).

CAFE LAGO [S] 25 | 18 | 21 | $25
2305 24th Ave. E. (bet. Lynn & McGraw Sts.), 206-329-8005
■ There are "long lines" and "great smells" at this "intimate and 'in'" Montlake Italian; regulars arrive early to get the most from the "limited" menu, which includes "wonderful antipasti", "excellent lasagna" and pizza raised "to an art"; a "friendly" staff adds to the charm, and if faultfinders grumble "pricey and crowded", for most "this is the real thing."

Cafe Langley [S] 21 | 17 | 20 | $25
113 First St. (waterfront), Langley, Whidbey Island, 360-221-3090
◪ Sited on the main drag in the Whidbey Island village of Langley, this convivial Mediterranean exudes "warmth"; seasoned diners suggest "stick with the Greek dishes", but that shouldn't preclude "excellent" options like the house specialty rack of lamb or the island-fresh seafood.

Cafe Nola [S]≠ 23 | 18 | 15 | $20
101 Winslow Way (Madison Ave.), Bainbridge Island, 206-842-3822
■ The "terrific breads" and "tasty pastries" are "unmatched for quality" at this "quaint brunch/lunch spot" on Bainbridge Island, which also offers a "limited menu" of "simply delicious" Northwestern dishes with Italian accents; early birds claim its "best for breakfast", but night owls often sell out the monthly wine-tasting dinners.

Café Septieme [S] 14 | 14 | 13 | $16
214 Broadway E. (bet. John & Thomas Sts.), 206-860-8858
◪ "Gen X slacker attitude prevails" at this "moody urban retreat" on Capitol Hill, where the French-American bistro fare takes a back seat to the "funky" atmo; anyone who's not into "blood-red walls" might better enjoy the "creative" breakfasts and "large variety of fab desserts" at a sidewalk table, albeit at the risk of experiencing "nonexistent service."

Café Soleil [S] ▽ 20 | 17 | 21 | $12
1400 34th Ave. (Union St.), 206-325-1126
■ Chef-owner "Kuri [Teshome] is a charming hostess" whose Madrona corner cafe provides a "lovely setting" for sipping latte over a "smashing breakfast" (with terrific pastries); it's every bit as appealing at night when the "funky" little room comes alive with "tasty" Ethiopian fare.

Cafe Starbucks [S] – | – | – | I
4000 E. Madison St. (E. 42nd Ave.), 206-329-3736
Pacific Pl., 600 Pine St. (6th Ave.), 206-652-4683
6500 California Ave. S. (Morgan St.), 206-935-7848
The biggest name in coffee is now conspiring to open a casual eatery (with boozy coffee drinks and table service, no less) on every corner in town; meanwhile, they're "working out the kinks" at a number of trial outlets, including the first in Madison Park, where soups, sandwiches and "great desserts" have been attracting hordes from the get-go.

Cafe Veloce [S] ▽ 17 | 13 | 14 | $18

12514 120th Ave. NE (bet. Totem Lake Blvd. & Totem Lake Way), Kirkland, 425-814-2972

◪ Kirkland's combination Italian eatery and biker museum fuels its fans with "huge servings" of pizza and pasta, but it's the motorcycle motif that packs the real "varoom" here; a mystified minority finds "motorcycles on the walls" a little "weird" and hints the "so-so" food and "lethargic" service are in need of a tune-up.

Caffe Ladro [S]⊘ 20 | 18 | 19 | $10

600 Queen Anne Ave. N. (Mercer St.), 206-282-1549
2205 Queen Anne Ave. N. (Boston St.), 206-282-5313

■ This Queen Anne coffee-bar couple provides an "un-Starbucks" alternative for "great espresso" and "beautiful desserts"; the style is "urban" "exotic", with an "eclectic crew" on hand to serve up "amazing" pastries and pies, as well as soups, salads and sandwiches; java junkies reckon it "one of the best" in its class.

Caffè Minnie's ◐[S] 11 | 9 | 9 | $13

101 Denny Way (1st Ave.), 206-448-6263
611 Broadway E. (bet. Mercer & Roy Sts.), 206-860-1360

■ Even "ear-shattering rock music" and "slacker service" don't deter seekers of "late-night grease", "breakfast 24 hours a day" or the "perfect cure for a hangover" from frequenting these Italianate all-nighters; some worry they "don't have enough pierced body parts to go in", though "at 3 AM" it's a nonissue; all in all, this is a "dingy" scene – "but they're open."

Calabria Ristorante Italiano [S] 20 | 16 | 18 | $24

132 Lake St. S. (bet. Kirkland & 2nd Aves.), Kirkland, 425-822-7350

■ All "feel welcome" at this "low-key" "little place" in Downtown Kirkland, where "big pasta" doused in cream or puttanesca sauce dominates a Southern Italian menu noted for its "value"; "window seats" are coveted, though an expansion has tripled the table capacity and is not reflected in the decor score.

CAMPAGNE ◐[S] 28 | 25 | 25 | $44

Inn at the Market, 86 Pine St. (bet. 1st Ave. & Post Alley), 206-728-2800

■ "Elegant" country French cooking (voted Seattle's No. 2 for Food) coupled with "impeccable service" make for a "superb dining experience" at this Pike Place Market "treasure", and "only the clank of *boules* could make it more Provençal"; chef James Drohmen "works miracles", and the "intimate setting" enhances both business and pleasure (even if you have to "mortgage your house for wine" from the "outstanding" list); bottom line: it still "sets the standard" for "class."

| **Seattle** | F | D | S | C |

CANLIS — 25 | 27 | 27 | $48
2576 Aurora Ave. N. (Halladay St.), 206-283-3313
■ The panoramic view of Lake Union remains "unmatched" and the "food has really improved" at this "old favorite", a "grand old lady" with a "marvelous" makeover; chef Greg Atkinson gives the Pacific NW "steak-and-seafood" menu a '90s twist", and the "superb service" is rated No. 1 in the Seattle *Survey*; "consistent luxury" is "expensive", though, and this is still "blue-blood" home turf.

Capitol Club S — 19 | 23 | 17 | $23
414 E. Pine St. (bet. Bellevue Ave. & Crawford Pl.), 206-325-2149
■ "Be sure to wear black" to this "hip", "happening" Capitol Hill hang, where the "unusual" Mediterranean food runs second to the "*I Dream of Jeannie*" decor; it's a chance to sample a Near Eastern bisque or vegetable couscous fired with harissa, or lean into "soft velvet cushions" and sip "generous drinks" in "exotic" but "intimate" style.

Carmelita S — 22 | 19 | 18 | $22
7314 Greenwood Ave. N. (bet. 73rd & 74th Sts.), 206-706-7703
◪ This "upscale" Greenwood entry "proves that gourmet Vegetarian is not an oxymoron", and the tofu troops pack the house to dig into "deliciously inventive" food in a "warm" environment; some suggest "bring a flashlight" and "crank up your hearing aid", but a plant-filled deck offers refuge from the "cavernous" dining room's "din"; skeptics snipe at "hit-or-miss" eating – "do you feel lucky?"

Cassis S — 22 | 21 | 22 | $30
2359 10th Ave. E. (E. Miller St.), 206-329-0580
■ The steak frites alone justify this "real" French bistro on Capitol Hill that combines a "classy atmosphere" with "traditional" fare; "simplicity" is evident on the "limited" menu and in the "understated elegance" of the room, which features a "cool" tin bar; everything from breads to desserts is made in-house, and the staff is mindful of "every detail."

Catfish Corner ⌽ — 20 | 10 | 16 | $12
2726 E. Cherry (Martin Luther King Way), 206-323-4330
■ It's a "little corner of the deep South" in Seattle's Central District, offering "no decor but great fish"; the Delta Soul Food makes it a "great spot" for "down-home" dining on Dixie delights like golden-fried catfish, and the hospitality has converts claiming they sho'ly do "want to come back."

Chandler's Crabhouse S — 19 | 19 | 19 | $29
901 Fairview Ave. N. (Mercer St.), 206-223-2722
◪ "Reliable" seafood and a waterfront view summon supporters to the Schwartz Brothers' indoor/outdoor Lake Union arena for "business-oriented" meals or group gatherings; inside, it "can be noisy" as fans clamor for "great fresh" fare, including oyster shooters and "superb" shellfish; a minority crabs about "boring", "pricey" fare.

Seattle

	F	D	S	C

Chanterelle Specialty Foods S ▽ | 22 | 15 | 15 | $17
316 Main St. (bet. 3rd & 4th Aves.), Edmonds, 425-774-0650
■ In the hands of a new owner and chef, this Edmonds "neighborhood restaurant" continues to find favor with its Eclectic menu and big country breakfasts; housed in a 1912 building with rural cafe-meets-deli decor, it satisfies with "good, quick" eats; N.B. the signature chilled tomato bisque, available by the quart, is a to-go favorite.

Charlie's Bar & Grill S | 13 | 10 | 15 | $15
Shilshole Marina, 7001 Seaview Ave., 206-783-8338
217 Broadway E. (John St.), 206-323-2535 ◐
◪ These "casual" saloons keep "late hours", which sums up their appeal; defenders of their American menus point to the steak and the "best wings in town", but those accustomed to "better choices" shrug and note at least "you can drink."

Chef Wang ◐S | – | – | – | M
2230 First Ave. (Bell St.), 206-448-5407
Bobby Wang's new Belltown Chinese cultivates a swank, urbane ambiance where patrons can down martinis with their moo shu or go gonzo over giant platterfuls of smoked frogs' legs and gussied-up lobster, garnished to qualify as works of art; inevitably, purists protest "Americanized Chinese food is not real Chinese food."

Chevys Fresh Mex S | 17 | 16 | 15 | $16
19920 44th Ave. W. (200th St.), Lynnwood, 425-776-2000
3702 S. Fife St. (S. 38th St.), Tacoma, 253-472-5800
■ Salsa-heads salute the "inventive" Tex-Mex at this microchain where the "fresh tortillas are a treat" (they're made on-site in a machine Rube Goldberg would envy); parents praise the "perfect family dining", while in the bar "big sombreros" and "powerful margaritas" reign; maybe it's "not real Mexican", but it's "not bad for a chain."

CHEZ SHEA S | 25 | 24 | 24 | $41
Pike Place Mkt., 94 Pike St. (1st Ave.), 206-467-9990
■ It must be the "orgasmic food and decor" – romantics regard this "sexy" Pike Place Market "hideaway" as the "perfect place" to "be proposed to" or "seduce" someone; skinflints flinch at "high prices", but the "adventurous" prix fixe New American menu and "impeccable" service are tops for a "quiet rendezvous"; N.B. chef Amy McCray signed on mid-*Survey,* but the kitchen is known for its consistency.

Chile Pepper, The ⇌ | 16 | 11 | 18 | $14
1427 NW 45th St. (Wallingford Ave.), 206-545-1790
◪ The "authentic" Mexican fare takes "no Americanized short cuts" at this modest Wallingford cantina, which has won a following with its "splendid chile rellenos" and other piquant fare; "friendly service" compensates for the "spartan" surroundings, and if foes sniff "mediocre" no one denies it's "cheap."

| **Seattle** | F | D | S | C |

China Gate ◐ S — 17 | 11 | 15 | $14
516 Seventh Ave. S. (S. King St.), 206-624-1730
■ Revived after a fire shuttered it last year, this International District Chinese has long been a destination for "a wide variety of dim sum" and a menu that presents "lots to choose from"; some of the Suzy Wong look has been renovated away, but the crowds still descend and karaoke still rules late nights in the lounge.

China Harbor S — 12 | 13 | 13 | $18
2040 Westlake Ave. N. (Fairview Ave.), 206-286-1688
◪ That hulking, black-tile façade on Lake Union conceals a monolithic Mandarin that offers "decent" if basic chow; boosters note that "most tables have a view", but critics contend "China should sue for defamation."

Chinoise Café S — 23 | 17 | 18 | $18
12 Boston St. (Queen Anne Ave. N.), 206-284-6671
■ Once an "unknown gem", this Queen Anne Pan-Asian is now "packed and noisy", and the "supremely crafted food" reveals why; as yupscale types mob the "super sushi bar", others settle in to sample "interesting", "tasty dishes", from pad Thai to yaki soba to General Tso's chicken; admirers announce that this "neighborhood place surpasses" the trendsetters for execution and "value."

Chinook's at Salmon Bay S — 19 | 18 | 19 | $21
1900 W. Nickerson St. (SW corner of Ballard Bridge), 206-283-4665
■ "Straightforward, no frills" finfare "fresh off the boat" lures loyalists to this "boisterous" Fisherman's Terminal powerhouse; the daily catch offers "variety galore", and the kitchen is "consistent" in its take on "really good workingman's seafood"; it's a place "to take visitors" and "watch the fishing fleet", with only one drawback: a "decibel level only slightly lower than a Boeing assembly plant."

Christina's S — ▽ 25 | 21 | 21 | $42
Porter Bldg., Main St., 2nd fl. (Horseshoe Hwy.), Eastsound, Orcas Island, 360-376-4904
■ Perched above a remodeled gas station, this waterside jewel is "worth the trip to Orcas" Island to indulge in "ample portions" of "excellent" Northwestern cuisine; chef-owner Christina Orchid builds her menu around quality seafood from area waters, matched with a worthy wine list; "wish it were closer" is the only lament.

Chutneys S — 20 | 16 | 18 | $20
519 First Ave. N. (Mercer St.), 206-284-6799
◪ Champions of this "classy" Queen Anne Indian tout the "tasty tandoori" and the "steal" of a lunch buffet; the unimpressed counter this is "typical" eating that could use "more imaginative specials", and a few worry that "quality is slipping."

Seattle

	F	D	S	C

Chutneys Bistro ⓢ   18 | 15 | 17 | $18
1815 N. 45th St. (Wallingford Ave.), 206-634-1000
◪ Delivering "better-than-average" Indian fare, this "cozy", casual Chutneys spin-off in Wallingford offers a "shorter menu" than its parent, featuring such items as "marvelous" mussels and an Indian-style pizza; detractors sense "expansion woes" and report an "uneven" act that doesn't reach the "standard of the original."

Chutneys Grille on the Hill ⓢ   19 | 17 | 16 | $20
605 15th Ave. E. (Mercer St.), 206-726-1000
◪ A bank of windows overlooks the Capitol Hill street scene at this "relaxed" "neighborhood" Indian where enthusiasts "swoon for the spicy dishes" ("succulent tandoori" is a house specialty) and "great breads"; the menu mimics that of the Queen Anne flagship, though detractors complain things are "not as consistent" here and cite "hit-or-miss" service.

Ciao Bella ⓢ   20 | 17 | 19 | $23
5133 25th Ave. NE (54th St.), 206-524-6989
■ "Sometimes good, sometimes great", this "charming, slightly funky" and definitely "not trendy" U-District Italian pushes a "big selection of pasta" and a list of "satisfying" standards; regulars hint "sit on the patio" and do without the "rather tired" decor.

Ciao Italia Ristorante ⓢ   ▽ 23 | 17 | 23 | $22
546 Fifth Ave. S. (Walnut St.), Edmonds, 425-771-7950
■ "Mamma mia, a bit of Italy without crossing the Atlantic", this "unassuming" trattoria, tucked away in an Edmonds strip mall, offers a "varied and interesting" Italian menu courtesy of the Gerardi brothers, who sling some "excellent" pastas and pizzas; candlelight and Chianti set the mood.

Circa Neighborhood Grill & Ale House ⓢ   ▽ 20 | 17 | 19 | $16
2605 California Ave. SW (Admiral Way), 206-923-1102
■ This "West Seattle watering hole" brings Eclectic pub grub to an area that's "starved for good food", with an "inventive menu" headlined by Oaxaca tacos and other global goodies; the "quaint", "cozy" "neighborhood tavern" setting is equally hospitable for "a few beers" or a lazy weekend brunch.

CJ's Eatery ⓢ   18 | 12 | 18 | $13
2619 First Ave. (Cedar St.), 206-728-1648
■ It may be the eatery formerly known as A. Jay's, but this is still where Belltown breakfasts on "fast, hot and tasty" faves, including thin pancakes, blintzes and sweet rolls; the NYC-style eats are served at lunch and dinner too, and the "pretty plain decor" comes "as close to a deli as possible."

Claim Jumper [S] 17 | 20 | 19 | $19

Redmond Town Ctr., 7210 164th Ave. NE (Bear Creek Pkwy.), Redmond, 425-885-1273

■ "Portions shock" at this rambunctious Redmond link of a Wild West–themed chain where the American menu runs to steaks, ribs, mile-high sandwiches and six-layer chocolate cake; if the "food's not super", it's a surefire "value", so take a number and get in the "long waiting line"; kids of all ages love it.

Cliff House [S] 21 | 23 | 21 | $30

6300 Marine View Dr. NE (Slaydon Rd.), Tacoma, 253-927-0400

■ A "spectacular setting" overlooking Commencement Bay lends this Tacoma Continental a "heavenly" ambiance; the formal upstairs room boasts an "interesting menu" with "creative presentations", and if hedgers find it "not quite up to the price", the more relaxed lower level offers a bistro alternative at a "real value" with the same "killer view."

Coastal Kitchen ◐ [S] 20 | 17 | 17 | $21

429 15th Ave. E. (Republican St.), 206-322-1145

◪ At this "loud, bustling" Capitol Hill "joint", the "innovative" International menu "changes quarterly" to highlight the cuisine of a coastal region (Morocco, Brazil, Tuscany, Yucatán, etc.); many "like the variety", though spoilers claim the results can be "disappointing"; it's also a hit with the "breakfast crowd", and "lines are long" for "housemade granola" and "coffee cake to die for."

Cool Hand Luke's Cafe [S] ⊄ 18 | 11 | 18 | $14

1131 34th Ave. (E. Union St.), 206-324-2553

■ What we've got here is "something for everyone"; the "handwritten chalkboard menu" at Sharon and Curtis Luke's "homey" Madrona "neighborhood dive" lists "unique" Eclectic fare, including "unusual" stir-fries; the "funky" space is "not much to look at", but it attracts a "hip crowd" and a "long weekend wait" is a given.

Copacabana Cafe [S] 16 | 14 | 15 | $16

Pike Place Mkt., 1520½ Pike Pl. (1st Ave.), 206-622-6359

◪ The cuisine is South American at this Pike Place veteran, but "the view and the bustle" are pure Seattle; supporters say "when you want something different" there's "nothing like corn pie" and "spicy shrimp soup", best enjoyed "on the balcony" overlooking the market; cynics snap "too bad you can't eat the view."

Costas Greek Restaurant [S] 15 | 12 | 13 | $17

4559 University Way NE (47th St.), 206-633-2751

◪ "You won't go hungry" at this "decent" Greek, long "a fixture" in the University District, so follow the "garlic smells" for "well-priced" spanakopita, gyros and the like; tough customers contend the cooking's "nothing to write home about", suggesting "try harder."

Costas Opa [S] | 16 | 14 | 16 | $18

3900 Fremont Ave. N. (34th St.), 206-633-4141

◪ "Skillful [Hellenic] cooking" and "old-country" charm win applause for Costas Greek's "better" Fremont sibling, where the dishes arrive in "generous portions" and the "fun" atmo reflects the "kooky neighborhood"; on the downside, service can be "scatterbrained" and the food "a little too American."

Coyote Creek Pizza Co. [S] | 18 | 15 | 16 | $16

15600 NE Eighth St. (156th Ave.), Bellevue, 425-746-7460
228 Central Way (2nd St.), Kirkland, 425-822-2226

■ Pizza partisans are "howling" for the "designer" pies from these "avant-garde" twins out in Bellevue and Kirkland; the "innovative combos" include "the North by Northwest pizza: apples, hazelnuts and Gorgonzola" on a thick, crispy crust – definitely "not your father's pizza."

Crab Cracker [S] | 19 | 17 | 19 | $30

(fka Franco's Crab Cracker)
452 Central Way (Lake Ave.), Kirkland, 425-827-8700

◪ Ichthyophagous partisans praise the "wonderful treatment of seafood" at this casual, "noisy" Downtown Kirkland entry, where bisque and "fresh crab cocktails" lead off a menu dominated by crustacean classics; a few doubters dismiss it as an "overpriced fried-fish house."

Credenzia's Oven | – | – | – | M

10 Mercer St. (Queen Anne Ave. N.), 206-284-4664

This Lower Queen Anne bakery and cafe recently morphed into a full-fledged Mediterranean overseen by chef Laura Dewell (ex the now defunct but much praised Pirosmani); artisanal breads, soups, pizza, panini and pastries satisfy by day, while more substantial dishes (seafood paella, hearty stews) dominate at dinner; a pair of stunning stone ovens and hand-hewn wood furnishings evoke the intended Eastern European village atmosphere.

Crêpe de Paris | 19 | 16 | 18 | $27

Rainier Sq., 1333 Fifth Ave. (Union St.), 206-623-4111

◪ They're open for lunch during the week, but twilight dining and the "usually hilarious" "cabaret shows" are the "real treat" at this French Downtowner; fans cheer for "yummy crêpes" and "fantastic desserts" – even if a few phobes muse "like France, it's seen better days."

Crocodile Cafe [S] | 14 | 13 | 12 | $12

2200 Second Ave. (Blanchard St.), 206-448-2114

◪ It's the "hip environment", "neat art" and live bands that capture Gen Xers at this "fun and funky" Belltown Eclectic, where scenesters show up for "breakfast/brunch" and slouch back later for "stiff drinks" and "decent bar food"; wholesome options like a veggie Reuben are featured on the "earthy" menu, but detractors still grumble about more "grease than you can shake a french fry at."

Seattle | **F** | **D** | **S** | **C** |

Cucina! Cucina! S | 15 | 16 | 15 | $19 |
Chandler's Cove, 901 Fairview Ave. N. (Mercer St.), 206-447-2782
Bellevue Pl., 800 Bellevue Way (NE 8th St.), Bellevue,
425-637-1177
Carillon Point, 2220 Carillon Point (Lakeview Dr.), Kirkland,
425-822-4000
Redmond Town Ctr., 16499 NE 74th St. (166th Ave.),
Redmond, 425-558-2200
Southcenter Mall, 17770 Southcenter Pkwy. (S. 180th St.),
Tukwila, 206-575-0520
2031 S. 316th St. (off 320th St.), Federal Way, 253-941-4800
Pickering Pl., 1510 11th Ave. NW (56th St.), Issaquah,
425-391-3800
4201 S. Steele St. (opp. Tacoma Mall), Tacoma, 253-475-6000
◪ The "party atmosphere" at these "kid-friendly", "formula Italians" is spurred on by loud decor, "sassy servers" and "bowling alley" acoustics; "nutty" doings notwithstanding, they're "reliable" for pastas, pizza and "great chopped salad", though dissenters detect "more scene than cuisine" and chant "inconsistent! inconsistent!"

Cutters Bayhouse S | 19 | 20 | 19 | $26 |
Pike Place Mkt., 2001 Western Ave. (Virginia St.), 206-448-4884
■ Adjoining Pike Place Market, this seafood-centric Elliott Bay "institution" can get "very touristy", but Brad Komen's "consistent", globally influenced American cuisine is capturing locals' attention too; good for "all ages", it draws a majority "yup" crowd in to admire the "bay view" (and one another) over "drinks and appetizers"; depending on your taste, the recent remodel either "looks great" or is "garish" enough to "scare the fish."

DAHLIA LOUNGE S | 26 | 24 | 23 | $34 |
1904 Fourth Ave. (Stewart St.), 206-682-4142
■ Chef-restaurateur Tom Douglas' firstborn is in full bloom, with a menu of "flavorful, Asian-influenced" Northwest cuisine that extends the "food as art" philosophy from "innovative entrees" to "incredible daily specials"; the "eccentric, stylish" Downtown room exudes "comfort and elegance", and the "top-notch" staff pays "amazing attention to detail"; overall it's "one classy joint" that can deliver "a sublime experience."

Daniel's Broiler S | 24 | 23 | 23 | $37 |
200 Lake Washington Blvd. (Alder St.), 206-329-4191
10500 NE Eighth St. (Bellevue Way), Bellevue, 425-462-4662
■ "Steaks as good as they get" and "beautiful views" from opposite shores of Lake Washington distinguish this couple of "elegant" cow palaces; whether for a quick "steak and martini" or a "special occasion", they follow through with "excellent service" and a winning wine list; it's all "a tad pricey" and "a little stuffy", but the meat-eating majority "continues to be impressed."

Seattle

| | F | D | S | C |

Dash Point Lobster Shop S | 20 | 20 | 20 | $32
6912 Soundview Dr. NE (Dash Point Rd.), Tacoma, 253-927-1513
Lobster Shop South S
4013 Ruston Way (McCarver St.), Tacoma, 253-759-2165
◪ These Tacoma siblings are known for their "delicious lobster bisque", though voters are split like an Australian lobster tail as to whether the "great seafood at charming Dash Point" is superior to the larger Ruston Way branch, which dissenters declare is "better than the original"; a few crabs complain that, at both, the tab is too "expensive."

Da Vinci's Flying Pizza S | 13 | 12 | 13 | $18
89 Kirkland Ave. (Lake St.), Kirkland, 425-889-9000
◪ "People-watching" and "pizza on the patio" are why the young and the restless frequent this waterside Kirklander, even if some snort "they call that pizza?"; after dark, it becomes a "dance bar" that attracts a "twentysomething pickup crowd" who do not live by mozzarella alone.

Delcambre's Ragin' Cajun | 19 | 11 | 19 | $14
1523 First Ave. (bet. Pike & Pine Sts.), 206-624-2598
■ At this taste of N'Awlins near the Pike Place Market, "inspirational" chef-owner Danny Delcambre dishes up Cajun cookin' in a casual cafe staffed by the deaf, who "all know sign language" (Delcambre himself is hearing- and sight-impaired); regulars rate the jambalaya "top-shelf."

Delfino's Chicago Style Pizzeria S | 20 | 12 | 15 | $14
2675 NE University Village (NE 45th St. & 25th Ave. NE), 206-522-3466
■ Devotees declare this bustling University Village entry "different from the average pizza place" on evidence of its "excellent" "Chicago-style" deep-dish pies; but the chewy stuffed spinach number is the connoisseur's choice.

Deluxe Bar & Grill ●S | 13 | 10 | 13 | $15
625 Broadway E. (Roy St.), 206-324-9697
◪ A "vibrant Capitol Hill crowd" hangs at this decades-old "greasy spoon" where such American basics as burgers send everyone away "feeling full"; it's "funky" "fun" for the "casual and young", but old-timers gripe about "the noise and the smoke" and observe it "needs a good scrubbing."

Desert Fire S | 18 | 21 | 17 | $21
Pacific Pl., 600 Pine St. (6th Ave.), 206-405-3400
Redmond Town Ctr., 7211 166th Ave. NE (Bear Creek Pkwy.), Redmond, 425-895-1500
◪ The "beautiful" sand-hued decor at these Southwestern newcomers gives the room a "pleasant" sun-bleached feel, but the cuisine gets a mixed reaction; supporters cite "innovative" items, including "light" sandwiches and salads, while dissenters dismiss the "formula menu" as "limited" ("chicken, chicken or chicken").

Seattle | F | D | S | C |

Dick's Drive-In ●S⊟ | 15 | 9 | 15 | $6 |
12325 30th Ave. NE (Lake City Way), 206-363-7777
500 Queen Anne Ave. N. (Republican St.), 206-285-5155
9208 Holman Rd. NW (12th Ave.), 206-783-5233
111 NE 45th St. (bet. 1st & 2nd Aves.), 206-632-5125
115 Broadway E. (bet. Denny Way & John St.), 206-323-1300
■ "Cheap, quick and open late", these hamburger havens provide "instant gratification" for "starving students" and seekers of "late-night eats", rating No. 1 for Bang for the Buck in the Seattle *Survey*; fans are fervent about the "greasy burgers" chased with the "best fries on earth" and "best shakes in the universe", affirming this "quintessential" fat food "puts fast food to shame."

Dimitriou's Jazz Alley S | 13 | 17 | 15 | $28 |
2033 Sixth Ave. (Lenora St.), 206-441-9729
■ Music lovers advise "feast with your ears" at this "cool", spacious Downtown club where the "overpriced" Eclectic "food is only fair but the jazz that follows is the best"; keeping in mind that "music is the main ingredient" here, regulars stick to "cocktails and the pizza-type snack that's unbeatable."

Dish, The S⊟ | ▽ 21 | 18 | 21 | $10 |
4358 Leary Ave. NW (8th Ave.), 206-782-9985
◪ This "pint-sized" Fremont "breakfast spot" does lunch too, so late risers can order up an all-American spread featuring a well-built BLT, potato salad with plenty of egg, corned beef hash and "delicious spuds"; it aims to appease the hungriest, even if hedgers grouse it has yet to "live up to" its promise; future plans call for a patio.

Duke's Chowderhouse S | 16 | 15 | 16 | $21 |
7805 Greenlake Dr. N. (78th St.), 206-522-4908
901 Fairview Ave. N. (south end of Lake Union), 206-382-9963
23 Lake Bellevue Dr. (NE 8th St.), Bellevue, 206-455-5775
◪ "Dependable" seafood and "decent value" draw loyalists to these "after-work" or "post-game" "standbys" for "chowder and cheeseburgers", salads and "terrific fries"; there's "no decor" to admire, though the lakeside locations boast "great" views; a disenchanted minority mutters about the "generic" "heart attack menu."

Dulces Latin Bistro S | 19 | 19 | 19 | $28 |
1430 34th Ave. (bet. E. Pike & E. Union Sts.), 206-322-5453
◪ A "dark", "romantic" setting qualifies this "cozy Latin bistro" in Madrona as "a real escape", with a seasonal menu listing a "wonderful variety" of "lovely" Mediterranean fare from paella to cassoulet; critics counter that it's "overrated and too expensive" and even the "very good service" can "falter"; puffers can repose in the clubby, fireplace-equipped cigar room.

Eating Factory, The [S] | 15 | 12 | 13 | $18
Gelati Pl., 10630 NE Eighth St. (106th Ave.), Bellevue, 425-688-8202
◪ "It really is a factory" say those who line up for the Japanese eats at this Bellevue buffet; maybe the sushi is just "ok", but it's "a good deal" and the all-you- can-eat format is "popular with students"; regulars simply advise "go hungry!"

Eggs Cetera's Blue Star Cafe & Pub [S] | 17 | 14 | 16 | $14
4512 Stone Way Ave. N. (bet. 45th & 46th Sts.), 206-548-0345
◪ Griddle gourmands can start their day with a "good breakfast" at this spartan Wallingford American; later on, a "pub grub" crowd comes to check out the "great choice of beer"; however, a few cynics gaze at this star and shrug "nothing shines."

El Camino ◐ [S] | 21 | 19 | 17 | $21
607 N. 35th St. (Fremont Ave.), 206-632-7303
■ The heart of funky Fremont pumps to the "hopping bar scene" and "fresh and authentic" fare at this "always lively" cantina; the "range of titillating dishes" is "not your typical Mexican", and those who mourn the "haphazard service" are outnumbered by devotees who love the "flair"; sipping "killer" "margaritas on the deck" is a local pastime.

EL GAUCHO ◐ [S] | 23 | 23 | 24 | $46
2505 First Ave. (Wall St.), 206-728-1337
◪ "Power steaks" coalesce with cigars, martinis and a piano bar in a "sexy" "supper club" setting to make this Belltown American a favorite for "show-off dinners"; flaming entrees, "tableside salad and dessert preparation", and "unparalleled" service all add to the "retro" effect; the scene strikes some as "pretentious", though, and the penny-wise warn "better be on an expense account" – "El Gouge-o is more like it."

El Greco [S] | 23 | 18 | 19 | $18
219 Broadway E. (bet. John & Thomas Sts.), 206-328-4604
■ Thomas and Carol Soukakos stress "attention to detail" at their petite, "lovely" Capitol Hill Mediterranean, and the payoff is some of the "best food on Broadway"; "interesting" ways to go include Hellenistic specialties, a "great veggie combo plate" and a well-attended weekend brunch.

Elliott's Oyster House [S] | 21 | 19 | 20 | $28
Pier 56 (Alaskan Way & Spring St.), 206-673-4340
■ It may be a "typical Seattle" fish house on the Downtown waterfront, but it delivers the goods with "fabulous fresh oysters, great Dungeness crab" and other "quality seafood (and plenty of it)" served by a "friendly" staff; in "summer, the tourists take over", but natives go year-round to indulge in oyster slurping and 'tini tippling dockside or in the handsome bar; N.B. an interior remodel is planned for '99.

Seattle   F | D | S | C

El Niño Restaurant & Tequila Bar S   15 | 18 | 16 | $20
113 Virginia St. (bet. 1st & 2nd Aves.), 206-441-5454
■ The kitchen is still finding its footing at this "trendy" Mexican "hot spot" near the Pike Place Market that offers "numerous tequilas" (more than 30); lunch is low-key, dinner dynamic and late-night a fiesta when a DJ takes over, turning the contempo space into an impromptu disco.

El Puerco Lloron S   21 | 14 | 13 | $11
1501 Western Ave. (Pike Pl. Hillclimb), 206-624-0541
■ This "rustic dive" is the "people's place" for "knockout" Mexican on the Pike Street Hillclimb; grab a tray and get in line for "terrific handmade tortillas" and taquitos that connoisseurs call "the real thing" – meaning "cheap" as well as "tasty."

Emmett Watson's Oyster Bar S ⊄ 18 | 13 | 15 | $14
Pike Place Mkt., 1916 Pike Pl. (bet. Stewart & Virginia Sts.), 206-448-7721
◪ "Delicious chowder", "better fish 'n' chips than Ivar's" and, of course, "great oysters" draw the faithful to this "very casual" Pike Place Market "hole-in-the-wall" named for the H. L. Mencken of the Jet City; spoilers howl "tourist trap" and say it merits attention for "historical reasons" only.

Entros World Grill S   16 | 20 | 16 | $24
823 Yale Ave. N. (bet. Aloha & Valley Sts.), 206-624-0057
◪ Cuisine plays a "supporting" role to the "carnival atmosphere" at this "adult amusement park" installed in a warehouse near Lake Union; although boosters maintain the "hearty" fusion fare is "better than you'd expect", detractors deem the grub "not great" and advise "the games are the real deal" – "eat somewhere else first."

Eques S   17 | 21 | 19 | $31
Hyatt Regency Hotel, 900 Bellevue Way NE (8th St.), Bellevue, 425-462-1234
◪ The formal dining room of Bellevue's glitz-and-glass Hyatt Regency puts up a "sophisticated" front that outclasses its "standard hotel" menu, which offers Northwestern takes on seafood and grilled meats; the food "tries to be really great and sometimes makes it", and early birds chirp over the "solid" morning fare ("wonderful pecan French toast"), but critics complain of "small portions" and cry "overpriced."

ETTA'S SEAFOOD S   25 | 21 | 22 | $30
2020 Western Ave. (bet. Lenora & Virginia Sts.), 206-443-6000
■ "Tom Douglas does seafood" at this "upbeat" eatery "on the water" that's noted for its "daring", "innovative approach" and "first-class ingredients" – the "exquisite salmon" is pit-roasted and spice-rubbed, and the sashimi and crab cakes are "unsurpassed"; too "trendy" for some, its proximity to Pike Place Market makes it "hard to get in" and, inevitably, "touristy."

Seattle

| | F | D | S | C |

Ezell's Fried Chicken S ⊄   22 | 7 | 13 | $9
7531 196th St. SW (76th St.), Lynnwood, 425-673-4193
501 23rd Ave. (E. Jefferson St.), 206-324-4141
■ "Colonel who?"; with the opening of a Lynnwood fledgling, the Central District's "in spot" for the "juiciest" crispy "finger lickin'" chicken ("spicy is the best"), sweet potato pie and popovers is now twice as "damn tasty"; so what if they "need atmosphere" and service is "uneven" – this is "the real thing"; N.B. takeout only.

Famous Pacific Dessert Co. S   20 | 12 | 13 | $10
516 Broadway E. (Republican St.), 206-328-1950
127 Mercer St. (Warren Ave. N.), 206-284-8100
◪ "Skip supper and celebrate" at these twin peaks of "sensual indulgence" where linzertorte, New Orleans cake and the chocolate velvet dome are just a few of the temptations "to die for"; they're designated "after-theater stops" for seekers of a "sugar high", and late arrivals risk "slim pickings"; skeptics are sour on the "slow" service, however, and argue these sweets are "overrated."

Figaro Bistro S   – | – | – | M
11 Roy St. (Mercer St.), 206-284-6465
Devotees of this "blissful", "oh-so-French" Lower Queen Anne bistro are grateful for some "variety near the opera house"; the menu emphasizes "simple" fare like steak frites, bouillabaisse and cassoulet, served up in an arty, urban setting that's dim and romantic, though hard surfaces and high ceilings offset the intimacy; prices are *gentil*.

Filiberto's   18 | 13 | 16 | $20
14401 Des Moines Memorial Dr. (144th St.), 206-248-1944
■ "Now that'sa Italiano" say admirers of this "out-of-the-way" Des Moines trattoria serving authentic pasta and what some call the "best pizza" around; regulars report the patio is the primo spot to enjoy a little bocce and gnocchi.

Firenze Ristorante Italiano S   ▽ 19 | 15 | 17 | $23
Crossroads Mall, 15600 NE Eighth St. (156th Ave.), Bellevue, 425-957-1077
◪ "Don't let the mall address fool you" say supporters of this Bellevue Italian – the setting may be modest, but plenty of pride surfaces in the Med-style meats and pastas; even so, nonfans sniff it's "adequate but nothing special."

5 Spot ◐ S   18 | 18 | 17 | $17
1502 Queen Anne Ave. N. (Galer St.), 206-285-7768
■ "Down-home cooking" makes this "cool" American "a frequent lifesaver" for "Queen Anne's twentysomethings"; the "rotating" regional menu highlights a different part of the country every few months, and the "decor changes with the season"; it's a hit morning, noon and night, and "long lines" and "long waits" (especially for a "terrific large breakfast" of "way-out huevos") are standard.

Seattle

| | F | D | S | C |

FLYING FISH ●S 25 | 22 | 21 | $33
2234 First Ave. (Bell St.), 206-728-8595

☑ "Fish from all over the world" surface at this "super-trendy", "high-energy" Belltown seafooder where chef-owner Christine Keff works "Asian-inspired culinary magic" to create "crowd-pleasers" like whole fried snapper, wok-seared "crab by the pound" and other "magnificent" presentations of "superbly prepared" aquatics; it's a "fun and sophisticated" scene, but phobes frown on "uneven quality", "slow service" and "the din" – "what's the big deal?"

Foghorn S 17 | 16 | 17 | $28
6023 Lake Washington Blvd. (NE 60th St.), Kirkland, 425-827-0654

☑ It has "been there forever", and loyalists hold the seafood is "getting more creative" at this Kirkland "gem", whose "outstanding" waterfront view compensates for its "dated" decor; even so, a few naysayers knock the menu as "mediocre" and "overpriced"; P.S. this is your chance to get there "by boat."

Four Seas S 18 | 15 | 17 | $20
714 S. King St. (8th Ave.), 206-682-4900

☑ This enormous International District Chinese serves some of this town's "best dim sum" and has become a "standby" for hordes of aficionados; despite a "cooperative staff", some flee the chaotic main floor and "only eat in the bar."

14 Carrot Cafe S 17 | 12 | 13 | $14
2305 Eastlake Ave. E. (E. Lynn St.), 206-324-1442

☑ Morning people proclaim the "fabulous omelets", blueberry pancakes and coffee cake "worth the wait" at this "fantastic breakfast nook" and "health food cafe" in Eastlake; the "hippie wholesome cooking" and "beautiful view of Lake Union" are a "charming" combo, but a small band of opponents objects it's "packed, small, noisy and hot."

Frankfurter, The ∌ 15 | 8 | 12 | $6
226 S. Orcas St. (3rd Ave.), 206-763-9669
1023 Alaskan Way (bet. Madison & Spring Sts.), 206-622-1748 S
213 Marion St. (bet. 2nd & 3rd Aves.), 206-382-0897
Seattle Ctr., 305 Harrison St. (5th Ave. N.), 206-728-7243 S
Columbia Ctr., 709 Fifth Ave. (Cherry St.), 206-623-1653
11020 Eighth Ave. NE (Northgate Way), 206-367-7569 S
Crossroads Mall, 15600 NE Eighth St. (156th Ave. NE), Bellevue, 425-746-8607 S
Bellevue Sq., 215 Bellevue Sq., Bellevue, 425-455-4492 S

■ Hot "diggety dogs and lemonade Scarlett would've loved" draw "street food" fanatics to these "convenient" "hole-in-the-wall" nosheries; standouts include the "good kosher dogs", "awesome cheese dogs", handmade "spicy Italian" sausages, bockwurst "with all the trimmings" and even a "surprisingly good" low-fat "Thai chicken dog"; there's "quick service when you're in a hurry" too.

Seattle | F | D | S | C |

Fremont Classic Pizzeria S | 19 | 13 | 19 | $15 |
4307 Fremont Ave. N. (43rd St.), 206-548-9411

■ A "very small place" that's "big on friendliness", this "off-the-beaten-path" "neighborhood" Italian in funky Fremont is beloved for its thin-crust pies and comprehensive "selection of pizza toppings"; there's also pasta, calamari, a "garlicky Caesar" and tiramisu, all "cheap" and "unexpectedly good."

Fremont Noodle House S | 20 | 18 | 16 | $13 |
3411 Fremont Ave. N. (bet. 34th & 35th Sts.), 206-547-1550

■ "Oodles of good noodles" offer the most "for the money" at this "pleasantly dark", art-filled Fremont Thai with "authentic" "comfort food"; advocates come in to "warm up" with fragrant "bowls of broth" and "never pass up *meing kahm* [leaf-wrapped Thai chile]."

FULLERS | 27 | 25 | 25 | $46 |
Sheraton Hotel & Towers, 1400 Sixth Ave. (bet. Pike & Union Sts.), 206-447-5544

■ It's an "art gallery" exhibiting "top-flight" food say admirers of this Downtowner's "exquisite" style; celeb chef Monique Barbeau has passed the toque to her sous, Tom Black, but surveyors remain enthusiastic about the "dramatic" Northwestern meat-and-seafood menu and "gracious service"; a minority grumbles it's too "expensive", "stuffy and conservative", but it remains "a must for the self-respecting gourmet."

F.X. McRory's S | 17 | 18 | 17 | $24 |
419 Occidental Ave. S. (King St.), 206-623-4800

◪ "Proximity to the Kingdome" ensures this "highly charged" "jock bar" is often "crowded", "loud and boozy", with a "saloon feel" that extends to the dining room and its "uncomplicated", "macho" menu of "prime rib, whiskey" and "great oysters"; operating like a "well-run factory", it gets results ranging from "really good" to "a little bland."

Galerias S | 21 | 21 | 19 | $19 |
210 Broadway E. (bet. John & Thomas Sts.), 206-322-5757

■ Converts "want to move to Mexico" after sampling the "authentic" "regional" cuisine served in a "gorgeous" Spanish-style setting at this Capitol Hill Mexican; the "fabulous flavors" arrive in "good-sized portions", and a "helpful staff" adds to the charm; the second-floor venue makes it "hard to locate" but a real find.

Gaspare's Ristorante S | 20 | 16 | 20 | $26 |
8051 Lake City Way NE (15th Ave. NE), 206-524-3866

■ A "favorite neighborhood spot" on the North End for "terrific" Southern Italian specialties, this trattoria is known for the "family touch" of husband-and-wife team Gaspare and Diane Trani, who provide "genuine hospitality" in a "warm and cozy" "Little Italy" setting; it can get "crowded and noisy", but hey, that's Italian.

Seattle | F | D | S | C |

GEORGIAN ROOM S | 25 | 28 | 26 | $51 |
Four Seasons Olympic Hotel, 411 University St. (bet. 4th & 5th Aves.), 206-621-7889
■ "Guys, dust off your jackets", 'cause Downtown's "grande dame" is still unmatched for "elegant hotel dining"; it boasts "beautiful", ornate decor that scores No. 1 in the Seattle *Survey*, and new exec chef Gavin Stephenson oversees an "outstanding" Pacific NW seasonal menu complemented by a vast wine list; whether for "power breakfast" or to "celebrate an occasion", it's "pricey but worth it" for a "fabulous" dining experience in an oh-so-"civilized" milieu.

Gordito's S⊅ | – | – | – | I |
213 N. 85th St. (Greenwood Ave.), 206-706-9352
True believers "go hungry and go often" to this "healthy, unassuming" Mexican, a "bargain-priced" Greenwood cantina offering "quick" service and portions that verge on "too much"; word is spreading on the "outstanding" eats, so locals plead "don't tell a soul."

Gordon Biersch ●◑S | – | – | – | M |
Pacific Pl., 600 Pike St., 4th fl. (6th Ave.), 206-405-4205
An offshoot of a California chain, this sleek new Downtown brewpub in Pacific Place boasts a something-for-everyone, Asian-Western fusion menu running from upscale comfort food to casual bar bites; the space is split into a cavernous dining room and an out-front bar where singles mingle.

Grady's Grillhouse S | 14 | 9 | 12 | $14 |
(fka Grady's Montlake Pub)
2307 24th Ave. E. (McGraw St.), 206-726-5968
◪ So what if the all-American "pub grub" is only "average" at this "friendly" Montlaker?; and who needs "charm" when there's plenty of beer on tap and a "big-screen TV" to goggle at while munching on a house specialty prime rib sandwich?

Gravity Bar S | 18 | 17 | 12 | $13 |
Broadway Mkt., 415 Broadway E. (bet. Harrison & Republican Sts.), 206-325-7186
■ A "must" for "macrobiotics" or "raw food lovers", this Capitol Hill Vegetarian juice bar cultivates a "cool", "post-apocalyptic" look that appeals to a mostly "young crowd" that arrives ready to "get juiced"; "the food is reliable and interesting, and the service is at least interesting."

Grazie Ristorante Italiano S | 18 | 16 | 16 | $21 |
Factoria Shopping Ctr., 3820 124th Ave. SE (I-90 & I-405), Bellevue, 425-644-1200
23207 Bothell-Everett Hwy. SE (232nd St.), Bothell, 425-402-9600
16943 Southcenter Pkwy. (Strander Blvd.), Tukwila, 206-575-1606
◪ Regulars report the food at these "suburban" Italians is "sometimes fabulous, sometimes ho-hum", but always "oozes garlic"; they work best for a "relaxing" bite of "good pasta", but grow "noisy and crowded" at peak hours.

Seattle   F | D | S | C

Green Cat Cafe S   21 | 17 | 12 | $12
1514 E. Olive Way (Denny Way), 206-726-8756
◼ On the cusp where Capitol Hill meets Downtown, a "great mix of people" frequents this "crunchy granola" haven to dig into "delicious veggie fare"; early risers can stoke up on scones, caramel rolls and "breakfast potatoes worth getting out of bed for"; the cramped quarters have been expanded, beer and wine are available and there's now table service at dinner (though it may be "erratic").

Hale's Ales Brewpub S   16 | 16 | 15 | $15
4301 Leary Way NW (43rd St.), 206-782-0737
◼ This huge Fremont brewpub is a "fun place" "to kick back and enjoy" "good conversation", "some of the best ales" in town and "a quick bite"; the "hearty", "above-average pub grub" includes "great soups", "awesome pizza and must-have BBQ chicken sandwiches", but detractors say the "kitchen is an afterthought."

Hattie's Hat S   15 | 12 | 15 | $13
5231 Ballard Ave. NW (20th Ave.), 206-784-0175
■ A "favorite haunt of the music crowd", this "somewhat dreary dive" in Ballard is "great for what it is" – a "smoky" watering hole with "cheap drinks", live entertainment and "retro decor"; while the Traditional American menu (along with some Scandinavian specialties) is merely "filling", the food is worth ordering if only because "the cooks are real characters."

Herbfarm, The S   – | – | – | VE
32804 Issaquah-Fall City Rd. (328th Ave. SE), Fall City, 206-784-2222
"Legendary and awesome but not yet rebuilt" after a fire destroyed it in 1997, this fabled outpost will temporarily occupy a 40-seat wine-aging room at the Hedges Cellars Winery in Issaquah (15 miles from the farm site in Fall City) beginning in May; there, chef Jerry Traunfeld will once again create his "exquisite" "once-in-a-lifetime experience for the palate" for the few lucky gourmands who "can get a reservation" to indulge in a "superb" NW-accented New American prix fixe feast.

Heron Beach Inn   ▽ 22 | 21 | 22 | $41
at Ludlow Bay S
Heron Beach Inn, 1 Heron Beach Inn, Port Ludlow, 360-437-0411
■ Outside this sprawling inn on the Olympic Peninsula, stately verandas welcome diners inside to a cozy lounge with a fireplace and an airy dining room that's as gracious and relaxed as the smiling servers; chef Joseph Merkling's expertly prepared Pacific NW cuisine delights with vividly flavored Asian-accented meats, seafood and produce, much of it locally purveyed; only dinner is served and yes, it's expensive but worth it.

Seattle | F | D | S | C |

Hidden Harbour ▣ | 17 | 15 | 18 | $26 |
(fka Franco's Hidden Harbour)
1500 Westlake Ave. N. (Lake Union), 206-282-0501
◪ Those who contend this American seafooder on Lake Union has "been there for years" and "never changes" take note: new owner Petter Petterson has dropped Franco's name but is reviving some of his classic dishes, as well as adding some Scandinavian specialties; the retro chic, "smoky throwback to the '60s bar" carries on as before.

Hilltop Ale House ▣ | 20 | 16 | 18 | $15 |
2129 Queen Anne Ave. N. (Boston St.), 206-285-3877
■ "Primo pub grub" and a "great beer selection" distinguish this "blue jeans–chic" Queen Anne tavern that reminds some of *Cheers*; the gang swears that "everything's a hit" on the "honest" American-Eclectic menu, especially the "fabulous halibut cakes"; the tables are "crammed close", which may be what makes the place so "friendly."

Hi-Spot Cafe ▣ | 21 | 17 | 18 | $16 |
1410 34th Ave. (bet. Pike & Union Sts.), 206-325-7905
■ "Wear your Birkenstocks" to this "totally funky" Eclectic set in a "cool old" Victorian house in Madrona that's filled with "romantic nooks and crannies"; chef and co-owner Joanne Segura will "tantalize your taste buds" with "perfect" "homestyle breakfasts" of the "best scones in the universe" and "fantastic" omelets; "on a nice day, eat outside" on the "unbeatable patio."

Honey Bear Bakery ▣⊘ | 19 | 14 | 15 | $8 |
2106 N. 55th St. (Meridian Ave.), 206-545-7296
◪ "Artsy refugees from the '60s" and "UW students" are among the "granola bunch" that hang at this "quaint", "hippy-dippy" bakery and Vegetarian cafe in Wallingford; "scrumptious cakes", "killer pumpkin muffins", huge cinnamon buns and other "baked treats" join an array of "healthy" sandwiches and salads; foes, though, gripe about a staff that's "not customer-friendly."

Honey Court ◐▣ | 20 | 11 | 16 | $15 |
516 Maynard Ave. (Weller St.), 206-292-8828
■ "Long live the fresh salt-and-pepper prawns, crab and rock cod" at this "dependable", late-night Cantonese-Mandarin in the International District, one of "the best Asian seafood" houses in town; it's also renowned for "yummy" BBQ pork and the "set meals are a bargain for the price."

Hong's Garden ▣ | 21 | 14 | 19 | $15 |
64 Rainier Ave. S. (Airport Way), Renton, 425-228-6332
■ Opened five years ago by the original owners of the House of Hong, this modest Renton strip mall Chinese "satisfies cravings" for "outstanding dim sum"; "great for the family", this "favorite" also offers solid Cantonese and Szechuan entrees later in the day at inexpensive prices.

House of Hong [S] 17 | 13 | 16 | $16

409 Eighth Ave. (Jackson St.), 206-622-7997

◪ This large, bustling I-District Chinese features "fresh seafood", notably "wonderful whole sweet-and-sour rock cod", but it's the most "fun for dim sum" say locals, who like the "variety"; also "try the take-out counter near the front window – you can watch your BBQ pork being precision-cut"; foes, however, cite "greasy food" and a "pushy" staff.

Hunan Garden [S] 17 | 11 | 17 | $17

11814 NE Eighth St. (118th Ave.), Bellevue, 425-451-3595

◪ Champions think this Bellevue standby is "one of the best places for Chinese food on the Eastside", but critics claim the "mediocre" (albeit "dependable") fare – like the setting – is "reminiscent of a bygone era"; still, the prices are "average" and the takeout convenient.

HUNT CLUB [S] 25 | 24 | 24 | $42

Sorrento Hotel, 900 Madison St. (Terry Ave.), 206-343-6156

■ "Dark, romantic and cozy", the "understated elegance" of this "clubby" room on First Hill perfectly reflects the "old-world charm" of the "lovely Sorrento Hotel"; chef Brian Scheehser's "gourmet" Northwest cuisine, enhanced by "impeccable" Mediterranean flavors, is "a wild game lover's paradise"; while some say it's "stuffy", most maintain it's swell for "a special occasion."

icon Grill ◐ [S] 17 | 21 | 18 | $29

1933 Fifth Ave. (Virginia St.), 206-441-6330

◪ The "sexy", pink gewgaw-strewn decor goes "a bit overboard" for some, but "tongue-in-cheek" excess is the point of this splashy, late-night Downtown newcomer; while some applaud "a smashing debut" with the "ultimate American comfort food", others point to "growing pains" among the staff in the dining room and the kitchen.

Il Bacio [S] 23 | 17 | 21 | $25

16564 Cleveland St. (164th St.), Redmond, 425-869-8815

■ Chef-owner Rino Baglio and his wife, Patsy, "pay attention to the details" at their "unpretentious" Northern Italian trattoria in Redmond; "don't be fooled by the exterior" or the "terrible" Eastside location, because behind the strip mall facade is "unrushed service", live music and "fantastic food that keeps you going back for more."

Il Bistro ◐ [S] 23 | 23 | 21 | $33

Pike Place Mkt., 93-A Pike St. (1st Ave.), 206-682-2154

■ "Still holding its own" after two dozen years, this "cave-like" "romantic" "hideaway" set in an alley below Pike Place Market serves "consistently" "wonderful" Italian food – the signature Caesar salad, seafood pastas and rack of lamb are "first-rate"; an "excellent bartender" oversees the "intimate", "smoky" bar, which locals keep "hoppin' till the late night."

il fiasco world bistro [S] ▽ 18 | 21 | 18 | $34

1309 Commercial St. (bet. Holly & Magnolia Sts.), Bellingham, 360-676-9136

■ Once the "gem of Bellingham", this "fine establishment" changed ownership post-*Survey* and replaced its menu with an International one; the atmosphere remains pleasant, so the drive up north is still worth considering.

Il Fornaio [S] – | – | – | M

Pacific Pl., 600 Pine St. (6th Ave.), 206-264-0994

Marble and murals adorn this Medici-esque chain outlet, which occupies a two-story corner of Pacific Place; it's outfitted with a bakery, a quick-service risotteria and an elegant dining room (plus a sandwich cafe in the center of the mall's atrium), covering the spectrum of fresh, rustic Italian fare.

Il Gambero 19 | 18 | 21 | $26

2132 First Ave. (Blanchard St.), 206-448-8597

◪ Made for "romance", this candlelit Belltown yearling charms with "authentic" Southern Italian specialties prepared by chef-owner Gaspare Trani and delivered by an "attentive" staff in a "comfortable", brick-walled room; but while some praise the fare as "exquisite and delicious", others yawn "nothing special."

I Love Sushi [S] 23 | 14 | 19 | $24

1001 Fairview Ave. N. (Mercer St.), 206-625-9604

11818 NE Eighth St. (116th Ave.), Bellevue, 425-454-5706

■ Sit at the "friendliest sushi bar in the city" and watch "phenomenally fresh fish" become sushi that's "as good as it gets"; "ask the sushi chefs" at these Bellevue and Lake Union Japanese twins "to make their own off-the-menu creations and you are in for" a "memorable" "treat"; "a finer spider roll you will never find", so forgive the "plain decor."

IL TERRAZZO CARMINE 26 | 24 | 24 | $38

411 First Ave. S. (bet. Jackson & King Sts.), 206-467-7797

■ Owner Carmine Smeraldo, "the godfather of Seattle's Italian food scene", is "always there to greet" the "sophisticated clientele" that frequents this "stylish", "festive" "standout" near Pioneer Square; expect "white-glove treatment all the way" and "few compromises on the authentic" menu, composed of "first-class" Northern specialties like "great venison farfalle"; "important dinner coming up and want to impress? – go here."

India House [S] 18 | 14 | 15 | $18

4737 Roosevelt Way NE (bet. 47th & 50th Sts.), 206-632-5072

◪ While this 30-year-old U-District Indian is "nothing fancy", disciples laud the staff's "warm hospitality" and the kitchen's "consummate knowledge of spicing"; delight in "excellent tandoori preparations", "chicken *korma* to dream about" and "great lamb" dishes, all "cooked with care."

Seattle

	F	D	S	C

INN AT LANGLEY   26 | 25 | 25 | $48
Inn at Langley, 400 First St. (Park Ave.), Langley, Whidbey Island, 360-221-3033

■ Open for dinner on weekends only, this relaxed Whidbey Island inn provides an "incredible" "adventure for palate and soul"; reserve at least two months in advance and hope for a seat at "the communal table", though all diners in the small room "get a cooking lesson" while watching talented chef Stephen Nogal prepare a "fabulous" five-course, prix fixe Pacific NW feast in the open kitchen; "plan for a long, leisurely meal and an educational experience."

Isabella Ristorante S   22 | 22 | 21 | $29
1909 Third Ave. (Stewart St.), 206-441-8281

◪ A change in owners and chefs has almost gone unnoticed at this Downtown Italian, which remains a "top-notch", "romantic spot" to enjoy "superior pastas" and other "satisfying" dishes in a "beautiful", high-ceilinged room; though a few complain about a "dark interior" that's "too noisy", many "love the martinis" and the live jazz that contributes to the "good times."

Italianissimo   ∇ 19 | 15 | 18 | $26
Woodinville Town Ctr., 17650 140th Ave. NE (175th St.), Woodinville, 425-485-6888

◪ Despite its "unlikely suburban location" in a Woodinville strip mall, this "family-operated Eastside treasure" is a "sophisticated" Northern Italian that impresses regulars with "great" "waiters who have very good memories" and a chef who turns out "wonderful", "delicious food"; detractors, however, find the fare merely "average."

Ivar's Acres of Clams S   16 | 15 | 15 | $17
Pier 54, 1001 Alaskan Way (bet. Madison & Spring Sts.), 206-624-6852

◪ Veterans of this "classic", if "touristy", fish house on the Downtown waterfront say no "blue-collar" joint in Seattle dishes up better seafood; Barbara Figueroa has signed on as the corporate executive chef of Ivar's Inc. to update the menu, but most come to this "institution" – as they have since 1938 – for "wonderful clam chowder" and "great" halibut 'n' chips.

Ivar's Mukilteo Landing S   17 | 16 | 19 | $20
710 Front St. (Whidbey Island ferry dock), Mukilteo, 425-742-6180

◪ "Grab a bite at the outside counter" at this Mukilteo seafood house and "eat on the ferry line" while enjoying a view of the Sound; it's much younger than its Seattle cousin, but this place also features "good, fresh fish" and "friendly service", as well as a "great happy-hour menu" in the bar that's half-priced.

Seattle | F | D | S | C |

Ivar's Salmon House 🆂 | 18 | 19 | 16 | $22 |
401 NE Northlake Way (north shore of Lake Union), 206-632-0767

▣ Perched on the north shore of Lake Union with a "good view of the city", this "local legend lives on" in an authentic replica of an Indian longhouse decorated with native artifacts; expect busloads of tourists who descend for a "fun Seattle experience" highlighted by "outstanding alder-smoked salmon" and "excellent clams" (the menu is "otherwise mediocre").

Izumi 🆂 | 22 | 18 | 21 | $20 |
Totem Lake West Ctr., 12539 116th Ave. NE (124th St.), Kirkland, 425-821-1959

■ "Very fresh fish" served in a clean, contemporary setting makes this casual, suburban Kirkland Japanese a "favorite" for sushi; regulars smile "since we go often, we're frequently given lots of unrequested things to try" by the "pleasant" sushi chefs.

Jack's Fish Spot 🆂 | 21 | 10 | 15 | $9 |
Pike Place Mkt., 1514 Pike Pl. (Post Alley), 206-467-0514

■ Even if you have to stand and get rained on, "you gotta try" the "cheap eats" at this tiny Pike Place Market seafood bar, which is partially exposed to the elements; "Jack is the king of seafood" and turns "fresh-as-it-gets" fruits de mer into terrific cioppino, clam chowder, crab cocktails and fish 'n' chips; there's "hardly a better place to grab a quick lunch at the Market."

JaK's Grill 🆂 | 23 | 18 | 21 | $24 |
14 Front St. N. (Sunset Way), Issaquah, 425-837-8834

■ The secret to the success of this small, "friendly" steakhouse in Issaquah – one of the "best on the Eastside" – is simple: "great grilled steaks, garlic mashed potatoes" and a "good bottle of wine", all "reasonably priced"; N.B. dinner only.

Jalisco | 16 | 12 | 16 | $15 |
1715 228th St. SE (bet. 15th & 18th Aves.), Bothell, 425-481-3931 🆂
115 Park Ln. (Lake Washington Blvd.), Kirkland, 425-822-3355 🆂
129 First Ave. N. (bet. Denny Way & John St.), 206-282-1175 ◗🆂
1467 E. Republican St. (15th Ave.), 206-325-9005
122 First Ave. N. (bet. Denny Way & John St.), 206-283-4242 🆂
12336 31st Ave. NE (Lake City Way), 206-364-3978 🆂
8517 14th Ave. S. (Cloverdale St.), 206-767-1943

▣ "Busy, bright, fast and cheap" sums up these "basic bean-and-cheese" chain Mexicans; aficionados insist that "the chicken mole can't be beat" and praise the "fast, courteous service", but opponents say that though the "greasy food comes in huge portions", it's "average."

Seattle

| F | D | S | C |

Jitterbug Café S | 21 | 18 | 18 | $18 |
2114 N. 45th St. (bet. Bagley & Meridian Aves.), 206-547-6313
■ Locals in Wallingford "just love" this "comfortable", "cute place", which is why it's "always busy"; working from an Eclectic (some say "odd") "rotating" menu that changes "regional" "themes" monthly, "personable" (or "sassy"?) waitresses deliver "substantial" plates of "inventive" fare, from the "excellent breakfasts" to the "euphoria-inducing dinners", all "artistically presented."

Julia's of Wallingford S | 17 | 14 | 14 | $14 |
4401 Wallingford Ave. N. (44th St.), 206-633-1175
◪ This "casual" cafe in Wallingford is famed for its "yummy", "bountiful breakfasts" (we "love their scrambles" and "wonderful breads and pastries"), but oh, "the wait"; it's less hectic at lunch and dinner, when the "healthy" Eclectic menu runs to "mmm good soups", "fresh salads" and "delicious stir-fries"; a vocal minority, however, cites "unimaginative" food and "rude" service.

Kabul Afghan Cuisine S | 21 | 14 | 19 | $19 |
2301 N. 45th St. (Corliss St.), 206-545-9000
■ "Authentic", "well-prepared" Afghan cooking, live "sitar music" and crisp "white linens" on the tabletops make this "modest" Wallingford storefront an "unusual" "ethnic treat"; the "wonderful vegetarian dishes and kebabs" rate special mention, and the "attentive owner and staff" add to the charm of this "consistently underrated", dinner-only spot.

Kaleenka, The | 18 | 15 | 16 | $17 |
1933 First Ave. (bet. Stewart & Virginia Sts.), 206-728-1278
■ "A pleasant surprise", this "hideaway" cafe near Pike Place Market makes "yummy piroshki" and other "hearty" "Russian soul food" that warms on "a cold, rainy day" "like a hug from grandma"; "consistently delicious" "home cooking", "good service" and affordable prices make it "worth a visit."

Kamon on Lake Union S | 18 | 20 | 17 | $26 |
1177 Fairview Ave. N. (Lake Union), 206-622-4664
◪ With its "wonderful location" off Lake Union, this palatial Asian lures with "sparkling" "views of the city lights at night" and a "pleasant atmosphere"; its extensive, "well-prepared" East-meets-West menu offers "something for everyone", and a meal of "excellent" "sushi out on the deck is heavenly"; N.B. there's a piano bar too.

Karam's   ∇ | 22 | 11 | 19 | $19 |
340 15th Ave. E. (bet. Harrison & John Sts.), 206-324-2370
■ "An ethnic pearl", this petite Capitol Hill Lebanese is a garlic lover's paradise and offers "amazing food", such as "incredible goat cheese" and the house signature, charbroiled *kibbeh* prepared with lamb or pumpkin; N.B. dinner only.

Seattle | F | D | S | C |

KASPAR'S 26 | 22 | 24 | $39
19 W. Harrison St. (1st Ave. W.), 206-298-0123

■ "Wow!" – "sit back, relax, drink, eat and enjoy" "outstanding chef" Kaspar Donier's "exceptional" Pacific NW cuisine; he clearly "knows what he's doing" and turns out "artistically arranged" "gourmet feasts" that are "innovative", "festive" and "always a delight"; the freshly renovated room in a "classy" Queen Anne locale feels even more welcoming due to the "warm hospitality" of the "professional" staff; P.S. the "fabulous wine bar" is "an excellent deal" with its short menu of small bites.

Kells S 16 | 17 | 17 | $20
Pike Place Mkt., 1916 Post Alley (bet. Stewart & Virginia Sts.), 206-728-1916

■ "Everyone becomes Irish" at this "hidden treasure" tucked away in Post Alley at Pike Place Market; it's "worth finding" for the "fun" "Celtic atmosphere" and "authentic" fare, especially the "wonderful soda bread"; it's "ominously dark" in the back room, but the "loud" gang downing pints of Guinness doesn't seem to mind.

Kidd Valley S⌀ 16 | 9 | 12 | $8
5502 25th Ave. NE (behind University Village), 206-522-0890
14303 Aurora Ave. N. (145th St.), 206-364-8493
135 15th Ave. E. (John St.), 206-328-8133
531 Queen Anne Ave. N. (Mercer St.), 206-284-0184
4910 Green Lake Way N. (50th St.), 206-547-0121
15259 Bellevue-Redmond Rd. (near NE Northup Way), Bellevue, 425-643-4165
6434 Bothell Way NE (61st Ave.), Kenmore, 425-485-5514
5910 Lake Washington Blvd. NE (near Houghton Beach Park), Kirkland, 425-827-5858
1201 Lake Washington Blvd. (Coulon Park), Renton, 425-277-3324

◪ "Why support the national chains when you can support these local grease joints" where "heart-stopping" burgers, "fried mushrooms" and "fab fresh fruit shakes" are "not just for kids"?; gone is the old look and the Kidd's infamous, leggy, oh-so-'70s, gal-in-platforms signage, but the "newly remodeled" "*Jetsons* surroundings" don't move chauvinists who carp: "to hell with being PC", "they should never have changed the logo."

Kikuya ∇ 22 | 15 | 16 | $20
8105 161st Ave. NE (Redmond-Kirkland Way), Redmond, 425-881-8771

■ It's "the simplest food [that offers] maximum flavors" at this Redmond strip mall Japanese where the name translates as 'chrysanthemum'; yet a dearth of respondents proves that mum's the word in more ways than one when it comes to this "hidden gem."

Seattle

| | F | D | S | C |

KINGFISH CAFÉ S⊘ — 26 | 23 | 21 | $22
602 19th Ave. E. (Mercer St.), 206-320-8757
■ The "beautiful" "Coaston sisters have taken Soul Food to another level" at their Capitol Hill hitter where chef Tracey McRae's "big portions" and "lovely interpretation of Southern standards" help make this "unique" spot with the "artsy-funky" atmo every bit "as good as the buzz"; "get there a half-hour before the place opens" say regulars who "hate the wait."

Kirkland Roaster & Ale House S — 13 | 14 | 14 | $21
111 Central Way (Lake St.), Kirkland, 425-827-4400
☑ A "young crowd" pumps up the volume inside and out at this Kirkland Downtowner, bending an elbow over a "good selection of microbrews"; but despite praise for the spit-roasted chicken, most gourmands gripe about the "predictable" and "generic" American-Eclectic fare.

Kokeb S — 18 | 12 | 12 | $14
926 12th Ave. (bet. Marion & Spring Sts.), 206-322-0485
☑ Surveyors are split over this pioneer near Seattle U: some say it's "the best Ethiopian food I've had", while others cry that "vast quantities of mediocre" fare, "dreary surroundings" and "unbearably slow service" make this once-popular ethnic hot spot a "sad shadow of its former self."

Krittika Noodles & Thai Cuisine S — – | – | – | I
6411 Latona Ave. NE (65th St.), 206-985-1182
A short walk from Green Lake, this "friendly, family-owned" "neighborhood" Thai is being discovered; take-out business is brisk at the sleek little newcomer, which offers a menu as long as it is interesting, with "good-sized portions" of noodles swimming in exotic gravies, crisp vegetables, aromatic curries, and seafood and meats stir-fried with a practiced hand.

La Buca S — 17 | 17 | 16 | $26
102 Cherry St. (1st Ave.), 206-343-9517
☑ This Pioneer Square Southern Italian provokes debate: admirers enthuse about "fine food" served in a "fun, lower-level" "cozy cavern" with "lovely lighting", but critics counter that while it was "good when it first opened", it's "a disappointment lately", adding that the "basement" setting is "drafty" and "dungeon-like."

La Fontana S — 22 | 21 | 22 | $26
120 Blanchard St. (bet. 1st & 2nd Aves.), 206-441-1045
☑ Fans beg "don't tell anyone" about this soulful Southern Italian where owner Mario Fuenzalina "is like family"; most say the eats are "consistently good", though some say they "vary from mediocre to inspired"; all agree that a repast here is best enjoyed in the "fabulous courtyard" "hidden" just off Belltown's more heavily trafficked Restaurant Row.

Seattle　　　　　　　　　　　　　F | D | S | C

Lake Washington Grillhouse ⓢ　　14 | 18 | 15 | $22
Kenmore Marina, 6161 NE 175th St. (Lake City Way), 425-486-3313

☒ "If you have a boat on Lake Washington, it's the place to dock", but a "wonderful view" and "location by the lake and the Burke-Gilman Trail" fail to excite critics who claim that Kenmore's "typical" steakhouse and seafooder "has gone downhill"; still, it remains "popular with the younger set" who obviously don't mind "marginal" fare and "average service."

La Medusa　　　　　　　　　　　22 | 18 | 21 | $24
4857 Rainier Ave. S. (Edmonds St.), 206-723-2192

■ Expect "authentic" "Sicilian soul food at its finest" courtesy of chef-owners Sherri Serino and Lisa Becklund whose "limited but tasty menu" offers "a nice twist" on Italian at their "bustling", "friendly" storefront; some lament that it's "a little pricey" and "loud when it's crowded", but all applaud "great pastas" and "creative" pizzas, making this "most exciting newcomer" "worth the jaunt" to Columbia City.

LAMPREIA　　　　　　　　　　　25 | 21 | 22 | $48
2400 First Ave. (Battery St.), 206-443-3301

☒ Much applause for owner Scott Carsberg, a "near perfectionist" whose seasonal Pacific NW menu features "absolutely simple, perfect food" that's "exquisite"; "tiny, delectable portions" wow loyalists, as do the "elegant, romantic atmosphere", "beautiful tableware", "refined service" and a "great cheese course"; a minority calls the setting "sparse", claiming this "way overpriced" Belltowner is "the most overrated, pretentious restaurant in Seattle."

La Palina/Duke's Italian Kitchen　　– | – | – | M
(fka Duke's)
236 First Ave. W. (bet. John & Thomas Sts.), 206-283-4400

Duke Moscrip's original chowderhouse is now a born-again Italian, but white linens, candlelight and a Tuscan-yellow paint job don't quite annul the bar-and-grill ambiance of old; chef Dino D'Aquila turns out noteworthy pastas, seafood, osso buco and his signature rack of lamb, but rumor has it the kitchen is more polished than the service.

LA PANZANELLA ⌀　　　　　　　25 | 21 | 19 | $11
1314 E. Union St. (14th Ave.), 206-325-5217

■ "Bread just doesn't get any better than this" say those who claim that Ciro Pascuito's "authentic, rustic" Italian loaves are the "best in town"; this Capitol Hill bakery/cafe's ebullient owner "has a million entertaining stories", best told over soup and "great focaccia sandwiches" at his big, wooden, communal table where you'll be "transported to Italy without the effort."

Seattle | F | D | S | C |

Latitude 47 S | 15 | 17 | 16 | $25 |
1232 Westlake Ave. N. (Valley St.), 206-284-1047
■ This Westlake waterfront steakhouse/seafooder's "great location" offers a "fine view" of Lake Union, but that's not enough for some surveyors who find the food "so-so"; still, movers and shakers stuck in Donna Summertime groove here to a disco beat, making this a "fun place on weekends."

L'Auberge S | - | - | - | M |
417 Main St. (5th Ave.), Edmonds, 425-775-5500
This staid, handsomely appointed cafe suits the sedate Edmonds scene, offering an "imaginative" Eclectic menu that traverses the globe for inspiration; the chef is most at home with Med-style dishes like chicken in Madeira cream sauce; service is more amiable than graceful.

Le Bonaparte S | ▽ 21 | 19 | 18 | $31 |
S. 216th St. (Marine View Dr.), Des Moines, 206-878-4412
■ Fine dining restaurants are few and far between South of the city, but this converted old house in Des Moines appeals (mainly) to Southenders who contend that the Classic French fare is "always good, no matter what you order"; but a few complain that it's "barely above-average."

LE GOURMAND | 26 | 20 | 24 | $46 |
425 NW Market St. (6th Ave. NW), 206-784-3463
■ "Caring, intelligent" chef-owner Bruce Naftaly is a "treasure" who "prepares everything with love" at this "classic" "fine French restaurant in an unlikely Ballard location"; there's "nothing trendy" about this unassuming house where "the freshest ingredients" often come from the chef's own trees, vines and garden; "great sauces" are key to his seasonal, prix fixe menu, which is "unbeatable for the money – hell, almost unbeatable, period."

LeoMelina Ristorante di Mare S | 21 | 22 | 20 | $32 |
Pike Place Mkt., 96 Union St. (1st Ave.), 206-623-3783
■ "Love the food and Friday night opera" trill fans of this "romantic" Pike Place Market Italian with a seafood-centric menu; "ask for a table overlooking the lively kitchen" in the "gorgeous dining room", but note that if the weather's warm, "there's nothing better than sitting on the deck" with its "great view" of the Sound; while a few critics cry it's "too expensive", they're drowned out by enthusiasts who insist that the "delicious experience" is worth it.

Leschi Lakecafe S | 16 | 18 | 16 | $22 |
102 Lakeside Ave. (Alder St.), 206-328-2233
■ "The location makes the experience" at this "yuppie joint" with "average" seafood and a "stunning view of Lake Washington", where "good fish 'n' chips" "out on the patio" are particularly "nice on a summer day or evening"; the "casual" "pub atmosphere" inside also makes this a "neighborhood magnet."

Seattle | F | D | S | C |

Lockspot Cafe S   ▽ | 15 | 11 | 13 | $15 |
3005 NW 54th St. (south of Market St.), 206-789-4865
◪ Longstanding (1917) seafooder near the Locks with middling ratings that's "an institution, but no *Michelin* stars are looming anytime soon"; while you'll find such inexpensive dishes as fish 'n' chips, if you're looking for ambiance, you'd do better to keep on driving south to the far-more-glam seafooderies that line this waterside Ballard/Shilshole stretch.

Lombardi's Cucina S | 18 | 15 | 17 | $20 |
2200 NW Market St. (22nd Ave.), 206-783-0055
1620 W. Marine View Dr. (Port Gardner), Everett, 425-252-1886
Gilman Sq., 695 NW Gilman Blvd. (7th Ave.), Issaquah, 425-391-9097
■ "When people smell garlic, they know you've been to Lombardi's", "your neighborhood family restaurant" with a new, third location way up north in Everett; "good, standard Italian food", "awesome marinara", "friendly service" and the "excellent garlic festival" held each year help explain why these "reliable" spots "are always crowded."

Longshoreman's Daughter S | 17 | 14 | 13 | $15 |
3508 Fremont Pl. N. (Fremont Ave.), 206-633-5169
◪ Expect "funky food and funky service at this funky Fremont" American where you're better off if you "stick to breakfast" ("fluffy buttermilk pancakes"); those unmoved by the "innovative" menu claim that this place is "up to its armpits in granola" and the setting is pure "Seattle grunge"; but both friends and foes warn: "go now, so you can get your food before the millennium", since the "slow service" is "absolutely pathetic."

Louie's Cuisine of China ●S | 18 | 16 | 17 | $18 |
5100 15th Ave. NW (Ballard Bridge), 206-782-8855
◪ "Dependable" "standard Cantonese fare" and "good service" make this "a favorite non-Chinatown restaurant" for denizens of Ballard; still, some voters claim this pioneer is "past its prime", having "slipped in recent years"; for those who liken the "windowless" atmosphere to "entering a cave", one surveyor has a cure: "we usually take out."

Louisa's Cafe & Bakery S⊅   ▽ | 20 | 13 | 16 | $10 |
2379 Eastlake Ave. E. (Louisa St.), 206-325-0081
■ Eastlake's "great neighborhood bakery" features a world of "tasty pastries" and "sandwiches on homemade bread", but this woody hangout (formerly called Tio's) is primarily a coffee-klatcher's haven where you line up, ante up, then settle in to read the paper, cram for exams (it's on the quick-route to UW) or have a schmooze fest over a latte or three.

Luau Polynesian Lounge [S] 20 | 20 | 19 | $21

2253 N. 56th St. (Kirkwood Ave.), 206-633-5828

■ Gonzo barman Thomas Price and his charming waitress/wife, Jessica, opened this "cool, campy" Hawaiian near Green Lake that devotees dub "one of the best new places" in Seattle; you'll have "fun", "fun", "fun" inhaling the aloha atmosphere and "wonderful drinks" dolled-up with plastic parasols and mermaids; the Polynesian-inspired menu – with its pupu platter and other "creative taste combinations" – makes this a hip take on the Trader Vic's theme.

Luna Park Cafe [S] 16 | 17 | 15 | $12

2918 SW Avalon Way (Spokane St.), 206-935-7250

◪ "The milk shakes alone are worth the trip" to this West Seattle American where the burgers and "great big breakfasts" are sometimes "hit-or-miss"; this "greasy '60s place" recalls a "Seattle that time forgot", where a jukebox and "collection of vintage lunchboxes" add up to "fun."

Lush Life [S] 22 | 22 | 21 | $29

2331 Second Ave. (Bell St.), 206-441-9842

■ "There *is* something luscious" about this "sexy", "dark and mysterious" "fabulous" Italian that's "noisy but swoony" just like its nearby sib, Marco's Supperclub; look for Belltown's "beautiful people" dining on grilled meats or "drinking martinis" in the "hip, artsy bar"; a "caring staff" that generates "good energy" is another plus.

Machiavelli 19 | 14 | 16 | $21

1215 Pine St. (bet. Boren & Melrose Aves.), 206-621-7941

◪ "Cute", "cozy" and "comfortable", Capitol Hill's living room serves "simple Italian food" – "tasty pastas", pizzas and "inventive specials" – to standing-room-only crowds; though a few foes feel that the joint "needs more staff and less 'tude", most maintain that it's a "sweet experience."

Macrina Bakery & Cafe [S] 24 | 17 | 17 | $14

2408 First Ave. (bet. Battery & Wall Sts.), 206-448-4032

■ "Unsurpassed", "inspirational" and "undoubtedly the best bakery in all of Seattle" say baker Leslie Mackie's fervent fans, who swear by her "tiny place" in Belltown; "delectable meze plates, artful decor and a flirty staff" make this "small gem" "a perfect lunch spot", though it appeals to the breakfast/brunch crowd too.

Mac's Smokehouse 16 | 8 | 13 | $11

1006 First Ave. S. (Royal Brougham Way), 206-628-0880 [S]

10315 E. Marginal Way (158th St.), Tukwila, 206-763-4645 ◐

◪ This "dingy hole-in-the-wall" near the soon-to-be-demolished Kingdome is a popular "pre-Mariners hangout" whose "pretty good Texas brisket" is "better than the food in the park" say some, despite the fact that it's "fatty, fatty, fatty" according to others; fans who feel "naked without a baseball cap" might also like Mac's Tukwila pit stop.

Seattle | F | D | S | C |

Madison Park Cafe S | 18 | 16 | 16 | $19 |
1807 42nd Ave. E. (E. Madison St.), 206-324-2626
■ The "casual atmosphere" at Madison Park's "reliably homey" cafe appeals to locals who have found this "quiet cottage", with a warm-weather courtyard, "charming" and "restful" for over 20 years; they come for weekend brunch, plus the "reasonably priced" French bistro menu and new liquor license draw a dinner crowd.

Mad Pizza S | 19 | 12 | 15 | $11 |
3601 Fremont Ave. N. (36th St.), 206-632-5453
1314 E. Madison St. (bet. 13th & 14th Aves.), 206-322-7447
4021 E. Madison St. (bet. 41st Ave. & McGilvra Blvd.), 206-329-7037
☑ "A noble attempt in a pizza wasteland" enthuse fans who sample the "interesting" pies with "fresh ingredients" and a "good, chewy crust" at this local chain, then crow they're "mad about it"; others who've lifted a slice or two are mad *at* it, citing "weird combos", crust that "needs work" and "maddeningly slow service."

Mae's Phinney Ridge Cafe S | 17 | 15 | 15 | $12 |
6412 Phinney Ave. N. (65th St.), 206-782-1222
☑ Like "fun, kitschy decor" that's big on the bovine?; "take the kids and out-of-towners" and "moo-sey on over" to this American, a "funky, friendly" Phinney fave for "great big breakfasts" with "a milk shake on the side", and don't miss the "cinnamon rolls, a must"; however, critics contend it's become "a victim of its own success" and that "lines out the door on weekend mornings show that yuppies have no taste."

Maggie Bluffs S | 16 | 17 | 17 | $16 |
Elliott Bay Marina, 2601 W. Marina Pl. (Smith Cove), 206-283-8322
☑ Though it's tucked beneath its far fussier sibling, Palisade, this "cute" and casual "hamburger joint" with a "stunning location at Elliott Bay Marina" offers an "awesome view from its outdoor patio" where you can "bring the kids" and "watch the boats sail by"; while there are "good" burgers and beer, the rest of the "standard pub chow" is only "so-so."

Malay Satay Hut S | – | – | – | I |
212 12th Ave. (Spruce St.), 206-324-4091
Sure it's a hole-in-the-wall tucked into a Vietnamtown strip mall, but its "authentic Malaysian" fare is earning big-time kudos thanks to cheap-eats prices for items like fresh-grilled roti, unusual curries and exceptional seafood dishes, proving that "a different twist on the usual Asian stuff" all but guarantees "a loyal following."

Seattle | F | D | S | C |

Maltby Cafe | 21 | 16 | 18 | $14 |
8809 Maltby Rd. (bet. Hwy. 522 & Hwy. 9), Maltby, 425-483-3123
■ Expect "service with a smile" and a "long wait" at this "quaint", "historic" and "crowded" Maltby American, a former school cafeteria; whatever you do, "come hungry" because "the best home-cooked breakfast on earth" is an "artery clogger" "so big and rich it comes with an ambulance on the side"; "burp!" add those who know it "takes two to carry one of those enormous cinnamon rolls."

Mama's Mexican Kitchen S | 17 | 15 | 15 | $14 |
2234 Second Ave. (bet. Bell & Blanchard Sts.), 206-728-6262
◪ "Great cheap margaritas", "big portions" of "decent-quality Americanized Mexican food" and the "kitschy" "Elvis Room" add up to one "crowded" Belltown hangout for the "hip", where "fashion over food" is the rule; amigos announce that it's a "blast" and great for "people-watching", but enemigos simply shrug "what's all the fuss?"

Mamma Melina S | 19 | 15 | 18 | $23 |
4759 NE Roosevelt Way (50th St.), 206-632-2271
◪ Though some say this U-District spot is just "so-so", more claim Melina Varchetta's eponymous Southern Italian with a seafood slant is "wonderful"; sons Salvio and Leo (respectively) operate the popular Ristorante Buongusto in Queen Anne and LeoMelina in the Market, while brother Roberto's cooking here; lucky soul-o-mios might enjoy "great opera" via Papa Varchetta.

Mandalay Café S | 20 | 14 | 19 | $16 |
(fka Janny's Curry House)
1411 N. 45th St. (Stone Way Ave. N.), 206-633-0801
■ Its name has been changed, but this tiny, "homey" and "hot" Southeast Asian "find" set in a "cute" "old house" in Wallingford retains the same owners, chef and – thankfully – menu; the kitchen specializes in "all kinds of" "serious", "delicious curries that are much different than expected."

Mangoes Thai Cuisine S | 18 | 12 | 16 | $17 |
1841 42nd Ave. E. (Madison St.), 206-324-6467
◪ "If only the restaurant layout had been better planned" sigh fans of this "respectable" Asian in Madison Park – it's a "great little neighborhood joint" except for the "crowded seating"; still, it's the only Thai in these parts and garners raves for the "best spring rolls around."

Maple Leaf Grill S | 19 | 15 | 18 | $18 |
8909 Roosevelt Way NE (89th St.), 206-523-8449
■ "The welcoming attitude is tops" at "the best-run pub in town", where host David Albert and his "friendly staff" serve up rabbit and other Eclectic eats; locals often raise a pint to this "nonsmoking", "funky old tavern" in Maple Leaf that "fits like a shoe"; N.B. plans to move up the street to 8929 Roosevelt Way in '99 were in the works at press time.

Seattle | F | D | S | C |

MARCO'S SUPPERCLUB S | 23 | 20 | 21 | $28 |
2510 First Ave. (bet. Vine & Wall Sts.), 206-441-7801
■ An "electric crowd" and Eclectic menu (signature dishes like "must-try jerk chicken", a "creative fried sage leaves appetizer" and "desserts to die for") make "the sister restaurant to Lush Life" "a real Belltown find"; "Marco treats his customers well" and runs what many agree is "still the hippest" spot in Seattle; "romantic", "always loud" and decidedly "dark and smoky" ("wish they'd wall off the bar section"), this jazzy joint is "long on atmosphere" and "great for people-watching."

Matt's Famous Chili Dogs ⇗ | ▽ 18 | 8 | 11 | $7 |
6615 E. Marginal Way S. (4th Ave. S.), 206-768-0418
699 110th Ave. NE (8th Ave. NE), Bellevue, 425-637-2858
■ It's "worth a trip" south to this Boeing boys' hangout where Matt Jones "puts the hot in the dog", dishing out Chicago comfort food to Windy City wanna-bes; tube steaks aren't the only thing he's pushing: Italian beef-and-sausage sandwiches are a mess-and-a-half, but always "worth the fat calories" at this stand-and-eat or take-it-to-go joint; N.B. the new Bellevue branch stays open later.

Matt's in the Market | - | - | - | M |
Pike Place Mkt., 94 Pike St. (1st Ave.), 206-467-7909
Once the "best-kept secret in town", this "tiny" seafood bar atop Pike Place Market is gaining ground with a "beautiful view" of the Sound and some of the freshest, cheapest finfare around; chef Erik Cannella dazzles with "incredible combinations" and vivid flavors, while owner Matt Janke, "an up-and-coming star", doubles as waiter and triples as wine steward – just trust him.

Maximilien S | 19 | 20 | 19 | $25 |
Pike Place Mkt., 81-A Pike St. (1st Ave.), 206-682-7270
■ After 20 years, chef-owner Francois Kissel bade 'adieu' to this Market veteran, which evokes "the Paris Hemingway wrote about", and it's now in the hands of "young owners" and former employees Axel Mace and Eric Francy; this French bistro with "great views" of Elliott Bay and the Olympics remains a "solid choice" "for out-of-town guests" and a "best-kept secret for [weekend] breakfast."

McCormick & Schmick's ☽ S | 21 | 19 | 19 | $27 |
1103 First Ave. (Spring St.), 206-623-5500
■ Even though "there are too many lawyers, the food is good" at this Downtown "landmark eatery" that offers a "reliable steakhouse-and-seafood experience"; get comfy in the spacious "wood-and-brass" dining room where "the fresh sheet always offers delicious seafood options"; "cheap appetizers" and "good martinis" also make for a "lively" "after-work happy hour."

Seattle | F | D | S | C |

McCormick & Schmick's Harborside ●S | 17 | 20 | 17 | $26 |
1200 Westlake Ave. N. (Highland Dr.), 206-270-9052
◪ The newer Harborside branch of this seafooder boasts "big, glamorous rooms", a "terrific location" and a "wonderful outdoor patio" on Lake Union; but while pros praise the "solid", "fresh" fare, others call the cooking "mediocre" and say you "can do better for the price."

McCormick's Fish House S | 21 | 18 | 20 | $28 |
722 Fourth Ave. (bet. Cherry & Columbia Sts.), 206-682-3900
■ Mick & Schmick's Midtown seafooder offers "consistently good" "fish prepared anyway you want it", as well as "great happy-hour specials"; an "enjoyable atmosphere" and a "knowledgeable staff" add to its appeal.

Mediterranean Kitchen S | 22 | 13 | 20 | $19 |
366 Roy St. (4th Ave.), 206-285-6713
103 Bellevue Way NE (1st St.), Bellevue, 425-462-9433
■ These Lebanese twins "do more with chicken, lemon and garlic than you would think possible" cluck believers who "waddle home" after downing "big portions" of everything; those who like the "new setting" are glad that the Seattle branch "moved closer to the Opera House" – across the lake from the Bellevue kitchen.

METROPOLITAN GRILL S | 25 | 22 | 24 | $39 |
820 Second Ave. (Marion St.), 206-624-3287
■ "Wanna impress? go here" declare devotees of this "dark", "clubby" meatery that garners raves for "the best steaks in town, year-in and year-out"; its Downtown location is "great for a power business lunch", and most maintain that this "classic" with "professional service" is "what all other steakhouses should be measured by."

Moghul Palace S | 17 | 15 | 19 | $19 |
University Bookstore Mall, 10301 NE 10th St. (Bellevue Way), Bellevue, 425-451-1909
◪ Kudos for "pleasant service" and tandoori dishes that are "among the best" of the "good, solid Indian food" served here; a lunch buffet and "bargain" prices reputedly draw both the richest man in the world ("Bill Gates eats here") and Bellevue's wallet-watchers; however, critics complain that the "quality has been slipping in the past year."

Mona's Bistro & Lounge S | 22 | 22 | 22 | $27 |
6421 Latona Ave. NE (65th St.), 206-526-1188
■ "I hate to rate it so high because then it will be even harder to get in" says one fan of this "dark, romantic" Green Lake "comer", "another great neighborhood place" that wins praise for service – "especially when the owners are there"; the "out-of-the ordinary" Eclectic menu is "tantalizing" and the "small, seductive bar" garners raves for its tapas and other "fun" eats.

Seattle

| | F | D | S | C |

Mondo Burrito S   18 | 15 | 15 | $10
2121 First Ave. (bet. Blanchard & Lenora Sts.), 206-728-9697
■ "Don't let the white linen tablecloths fool you" – this Belltown Mexican with a serious following is a "fun place" known for "big", "creative", "internationally flavored" burritos and "delightful seasonal specials"; a "late-night" weekend "standby" (open till 3 AM Friday–Saturday), it offers "excellent value for the money."

Musashi's ⊄   – | – | – | I
1400 N. 45th St. (Interlake Ave.), 206-633-0212
"Be prepared to wait" at this "friendly", "family-owned" "bargain Japanese", a "crowded" Wallingford "hole-in-the-wall" known for its "great, fresh, cheap sushi" and "excellent" bento boxes; the "taste treats" have made standing in line a local pastime.

My Favourite Piroshky S   15 | 8 | 13 | $8
122 Broadway E. (bet. Denny Way & John St.), 206-322-2820
Bellevue Sq., 1010 Bellevue Sq. (Bellevue Way), Bellevue, 425-646-9354
■ For "quick, warm snacks" of "homey, filling" "savory pastries prepared by real Russians", loyalists head for this "cozy", minuscule Broadway bakeshop and its bigger Bellevue Square branch; but the unimpressed sniff "small portions" and "no service."

My Friends Cafe S   ∇ 16 | 9 | 11 | $11
310 NE 72nd St. (bet. Green Lake Dr. & Woodlawn Ave.), 206-523-8929
■ At this "simple storefront" Eclectic, "excellent omelets, scones" and other, more "healthy food" appeal to Green Lake's joggers and coffee-klatchers; not so the "unappealing ordering system", which causes critics to carp "God forbid you should sit before ordering" and explains the less-than-enthusiastic service scores.

Neo Bistro S   – | – | – | M
14053 Greenwood Ave. N. (bet. 140th & 143rd Sts.), 206-366-0104
A "welcome newcomer" to the "North End restaurant desert", this "family-owned" Mediterranean attracts the "neighborhood" trade with its ambitious menu of meat, seafood, pasta and pizza, delivered by a pleasantly efficient staff; the multilevel space accommodates a cozy bar, a fireplace, and plenty of nooks and crannies for quiet dining.

New Jake O'Shaughnessey's S   16 | 15 | 16 | $23
Bellevue Sq., 401 Bellevue Sq. (Bellevue Way), Bellevue, 425-455-5559
■ "Adequate food, strange site" describes this lower-level Bellevue Square veteran known for "good seafood" and better beer; some say it's "ok for lunch", but more grouse that the "broad" American menu features "so-so" "chain fare" and the "miserable, dark" decor "needs sprucing up."

Seattle

| F | D | S | C |

New Orleans 🆂 | 14 | 13 | 13 | $17 |
114 First Ave. (bet. Washington St. & Yesler Way), 206-622-2563
◪ Foot-stomping, beer-lifting, zydeco-loving optimists like this "loud" Pioneer Square Cajun; while some come to "eat crawdaddies", most drop by "to drink" and listen to the "good jazz."

Nickerson Street Saloon 🆂 | 17 | 14 | 17 | $14 |
318 Nickerson St. (bet. Dexter & 4th Aves. N.), 206-284-8819
◪ A "super happy hour" and "a saloon burger dripping with cheese" get the nod from Fremontsters who step inside for a "sports bar atmosphere" or claim a patio table to enjoy the "unique combination of sitting next to the [Fremont] Bridge and the water, while you're practically in the middle of an intersection"; a few knock "bad service and warm beer."

Nikko | 24 | 24 | 21 | $30 |
Westin Hotel, 1900 Fifth Ave. (Westlake Ave.), 206-322-4641
■ Downtowner whose "beautiful space" in the Westin Hotel makes it one of the "prettiest restaurants in town"; pros praise the "sensational all-you-can-eat sushi lunch" (to say nothing of the spectacular Nikko Roll draped with seven different slices of fish), "super happy hour" and "fun atmosphere"; a few wallet-watchers warn that the "expense-account Japanese food" served here is "good, but no longer great."

NISHINO 🆂 | 26 | 22 | 22 | $33 |
3130 E. Madison St. (Lake Washington Blvd.), 206-322-5800
■ Tatsu Nishino (ex LA's Matsuhisa) serves "creative", "cutting-edge" cuisine at this "graceful" Madison Park Japanese; his "beyond description chef's-choice dinner" and "great sushi bar", where everything is "beautifully presented", are "impressive"; though some complain about "tiny", "overpriced" portions, most feel the food is "wonderful" and "can't wait to return."

Noble Court 🆂 | 22 | 14 | 16 | $19 |
1644 140th Ave. NE (Bellevue-Redmond Rd.), Bellevue, 425-641-6011
■ Overlake's neon-festooned "Hong Kong West" is home to "huge crowds, long waits, the best dim sum in town" and excellent seafood (much of it pulled from live tanks up front) according to acolytes who flock to this "family-friendly" Chinese; "get there early to beat the rush" on weekends.

Noodle Ranch | 21 | 16 | 16 | $15 |
2228 Second Ave. (bet. Bell & Blanchard Sts.), 206-728-0463
■ "Noodle-rific!" shout fans of this "aggressively hip" Pan-Asian with the "strange name" and the "great Belltown location"; "you'll never get bored" eating "yummy soups", "rockin' rice-and-fish bowls" and the other "amazing", "ridiculously cheap" fare here – "you can get a great healthy meal for $10."

Seattle F | D | S | C

Noodle Studio 20 | 14 | 18 | $14
209 Broadway E. (bet. John & Thomas Sts.), 206-325-6277
■ "Excellent food and fast service" impress voters who find "the noodle bowls hit the spot" at this Broadway Thai that's "always immaculate, authentic" and "cheap."

ObaChine 19 | 22 | 18 | $32
1518 Sixth Ave. (bet. Pike & Pine Sts.), 206-749-9653
☒ Voters are definitely divided over this flashy Downtowner that's Wolfgang Puck's first foray into Seattle: pros praise the "exotic" Pan-Asian menu, calling attention to "great presentations" and "fantastic desserts"; but a cadre of critics comes down hard on this "overpriced tourist stop", dissing Barbara Lazaroff's "overblown decor" ("better suited to LA") and an experience that's "all show, no substance."

Ocean City 19 | 12 | 16 | $20
609 S. Weller St. (6th Ave.), 206-623-2333
☒ Some say this "cavernous Chinese" is an International District "Sunday morning dim sum necessity" that's always "good for a large group"; hot tea cuts the grease when you're downing roast duck, but it's no help when it comes to the "greasy carpets" say those who sniff the place needs some spiffing up; N.B. its adjoining noodle shop/barbecue stop is handy for quick, cheap eats.

Olympia II Pizza & 18 | 10 | 15 | $14
Spaghetti House
4501 Interlake Ave. N. (45th St.), 206-633-3655
Olympia III Pizza & Spaghetti House
516 15th Ave. E. (bet. Mercer & Republican Sts.), 206-329-4500
☒ Independently owned "neighborhood pizza places" with "better-than-average pies" and "huge" house salads that some call "great" and others opine are "overrated"; they're short on decor, but they're "kid-friendly" and "cheap."

Original Pancake House 20 | 14 | 18 | $12
Park Place Ctr., 130 Park Place Ctr., Kirkland, 425-825-7575
■ "You gotta love a place that serves heavy cream for your coffee", "light, fluffy buttermilk pancakes" and "great crêpes"; a "good variety" of other "homestyle eats" helps make this "hearty, pleasant" and "busy" Kirkland pancake house (where service comes with a we-mean-it smile) the home of "breakfast, illustrated to perfection."

Oyster Bar on Chuckanut Drive 22 | 23 | 22 | $38
2578 Chuckanut Dr. (Estes Rd.), Bow, 360-766-6185
■ "The pearl of Chuckanut Drive" offers "excellent everything", including local oysters and other "well-prepared" NW seafood that's "worth the drive from Seattle"; this "beautifully located and appointed restaurant" with an "out-of-this-world" Samish Bay view also offers "top-notch service" and an award-winning wine list; N.B. no children under 10 permitted.

Seattle

| | F | D | S | C |

Oyster Creek Inn S   23 | 22 | 22 | $32
2190 Chuckanut Dr. (Estes Rd.), Bow, 360-766-6179
■ Bow's creekside "charmer" whose "incredibly tasty" NW seafood "menu is perfect for all types of appetites"; there's a "good wine list", as well as guest house "rooms to rent" to those who find it hard to leave the "great setting" of this "old-fashioned fish house" "nestled in the trees."

Pagliacci Pizza S   20 | 10 | 14 | $11
426 Broadway E. (Harrison St.), 206-324-0730
4529 University Way NE (45th St.), 206-632-0421
550 Queen Anne Ave. N. (Mercer St.), 206-285-1232
■ Pros praise the "consistently good" pies at Dorene Centioli-McTigue's pizza places and add "thank God they deliver"; the "seasonal pizzas are guaranteed to break your diet" and the "pesto primo is to die for" say devotees who've died and gone to "thin-crust heaven"; N.B. call the central number (206-726-1717) for takeout.

Painted Table, The S   24 | 24 | 22 | $37
Alexis Hotel, 92 Madison St. (1st Ave.), 206-624-3646
■ "Artsy and elegant", the Alexis Hotel's "calm" and "romantic" dining room is "great for a business meeting or an intimate dinner"; "talented chef" Tim Kelley's "innovative" and "imaginative menu" relies on "NW and Asian influences"; a few doubters cry "overrated", complaining of "tiny portions", but most maintain it's "well worth the price for that special occasion."

PALACE KITCHEN ◐ S   23 | 22 | 21 | $31
2030 Fifth Ave. (Lenora St.), 206-448-2001
◪ "Tom Douglas' restaurants are always fabulous", and this Downtown NW (his third) is no exception; the "flashy and fun" U-shaped bar is the center of the Palace's universe, where the "self-consciously hip" "cocktail set" comes to see and "be seen" in a "cool" setting; while fans feel the cooking's "worthy of adulation" and that Douglas and company are "not afraid to lead food trends", foes find the menu too meat-y, the room "very noisy" and the seats "hard and uncomfortable."

PALISADE S   22 | 25 | 22 | $36
2601 W. Marina Pl. (23rd Ave. W.), 206-285-1000
■ The "breathtaking view" of "mountain, water and skyline" from the base of Magnolia Bluff makes this grandiose "destination dining" spot worth seeking out; but the "great seafood", wood-fired NW specialties, "spectacular Sunday brunch" and "attentive service" also "impress"; those who cry "way too expensive!" should heed this advice: "go for lunch when there are fewer people, a lower bill, and the same food and ambiance."

Seattle

| F | D | S | C |

Palomino Euro Bistro S | 21 | 22 | 20 | $28 |
Pacific First Ctr., 1420 Fifth Ave. (Pike St.), 206-623-1300
◪ Its "casual elegance works well for business and pleasure", but its "trendy" Med menu appeals to "a clientele so good looking it's hard to focus on the meal"; for some it's a "reward after shopping at City Centre", for others a "fun after-work getaway" whose bar is the "perfect place for beer and appetizers"; yet critics of this "glamour formula restaurant" chant: "look chic, be chic, eat elsewhere."

Pandasia S | 18 | 10 | 15 | $16 |
1625 W. Dravus St. (16th Ave.), 206-283-9030
◪ Surveyors are split over this Interbay Pan-Asian; some say the "diverse", "fresh and delicious" menu (featuring "homemade spinach noodles like you never had before") is "satisfying, reliable" and available via "the best Chinese delivery ever"; critics claim that since breaking away from its Wedgwood sibling (now renamed Black Pearl), it "went downhill", and a slip in ratings supports this point of view.

Paragon Bar & Grill S | 18 | 16 | 16 | $25 |
2410 Queen Anne Ave. N. (Boston St.), 206-283-4548
◪ In this sleek bar and grill atop Queen Anne, "the food looks beautiful" as do the "beautiful people"; relax in the handsome dining area or join the "noisy yuppies on the prowl" up front in the bar; optimists insist that the "great" NW fare is "sometimes overlooked because the bar [scene] is so great", while detractors declare: "reduce the focus on drinks and increase the focus on food."

PASEO CARIBBEAN FOOD S⇍ | 25 | 8 | 14 | $10 |
4225 Fremont Ave. N. (bet. 42nd & 43rd Aves.), 206-545-7440
■ Cuban ex-pat Lorenzo Lorenzo (a name so nice he's got it twice) gives it all he's got at this Upper Fremont Caribbean "hole-in-the-wall" where a dozen customers mean a crowd; and what he's got is grilled chicken and scallops soaked in an "addictive" secret marinade that has fans begging "I want to know what's in that stuff!"

Pasta & Co. | 22 | 14 | 17 | $13 |
University Village, 2640 NE University Village (25th St.), 206-523-8594 ●S
Harvard Mkt., 815 E. Pike St. (bet. Broadway & Harvard St.), 206-322-4577 S
1001 Fourth Ave. Plaza (Spring St.), 206-624-3008
2109 Queen Anne Ave. N. (W. Crockett St.), 206-283-1182 S
10218 NE Eighth St. (102nd Ave. NE), Bellevue, 425-453-8760 S
■ Marcella Rosene's city-wide outlets for "gourmet on the run" "can always be counted on" for "totally terrific takeout"; "the smells lure you in, but the food keeps you coming back" for "inventive salads", "satisfying" pastas and "picnic supplies" that "beat cooking at home"; but wallet-watchers whine that the "quality takeout" and fancy packaged goods are "not for the budget-conscious."

Seattle | F | D | S | C |

Pasta Bella 🆂   18 | 15 | 17 | $19
5909 15th Ave. NW (bet. 59th & 60th Sts.), 206-789-4933
1530 Queen Anne Ave. N. (Garfield St.), 206-284-9827
■ While devotees of this Italian duo declare its "tasty food" a "good value", cynics snipe "Pasta Bada", citing "so-so" fare; still, Queen Anne fans favor the "cozy fireplace" and the "nonsmoking deck" at that branch.

Pasta Ya Gotcha   13 | 11 | 12 | $10
823 Third Ave. (Marion St.), 206-223-4788
123 Lake St. S. (Central Way), Kirkland, 425-889-1511 🆂
11025 NE Eighth St. (110th Ave.), Bellevue, 425-637-7019 🆂
■ Surveyors are split on this 'International pasta bar' trio; fans come for "cheap and quick" fare served in settings with "fun decor", but critics complain about "blah" pasta that "gives Italian a bad name."

Pazzo's ◐🆂   19 | 15 | 17 | $16
2307 Eastlake Ave. E. (Lynn St.), 206-329-6558
■ This "informal" pizza joint is a home away from home for Eastlake apartment-dwellers and U-Dubbers, just the ticket for a salad, a microbrew and some of the "best calzones around"; the brick and wood-beam accents lend a civilized feel, but it's "very kid-friendly" nonetheless.

Pecos Pit BBQ ⌿   24 | 7 | 16 | $9
2260 First Ave. S. (bet. Holgate & Lander Sts.), 206-623-0629
■ "When you can't resist messy beef" go for the brisket sandwich and expect a "religious experience"; tell smiling owners Ron and Debra Wise to 'spike it' (with a hot link) and you'll understand why "long lines" of "fans flock to the place" across from Starbucks headquarters for "the best damn barbecue in the state"; you can sit outdoors at picnic tables or take your 'cue to go.

Pegasus Pizza & Pasta 🆂   22 | 14 | 18 | $14
2758 Alki Ave. SW (bet. 61st & 62nd Aves.), 206-932-4849
12669 NE 85th St. (126th Ave. NE), Kirkland, 425-822-7400 ◐
4201 NE Sunset Blvd. (Union Ave.), Renton, 425-271-4510
■ Customers "get cravings for Tom's special pizza" – the Greek-accented house pie that pulls 'em in at branches in West Seattle, Kirkland and Renton; "humongous salads" and homey pastas are every bit as much of a draw; since "it's hard to get a table" at the Alki branch, which has a "view of the beach", do as the locals do: "call ahead" and get it to go.

Perché No 🆂   20 | 15 | 20 | $30
621½ Queen Anne Ave. N. (bet. Mercer & Roy Sts.), 206-298-0230
■ "Can an Asian couple run a good Italian restaurant? *Perché no*? [Why not?]" insist those who've tried this "charming" spot whose proximity to Seattle Center makes it "ideal before the opera"; the "personable owners" also provide "fast service for the theater crowd" (and "limos to Seattle Center"), so they "get you out in time for the show."

Pescatore [S] 20 | 23 | 20 | $27

5300 34th Ave. NW (54th St.), 206-784-1733

◪ Enjoy "excellent seafood and service" at this big, "bright and comfortable" Locks-side stop; though it's "changed chefs and management too often" (leaving critics crying "inconsistent"), most agree the place has "much improved" and "has evolved into a focused and friendly" fish house; nosh on appetizers in the bar or "ask for a seat on the patio" and "watch the passing boats on the Ship Canal."

Philadelphia Fevre Steak & Hoagie Shop ▽ 20 | 9 | 9 | $10

2332 E. Madison St. (John St.), 206-323-1000

◪ Former Philadelphian Renée LeFevre mans the grill at this stripped-down Madison Valley steak-and-hoagie house; her fries are crinkly, her cheese is appropriately Whiz-like and her steak sandwiches are served up sizzling; sit at the counter or grab a table in the dining room and order up; it's "not as good as the real thing, but it's close", and, of *course* there's TastyKake for dessert.

Phoenecia at Alki [S] 22 | 19 | 22 | $26

2716 Alki Ave. SW (bet. 60th & 61st Aves.), 206-935-6550

◪ Let the Mediterranean sun shine on you at Alki Beach, where Hussein Khazaal runs from table to table, offering "gracious service" and making his longtime fans "feel special"; "enjoy his generosity" and his menu, which ranges from Middle Eastern to Italian; if you don't know what to order "let the owner take over – he will anyway."

Piecora's [S] 17 | 9 | 12 | $12

1401 E. Madison St. (14th Ave.), 206-322-9411
Bridle Trails Mall, 6501 132nd Ave. NE (NE 70th St.), Kirkland, 425-861-7000

◪ It's "the closest thing to New York pizza" proclaim those who know that Piecora's "cheesiest" are "on cardiologists' top 10 hit list"; don't expect much when it comes to decor at the Capitol Hill digs (where it's "too smoky to breathe" and customers wonder "is that a nose ring or an olive slice on my pizza?"), and in Kirkland some say "logy service" leads to "missing ingredients."

Pink Door Ristorante 20 | 21 | 18 | $25

Pike Place Mkt., 1919 Post Alley (bet. Stewart & Virginia Sts.), 206-443-3242

■ "There's not a better place to be on a summer evening" than the Pink Door's rooftop deck, thanks to its "spectacular view" of Elliott Bay; "dark and sexy" with "occasional celebrity sightings", this "quirky" bar and restaurant offers "a reason to fight the crowds in Pike Place Market", who come for "simple pastas" as well as "jazzed-up Italian classics"; there's cabaret in the lounge and a "menu for late-night nibbles."

Seattle

| | F | D | S | C |

Place Pigalle — 24 | 23 | 22 | $33
Pike Place Mkt., 81 Pike St. (Pike Pl.), 206-624-1756
■ "Small and intimate" with a "dreamy view of the Sound", this "delightful" French bistro with a Northwest accent is "worth trying to find" (pssst: it's "behind the pig" in Pike Place Market); sure it holds much appeal for savvy tourists, but even locals are inclined to "skip work and play hooky at this romantic spot" with a "charming" little bar and clutch of outdoor tables; in sum, most say it's got the "perfect combination of food, decor, service and price."

Place Hollywood S — 8 | 16 | 11 | $20
1500 Sixth Ave. (Pike St.), 206-287-0001
■ "Ugh!" they "should have stayed in Hollywood" declare detractors who give a "thumbs down" to this "tourists-only" "blight on Downtown", where a "fun atmosphere" and "lively decor" can't make up for what many consider "some of the worst food I've ever had"; still, it's "great for kids" and the perfect place to "take people when you don't really want to talk to them."

Plenty Cafe S — 22 | 18 | 18 | $19
1404 34th Ave. (Union St.), 206-324-1214
■ "Great for eating in or taking out", "Madrona's best-kept secret" is "a true find" in a "comfortable", "country-store setting"; chef/co-owner "Jim Watkins is an artist with food" whose "inventive" dishes and "regularly changing [NW] menu" are "not as vegetarian" as some suspect.

Pogacha — 17 | 13 | 17 | $18
Bellevue Plaza, 119 106th Ave. (Main St.), Bellevue, 425-455-5670
120 NW Gilman Blvd. (Front St.), Issaquah, 425-392-5550 S
■ "Tasty" and "a little different", Bellevue's Croatian-influenced pizza, pasta and sandwichery (the name refers to a Croatian dinner roll, baked here in a wood-fired oven) recently changed hands and cloned itself in a newer, larger and more attractive Issaquah setting.

Pon Proem S — ▽ 22 | 15 | 21 | $16
3039 78th Ave. SE (bet. 77th & 78th Sts.), Mercer Island, 206-236-8424
■ Though "good restaurants are hard to come by on the Eastside", Mercer Islanders rely on this "authentic" Thai for "good-sized portions" of "fresh", "tasty" fare.

Pontevecchio — 19 | 14 | 19 | $24
710 N. 34th St. (Fremont Ave. N.), 206-633-3983
◪ In the shadow of the Fremont Bridge, Michele Zacco's "intimate" Southern Italian offers a "warm setting" and "homey atmosphere" with "good schtick" (flamenco dancers, Friday night opera); but while fans insist it "feels like Florence", critics counter "the food's mediocre" and "the sauces all taste the same."

Seattle   F | D | S | C

PONTI SEAFOOD GRILL S   24 | 24 | 22 | $34
3014 Third Ave. N. (Nickerson St.), 206-284-3000
■ "Romantic inside, delightful outside", this "elegant", Eclectic sib of Adriatica and Axis features "consistently well-prepared seafood" (including its shellfish-laden "Thai curry penne – addictive and illegal in 49 states"); the "lovely view of the Ship Canal", "great happy hour specials" in the bar, Sunday brunch and a "super wine list" make this the right choice "for all occasions", including "business or romance."

Poor Italian Cafe S   19 | 17 | 18 | $22
2000 Second Ave. (Virginia St.), 206-441-4313
◪ This "neighborhood bistro in the heart of Downtown" garners mixed reviews; some enjoy "yummy, authentic fare" ("love those meatballs!" and "the best puttanesca in town") that is modestly priced "in a town full of overpriced Italian food"; critics cite "undercooked pasta" and "inconsistent" meals, but fans say the "noisy" atmo and "informal service" "reminds us of the wonderful Italian restaurants in Italy and NYC."

Prego S   19 | 20 | 22 | $31
Madison Renaissance Hotel, 515 Madison St. (6th Ave.), 206-583-0300
◪ High atop the Madison Renaissance Hotel, this Italian caters to hotel guests who swoon over the panorama from the 28th floor; though the dining room is otherwise "not much on atmosphere", "the wonderful view" is almost worth the price of admission.

Provinces S   ▽ 21 | 15 | 18 | $18
Old Mill Town, 201 Fifth Ave. S. (Maple St.), Edmonds, 425-744-0288
◪ Owner "Ken Lee has a way with Oriental flavors" at his Edmonds antique mall haunt (big sib to the newer, flashier Shallots Asian Bistro in Belltown); this been-around-awhile Pan-Asian appeals primarily to the egg-drop soup crowd; smokers bend an elbow in the bar, while families and neighborhood business folk dine in a pastel-colored dining room that some find "depressing", its peekaboo Sound view notwithstanding.

Pyramid Alehouse S   16 | 17 | 15 | $16
91 S. Royal Brougham Way (1st Ave.), 206-682-3377
■ Proximity to the ill-fated Kingdome and its ballpark successor, Safeco Field, makes this "temple of butthead sports lovers" the perfect place for "grease and salt" standards and other "better-than-average pub food"; a "fun, open", "nonsmoking" "hangout", it features "excellent beer" ("tour the brewery while you're there"); some say "if you want service, avoid game days."

Seattle F | D | S | C

Queen City Grill Ⓢ 21 | 20 | 20 | $30
2201 First Ave. (Blanchard St.), 206-443-0975
■ This "high-energy" "Belltown landmark" is always "jam-packed", "lively" and "way too loud"; the "see-and-be-seen" crowd oozes "urban chic" as it "bellies up to the bar" or confabs at "intimate" booths, sipping "great wines" and taking advantage of the "consistently good" seafood-centric NW grill menu.

Queen Mary Ⓢ 20 | 23 | 20 | $17
2912 NE 55th St. (25th Ave.), 206-527-2770
■ "Classy" and "charming", this "quaint" Ravenna tearoom serves breakfast and lunch and is the perfect place to "take mom" for a veddy English "grown-up tea party"; you'll sup on "excellent pastries" and crustless cucumber sandwiches, sip a souchong and "feel like a lady", raising pinkies and eyebrows at those who cough "overpriced!"

Racha Ⓢ 19 | 16 | 18 | $15
537 First Ave. N. (Mercer St.), 206-281-8883
■ The "cheerful atmosphere, great service and above-average" Thai food have fans "eating their way through the menu" at "everybody's noodle house" – a popular "bargain"-priced "addition to the Lower Queen Anne theater district"; with "delicious pad Thai" and "duck noodle soup to die for", this "clean, fast" newcomer "is a delight every time."

Raga Ⓢ 19 | 16 | 17 | $20
555 108th Ave. NE (6th St.), Bellevue, 425-450-0336
◪ Fans call Kamal Mroke's Eastsider their "favorite Indian", praising the "enjoyable", "consistent" cooking, "the lightest of breads" and the "attentive service"; while a few wallet-watchers claim that it's "too expensive", most maintain the "lunch buffet is a real deal."

RAY'S BOATHOUSE & CAFE Ⓢ 22 | 23 | 21 | $33
6049 Seaview Ave. NW (near Shilshole Marina), 206-789-4130
◪ With its "incredible" Shilshole locale, "magnificent sunset view" and "excellent wine list", Ray's is still considered "one of the best" by some and the "definitive Seattle seafooder" by many; though "seen as touristy" – with fish that "ranges from fabulous to ok" – it remains a "must-do for out-of-towners"; all concur that "nothing beats the deck" or the "great happy hour" at its "fun" "upstairs cafe."

Red Door Alehouse Ⓢ 17 | 15 | 15 | $14
3401 Fremont Ave. N. (34th St.), 206-547-7521
■ "Pub grub at its finest" crow the "fraternity guys" and neighborhood salty dogs who claim this "always dependable" "corner hangout" and "Fremont institution" serves the "best bar food in town"; "excellent burgers", "great sandwiches" and steamed mussels go down better with one of many "good" brews on tap.

| Seattle | F | D | S | C |

Red Mill Burgers 🅢⊘ | 22 | 11 | 14 | $10 |
312 N. 67th St. (Phinney Ave.), 206-783-6362
1613 W. Dravus St. (16th Ave.), 206-284-6363
■ There's "always a line out the door" at these "upscale burger joints", but the end-product's "worth the wait" and even vegetarians "can't stop raving"; Babe and John Shepherd "raise hamburgers and shakes to an art form" and serve the "best onion rings on the planet"; when the lunch and dinner rush is going full-bore "don't count on being able to sit down to eat" at either the Phinney Ridge or newer Interbay branch.

Red Robin 🅢 | – | – | – | I |
3272 Fuhrman Ave. NE (Eastlake Ave. E.), 206-323-0917
1100 Fourth Ave. (Spring St.), 206-447-1909
Northgate Mall, 138 Northgate Plaza, 206-365-0933
Pier 55, 1101 Alaskan Way, 206-623-1942
11021 NE Eighth St. (110th Ave.), Bellevue, 425-453-9522
22705 Marine View Dr. S. (227th St.), Des Moines, 206-824-2214
1085 Lake Dr. (Pickering Pl.), Issaquah, 425-313-0950
With a flagship anchoring the Southern end of the University Bridge, this bright, cheerful "hamburger chain" is a hit for "family dining"; the youngsters love the all-American menu, and oldsters are content because they "can get a drink."

REINER'S | 25 | 24 | 25 | $39 |
1106 Eighth Ave. (bet. Seneca & Spring Sts.), 206-624-2222
■ "First-class food and atmosphere", "European charm" and "warm, professional service" add up to high scores all around for this "jewel" on First Hill; chef-owner Hanspeter Aebersold's "excellent Continental menu, with German specials" is far from cutting edge (which explains its appeal to the "blue hair set"), but his "little hideaway" is "cheaper than a trip" abroad and every bit as "special."

Relais | – | – | – | M |
(nka Hillside Bar & Grill)
17121 Bothell Way NE (96th Ave. NE), Bothell, 425-485-7600
This "unlikely [Bothell] spot" was long "a favorite under former owner Gerard Parrat", but became "a more relaxed fave" under new chef-owner Eric Eisenberg who, boosters say, "is improving this restaurant every day"; he's renamed and reenvisioned the place, turned the main dining room into a fireside lounge and added fancy burgers and bar food to a menu of well-received French bistro classics.

Restaurant, The 🅢 | 16 | 17 | 15 | $23 |
(fka Ernie's)
Hotel Edgewater, Pier 67, 2411 Alaskan Way, 206-269-4575
◪ New chef Scott Blackerby specializes in cooking with a Pacific NW twist at this waterfront Downtowner; the results are "good for guests" of the hotel, but the Sunday brunch buffet and a wide-open view of the Sound seem to be the main attractions for the typical native.

Rhododendron Café [S] 19 | 15 | 18 | $21
5521 Chuckanut Dr. (Bow Hill Rd.), Bow, 360-766-6667
◪ "Quaint and cozy", this "underappreciated discovery" with "zero pretentions" is like a visit "to your country aunt's" for "wonderful home-cooked meals and desserts" with an International accent; though spoilers cry "average food", the majority makes the trip to Bow just to eat "portobello burgers" at this beloved spot along scenic Chuckanut Drive.

Ristorante Buongusto [S] 21 | 18 | 20 | $26
2232 Queen Anne Ave. N. (McGraw St.), 206-284-9040
■ "Delicious" cuisine, "gracious hosts", "good service" and a "warm" atmosphere attract Queen Anne regulars to Salvio and Anna Varchetta's "great Italian neighborhood find"; "upper-class peasant food" is not an oxymoron here where they serve the "best bruschetta in town."

Ristorante Paradiso [S] 19 | 16 | 18 | $27
120-A Park Ln. (Lake Washington Blvd.), Kirkland, 425-889-8601
◪ "Make reservations or wait" for "reasonably priced" "solid [Southern] Italian food" in the heart of downtown Kirkland; loyalists like the "friendly staff", "excellent pasta" and "veal funghi that's a mouthwatering experience", but the less enthused exclaim that it's "better than ok but not great."

Ristorante Salute [S] 19 | 17 | 17 | $24
3426 NE 55th St. (35th Ave.), 206-527-8600
◪ "Never bad, never great, but always consistent", this "cute" Ravenna cafe with the Eastside sib (Salute of Bellevue) is "what Italian should taste like, smell like and look like"; expect "all-around good food at a good price", but don't expect Salute to be in its original, cozier location – it's now located up the block on the corner.

Romio's Pizza & Pasta [S] 15 | 9 | 13 | $13
8523 Greenwood Ave. N. (bet. 85th & 87th Sts.), 206-782-9005
12501 Lake City Way NE (125th St.), 206-362-8080
2001 W. Dravus St. (20th Ave.), 206-284-5420
3242 Eastlake Ave. E. (Fuhrman Ave.), 206-322-4453
917 Howell St. (9th Ave.), 206-622-6878
◪ "Quick, call Pizza Hut" cry critics of this minichain, who claim it serves "bland", "cardboard pizza" in settings with "no atmosphere" and "slow" staffers; but a few insist "try the G.A.S.P. pizza" – it's topped with garlic, artichoke hearts, sun-dried tomatoes and pesto and it's "good."

Rosebud Restaurant & Bar [S] 15 | 16 | 16 | $17
719 E. Pike St. (Harvard Ave.), 206-323-6636
◪ Fans feel this Capitol Hill eatery is a "great neighborhood cafe" that's "ok for food and coffee", though some Gen Xers "go for the atmosphere alone" (comfy booths in the dining room, couches in the lounge); that said, pessimists contend the Eclectic menu brings to mind "amateurs trying, but not making it."

Seattle | F | D | S | C |

Rosita's Mexican Grill 🅂 | 19 | 15 | 18 | $15 |
7210 Woodlawn Ave. NE (bet. 71st & 72nd Sts.), 206-523-3031
Holman Rd. Sq., 9747 Fourth Ave. NW (Holman Rd.), 206-784-4132

■ "The food is a step above the usual chains" at these "dependable" North End twins where "cheerful", "fast" service and a "fun atmosphere" make eating especially "great for kids"; dipsters and sipsters give a big nod to "flavorful salsas" and homemade tortillas and come here to relax over a "happy-hour super nacho plate with margaritas – the perfect Friday night meal."

ROVER'S | 28 | 24 | 27 | $65 |
2808 E. Madison St. (28th Ave.), 206-325-7442

■ "Gifted chef" Thierry Rautureau presides over "the best special occasion place in the Northwest", where you can "indulge all your senses" with "impeccable everything"; "is there an award he hasn't won?" ask surveyors who have voted this "charming" Frenchman's "romantic" Madison Park hideaway No. 1 for Food; "always superb", the "world-class" prix fixe menu is "spendy", but well worth the "splurge" for "ambrosia on a plate."

Roy's Seattle 🅂 | 22 | 20 | 21 | $34 |
Westin Hotel, 1900 Fifth Ave. (Stewart St.), 206-256-7697

◪ Surveyors are split over Roy Yamaguchi's "Hawaiian transplant" in the Westin Hotel; fans feel that this "newcomer ranks with the best as a great addition to the Seattle food scene", with a "clever menu" and "well-prepared", "imaginative" Euro-Asian cuisine; but critics counter that the cooking "is not as good as the reputation that preceded it" and the atmosphere "lacks the zip and electricity of Roy's other locations."

Roy St. Bistro 🅂 | 19 | 16 | 20 | $28 |
174 Roy St. (2nd Ave. N.), 206-284-9093

■ "Who said English food sucks?" ask fans of Patrick Conlan's "charming" bistro with an "interesting" Northern European menu; "good before the opera" and "convenient to the Rep", its "quaint", "low-key atmosphere" appeals to the Seattle Center crowd who also stop by post-event to wait out traffic over dessert and a nightcap.

Ruth's Chris Steak House 🅂 | 24 | 19 | 22 | $42 |
Seafirst Plaza, 800 Fifth Ave. (Columbia St.), 206-624-8524

◪ "Yeah, it's a chain – I don't care" sums up the attitude of those convinced this Downtowner is "the best of the gourmet steakhouses" and just the venue for "adult dining with not too much fuss"; some grumble the "men's club decor" is "lost in time" and warn "everything is à la carte and the bill really adds up", but most shrug: "go if you have low cholesterol and lots of money."

Seattle | F | D | S | C |

Sahib S | ▽ 23 | 17 | 21 | $24 |
101 Main St. (Ferry Terminal), Edmonds, 425-775-2828
■ Edmonds Indian with "lots of good choices", a bargain-priced lunch buffet, full bar and a "very personable staff"; there's a "nicely decorated dining room" with a view of the Olympics and the Sound, or you can dine out on the deck – but hold on to your naan: the train tracks are only feet away.

Saigon Bistro S | 21 | 9 | 14 | $11 |
1032 S. Jackson St. (12th Ave.), 206-329-4939
■ "Can't find a parking spot? that's because every Vietnamese in town who knows his onions dines here"; the "no-frills" atmo leads some to cry into their "fabulous soup" over "substandard surroundings", but not enough to keep them from the "fantastic" fare at this Jackson fave.

SALEH AL LAGO | 26 | 21 | 25 | $39 |
6804 Green Lake Way N. (1st Ave. NE), 206-524-4044
■ Saleh Joudeh "continues to produce outstanding food year after year" at this "small, out-of-the-way" "upscale [Northern] Italian" near Green Lake; a who's who of local luminaries dine on the "best veal in town" served by an "exemplary" staff ("take their recommendations"); but alas, a vocal contingent finds the "atmosphere sterile", insisting that "such good food demands more sophisticated decor."

SALISH LODGE S | 23 | 26 | 22 | $42 |
Salish Lodge & Spa, 6501 Railroad Ave. SE (Hwy. 202), Snoqualmie, 425-831-6550
■ A "destination restaurant with an A+ wine list" and a "pricey" NW-inspired menu, this "romantic getaway" with a "terrific view of Snoqualmie Falls" is a "special occasion spot" that's also "famous for its country breakfasts" (just "don't expect to move afterward"); though a meal's "worth the drive", why not "spoil yourself" and "stay at the lodge?"

Salmon Bay Café S | 16 | 11 | 16 | $14 |
5109 Shilshole Ave. NW (20th Ave.), 206-782-5539
■ "Fishermen eat here because of the [Ballard waterfront] location", "great greasy eggs", "excellent" oversized omelets and other Americana; "negative points on decor" don't keep them away from this "funky place" where the lines are always long on weekends.

Salty's S | 17 | 21 | 18 | $30 |
1936 Harbor Ave. SW (19th St.), 206-937-1600
28201 Redondo Beach Dr. S. (280th St.), Federal Way, 253-946-0636
◪ Despite the "outstanding Seattle skyline view" from Alki and a "delightful" vista in Redondo Beach, these waterside twins draw mixed reviews when it comes to their "high-priced", seafood-centric menus; while some laud "excellent salmon" and "the best Sunday brunch", critics contend the fare's "bland" and "doesn't equal the view."

Seattle | F | D | S | C |

Salute of Bellevue S | 16 | 16 | 16 | $25 |
10134 Main St. (bet. 101st & 102nd Aves. SE), Bellevue, 425-688-7613
☒ "Put some rugs on the floor, something to absorb the noise" cry critics after eating at this Eastside version of the "much better" Ravenna original; the red-gravy Italian food gets a thumbs-up from some (who cite "great antipasto" and "chicken Gorgonzola"), but a "ho hum" from others; some sniff that the "snotty help" merits no salutes.

Salvatore Ristorante | 22 | 18 | 20 | $24 |
6100 Roosevelt Way NE (61st St.), 206-527-9301
■ The "warm, welcoming ambiance", "broad menu of specialties" and "excellent wines at fair prices" help make Salvatore Anania's place near the U-District an "all-time pick for neighborhood Italian"; his "specials never fail to delight", nor do his servers, who will likely "recognize you on trip number two."

Sanmi Sushi S | 23 | 14 | 16 | $22 |
2601 W. Marina Pl. (Smith Cove), 206-283-9978
■ Snug in the shadow of Palisade, chef Misao Sanmi presides at this Japanese that shares space in a modest office complex at Smith Cove; though the service can be "indifferent" and the decor less than exciting (anything would pale next to Palisade), the "excellent", "impeccably fresh" sushi makes loyalists out of all who enter.

Santa Fe Cafe S | 20 | 16 | 17 | $21 |
5910 Phinney Ave. N. (bet. 59th & 60th Sts.), 206-783-9755
2255 NE 65th St. (23rd Ave.), 206-524-7736
■ "Comfortable, casual" sibs with "unique" "upscale" Mexican-Southwestern food that are definitely "not your standard nachos and burritos places"; the cooks have a "magical touch with chile peppers" and regulars know not to miss the "garlic custard (wow!)."

Sazerac S | 20 | 23 | 19 | $32 |
Hotel Monaco, 1101 Fourth Ave. (Spring St.), 206-624-7755
☒ Big Dawg Jan Birnbaum (Napa Valley's Catahoula) is "helping spice up Seattle" in the Hotel Monaco Downtown; the "gorgeous" space is "vibrant", thanks in part to a "great bar scene"; yes, "the Big Dawg has barked" with "bold" bites and "festive" Louisiana-accented Southern cooking, but some say the food "doesn't always work" and "isn't worth the hype", adding that the "service is slow."

Scarlet Tree S | 17 | 11 | 18 | $14 |
6521 Roosevelt Way NE (65th St.), 206-523-7153
☒ Though known primarily as a bluesy music venue, mornings mean "good greasy breakfasts" at Roosevelt's "pleasant-enough neighborhood dive"; the dinner menu offers diner-style Americana, but those in the know go the gimee-a-beer route come evening and call it a day.

Seattle | F | D | S | C |

Sea Garden ⓢ   20 | 12 | 16 | $20
509 Seventh Ave. S. (S. King St.), 206-623-2100
200 106th Ave. NE (2nd St.), Bellevue, 425-450-8833

☑ "Forget the NY atmosphere, just eat!" and " if you order right you can experience great Chinese food" at these seafooders in the I.D. ("open late at night") and Bellevue; some diners insist "the Seattle version is better than the Eastside", but most agree the big draw at either is the "wonderful crab in black bean sauce"; too bad the "facilities need attention" and "inscrutable waiters are no help."

Seattle Catch Seafood Bistro ⓢ   20 | 16 | 18 | $22
460 N. 36th St. (Dayton Ave.), 206-632-6110

■ "A great new addition" to the Seattle seafood scene, this "funky Fremonter with class" boasts a "beautifully restored bar"; "the freshest fish is simply prepared", as are "yummy pastas", but while there's overall "excellent value" here, some say that the "best deals are at lunch."

Serafina ⓢ   22 | 22 | 19 | $28
2043 Eastlake Ave. E. (Boston St.), 206-323-0807

☑ "Seductive lighting", "live jazz" and "terrace dining" that's "great in summer" mean this "romantic, intimate and delicious" "rustic" Italian Eastlake bistro is "always busy"; but for many, the "warm, inviting room and food are cooled by the wait and the staff."

74th St. Ale House ⓢ   17 | 14 | 15 | $14
7401 Greenwood Ave. N. (74th St.), 206-784-2955

■ "You can't lose" with "lunch and a brew" ("do a Thomas Kemper and a bucket o' mussels") at this ale house with "innovative" – although some say "overspiced" – pub fare; a "comfortable", "nice neighborhood setting" helps make this the equivalent of "*Cheers* in Seattle."

Shallots Asian Bistro   23 | 20 | 22 | $23
2525 Fourth Ave. (Vine St.), 206-728-1888

■ After much success at Provinces in Edmonds, chef Ken Lee brought his act to Belltown and the word's out: "this isn't just a poor man's Wild Ginger" – "the food is almost as good as the Ginger with no waiting!"; so it's no surprise that fans of this "small", "priced-right" Pan-Asian with "attentive service" say they "could eat here every night."

Shamiana ⓢ   24 | 18 | 21 | $21
Houghton Village, 10724 NE 68th St. (108th Ave.), Kirkland, 425-827-4902

■ "In Kirkland, this is exotic" – particularly considering the "shopping center setting" where locals come for Indian food "as it was meant to be: spicy and flavorful"; "delicious curries, lovingly prepared" by chef-owner Eric Larson (who was raised with his sister and co-owner, Tracy, on the subcontinent) are "authentic and tasty", and the "interesting menu" is as appealing as the budget-priced lunch buffet.

Shanghai Garden [S] | 25 | 13 | 16 | $19 |
524 Sixth Ave. S. (Weller St.), 206-625-1689
80 Front St. N. (I-90, exit 17), Issaquah, 425-313-3188
Shanghai Cafe [S]
Factoria Sq. Mall, 12708 SE 38th St. (bet. 126th & 128th Aves.), Bellevue, 425-603-1689
■ "A pleasure in the I.D., a jewel in Issaquah", this duo is the No. 1 rated Chinese in the Seattle *Survey*, "amazing" eats, including "sweet chile shrimp, yes!" and other "unique dishes not found elsewhere", mean it's "head-and-shoulders above" others of its ilk; sensitive sorts sigh that while the service is "efficient", it's "not always friendly"; N.B. the smaller Shanghai Cafe offshoot, which offers an identical menu, is new and unrated.

Sharp's Roaster & Ale House [S] ▽ | 19 | 18 | 19 | $18 |
18427 Pacific Hwy. S. (188th St.), 206-241-5744
◪ Its "great beer selection" and "a lot of roasted" meats and poultry on the menu characterize this American; while some say the fare is "bland", most maintain that the spot serves as a "good stop-off" if you're near Sea-Tac airport.

Shea's Lounge ◐ [S] | 24 | 24 | 23 | $24 |
Pike Place Mkt., 94 Pike St. (1st Ave.), 206-467-9990
■ "The ultimate romantic hideaway" is almost invisible from the Market below (pssst: stand under the clock, face the Corner Market Building, then look up), but those privy to its secrets find this lounge act adjoining Sandy Shea's elegant prix fixer "a great way to get the excellent food of Chez Shea without the expense"; "dark", "comfortable" and "cool", it's "the place for drinks and conversation" while nibbling on Mediterranean-inspired fare.

SHIRO'S SUSHI [S] | 27 | 17 | 21 | $31 |
2401 Second Ave. (Battery St.), 206-443-9844
■ Celebrated sushi chef Shiro Kashiba made his name at Nikko, but his followers now flock to his eponymous Belltowner for "sushi from heaven" that makes it Seattle's No. 1 for Japanese; "sit at the counter and watch an artist in action", but "get there when they unlock the door or you'll have to give people the evil eye" as you wait; the decor is "simple and classy", though "elbow-to-elbow" tables and "paper napkins disappoint."

SHOALWATER [S] | 26 | 23 | 23 | $37 |
Shelburne Inn, 4415 Pacific Hwy. (45th St.), Seaview, 360-642-4142
■ For a "very special" meal at Ann and Tony Kischner's "warm, cozy" restaurant in the 1896 Shelburne Inn, it's "worth a trip" to the Pacific Coast; though it's close to the beach, there's "no view" from the formal dining room, but the "NW ingredients are skillfully prepared" and the wine list is carefully composed; the adjoining Heron & Beaver Pub – a great rainy day spot – shares its kitchen.

Shuckers [S] 23 22 23 $30
Four Seasons Olympic Hotel, 411 University St. (4th Ave.), 206-621-1984
■ Anchoring a handsome corner in the Four Seasons Olympic Hotel, this "clubby, pleasant" "old-style grill" features the "friendliest oyster bar in town", as well as "excellent seafood and service"; its location makes it a prime place for lunch, "a good choice for an informal meal" and a convenient "pre-symphony" stop.

Shultzy's [S]🚫 21 10 16 $8
4112 University Way NE (bet. 41st & 42nd Sts.), 206-548-9461
■ Don Schulze's longtime U-District dive, where "a friendly bunch of guys" sat at the counter snarfing "the best sausages in town", is a dive no more – it's moved to much snazzier quarters just up the block, thus outdating the above decor score; you "always get your money's worth" here, plus you can now chug a brew or two with your chow.

Simpatico [S] 19 18 19 $23
4430 Wallingford Ave. N. (45th St.), 206-632-1000
■ Wallingford "old-school" Italian whose "broad menu", "good food", "polished staff" and "kid-friendly" atmosphere make it a "nice" "neighborhood place"; it's "cozy on winter evenings" and offers patio seating in summer.

Sisters European Snacks [S]🚫 19 11 12 $10
Pike Place Mkt., 1530 Post Alley (Pine St.), 206-623-6723
◪ The Jacobi sisters preside at this colorful Euro-style quick eatery in Pike Place Market, where an open-air Post Alley perch provides "a nice vantage point from which to people-watch"; "sit at the counter" and choose "good grilled panini" or "tasty side salads" from a rotating menu; still, some surveyors say that service is "not super friendly" and one insultee insists "the cashier yelled at me!"

Sit & Spin [S]🚫 14 20 14 $12
2219 Fourth Ave. (bet. Bell & Blanchard Sts.), 206-441-9484
■ The Gen X Laundromat of choice is this "loud and crazy" Belltown site, where scenesters watch their undies spin while they groove on "coffee, music" and a budget-priced, veggie-heavy menu; the "awesome juice bar" and "great [fermented] drink choices" are popular, and the live music is a hit with Tide-toting "groupies."

Six Degrees [S] 17 18 16 $19
7900 Green Lake Dr. N. (Ashworth Ave.), 206-523-1600
121 Park Ln. (Kirkland Ave.), Kirkland, 425-803-1766
◪ This Green Lake New American and its Kirkland kin have hit on a "great concept" – a "lively and colorful" tavern setting primed with a formidable "beer selection" and a "creative" pub menu offering "variations on popular themes"; critics cite "mediocre" eats and "noisy and hectic" dinner crowds ("I may be too old for this place").

Snappy Dragon [S] 21 | 12 | 17 | $16

8917 Roosevelt Way NE (bet. 89th & 90th Sts.), 206-528-5575

◪ "Sometimes uneven but often outstanding", the Maple Leaf answer to the I.D. is home to "tasty" Chinese (including chef-owner Judy Fu's "addictive" homemade noodles) that competes with "the best" in town; some say it's "lost its snap", though, and note the two "small rooms" are "not much to look at" ("great takeout" is an option).

Sostanza Trattoria 23 | 22 | 22 | $34

1927 43rd Ave. E. (Madison St.), 206-324-9701

■ Supporters sigh the "food is better than ever" at Lorenzo Cianciusi's "incredibly romantic" Northern Italian "favorite"; the "great neighborhood vibe" makes it a home away from home for Madison Park's movers and shakers, a "lovely place to have dinner outside" that's every bit as appealing for a rustic meal "by the fire on a cold night."

Space Needle Restaurant [S] 14 | 23 | 16 | $37

Seattle Ctr., 219 Fourth Ave. N. (Broad St.), 206-443-2100

◪ "The old adage about revolving restaurants proves true" at Seattle's signature "tourist trap": "the view's great, the food's mediocre"; the 360-degree vista from the Needle's 500-foot vertical vantage is "unsurpassed", but the consensus is the NW-inspired fare "needs some work"; still, many grant it's a winner when the time comes to bring "your mother-in-law" up for Sunday brunch.

Spazzo Mediterranean Grill [S] 19 | 21 | 19 | $26

Key Bank Bldg., 10655 NE Fourth St. (106th Ave.), Bellevue, 425-454-8255

■ With "cool decor" and a "wonderful view" from atop Bellevue's Key Bank building, this Med "favorite for casual dining" is as much an "all-ages" spot as it is a "date place"; come sunset, a "great happy hour" and a "two-page tapas menu" make it a hub for "grazing" and gazing.

Spirit of Washington Dinner Train [S] 17 | 24 | 20 | $45

625 Fourth St. (Burnett Ave.), Renton, 425-227-7245

◪ It's not just a view – it's "scenery"; this repast on rails offers "relaxation and pampering" along with a Northwestern menu that's "middling" but "better than you would expect" during a "bumpy" but "fun" jaunt along Lake Washington in a vintage dining car (the "dome cars" are "worth the extra bucks"); with a stop at the Columbia Winery for a tour, it's "great for out-of-town guests."

Stanley & Seafort's 22 | 21 | 22 | $30

115 E. 34th St. (Pacific Ave.), Tacoma, 253-473-7300

■ "A long drive" is rewarded with an "amazing" panoramic vista at this Tacoma surf 'n' turf veteran, a member of the well-run Restaurants Unlimited clan; it serves as a "reliable" "meeting place" with classic cooking, "deep, comfy booths" and a "romantic" backdrop.

Seattle　　　　　　　　　　　F | D | S | C

Stars Bar & Dining ◐ S　　　– | – | – | E
Pacific Pl., 600 Pine St. (6th Ave.), 206-264-1112
Jeremiah Towers' glamorous, glitzy pleasure palace is the jewel in Pacific Place's crown; the New American cuisine has to work hard to match the hip scene, and when everything clicks the combination is a winner, though the food and service do have their ups and downs; as evidence of its success, the room is always jammed after dark.

Stella's Trattoria ◐ S　　　14 | 14 | 14 | $17
4500 Ninth Ave. NE (45th St.), 206-633-1100
◪ "24 hours a day", this "Italian diner" in the U-District is "one of the few" open options for "cheap and passable food"; it can be "noisy" and "a bit cramped", but it remains popular with "late-night" pilgrims and Metro Cinemas regulars who say it "will suffice" when popcorn and Jujubes won't.

Still Life in　　　　　　　　19 | 16 | 12 | $11
Fremont Coffeehouse S ⌦
709 N. 35th St. (Fremont Pl.), 206-547-9850
■ "The coffeehouse of choice for Fremontsters", this Eclectic "original" specializes in "unique", "tasty, earthy" food along the lines of "hearty soups and sandwiches", "hippie granola", "amazing pastries", and "holistic coffee and desserts"; "surly" service aside, it's the "ultimate hangout" and "forever a classic" – "every city needs one."

Streamliner Diner S ⌦　　　20 | 14 | 16 | $14
397 Winslow Way (Bijune St.), Bainbridge Island, 206-842-8595
■ Fans set their alarm clocks and "take the ferry" early to tuck away a "memorably wonderful high-cholesterol breakfast" at this "always-packed" "Bainbridge fave"; the diner-style American comfort food is "worth the wait", and some sense service is "friendlier under the new ownership."

Sunfish S ⌦　　　　　　∇ 20 | 12 | 16 | $9
280 Alki Ave. SW (62nd Ave.), 206-938-4112
■ They "know how to do halibut" at this beachside Alki fish shanty where sun worshippers gather in appreciation of the "awesome" "fish 'n' chips (and a view to boot)"; caveat: this crunchy, batter-dipped finger food is your swimwear's worst enemy.

Sunlight Cafe S　　　　　17 | 10 | 12 | $12
6403 Roosevelt Way NE (64th St.), 206-522-0099
◪ Loyalists "love those whole-grain waffles" and "tasty organic salads" at this Vegetarian on Roosevelt, insisting "sometimes nothing else will do"; meanwhile, critics contend it's a "tired concept" living in the "shadow of its former glory" and suggest the cadre of "retired hippies" on staff should "put the bong down" and get to work.

Seattle | F | D | S | C |

Swingside Cafe | 21 | 16 | 19 | $23 |
4212 Fremont Ave. N. (42nd St.), 206-633-4057
■ Brad Inserra's "quirky", "crowded" "little" Italian is a "hidden treasure" in an "off-beat location" in upper Fremont; his "small menu is richly realized" whether he's tossing *aglio e olio* or venturing beyond the Boot to concoct his killer gumbo or Moroccan couscous for a captive audience that knows "this food is nurtured and loved."

SZMANIA'S S | 26 | 23 | 25 | $36 |
3321 W. McGraw St. (34th Ave.), 206-284-7305
■ "Out-of-the-way" Magnolia affords a chance to get "away from the trendy scene" and into chef Ludger Szmania's "fabulous food" at this "Northwest treasure" with a German accent; with its "delectable entrees" (the "half-portion concept is brilliant"), "romantic atmosphere" enhanced by a "subtle and warm remodel" and "highly professional" service, this "neighborhood" "gem" "has it all."

Taco Del Mar S | 15 | 7 | 12 | $8 |
615 Queen Anne Ave. N. (Mercer St.), 206-281-7420
12816 SE 38th St. (128th Ave.), Bellevue, 425-643-5675
1520 Broadway (Pike St.), 206-328-4868
90 Yesler Way (1st Ave.), 206-467-5940
Convention Ctr., 725 Pike St. (7th Ave.), 206-628-8982
1336 First Ave. (Union St.), 206-623-8741
3526 Fremont Pl. N. (35th St.), 206-545-8001
1815 N. 45th St. (Wallingford Ave.), 206-545-3720
13780 NE 175th St. (138th Ave.), Woodinville, 425-398-8183
12551 116th Ave. NE (north of 124th St.), Kirkland, 425-820-5763
☑ "You'll need a wheelbarrow" (well, "two hands" anyway) to manage the "humongous", "messy" "super burritos" at this "ubiquitous" "local chain"; the multitudes also appreciate the "quick fix for fish tacos", but a handful of holdouts alleges "these are *not* Mission-style burritos" and notes the goods are "served with attitude."

Tai Tung ●S | 19 | 8 | 13 | $17 |
655 S. King St. (Maynard Ave.), 206-622-7372
☑ This I-District "greasy chopstick" "hasn't changed much in decades", achieving "landmark" status with its "Chinese comfort food" in spite of "horrid decor" ("can't have everything"); enthusiasts advise "watch what the locals eat" and note the up-front "counter is great" for anyone squeamish about the "dark" interior.

Texas Smokehouse BBQ S | 19 | 14 | 14 | $14 |
14455 Woodinville-Redmond Rd. (NE 145th St.), Woodinville, 425-486-1957
■ "Someone's backyard in Texas" is the motif at this Woodinville "storefront", a down-home destination where 'cue connoisseurs can "take the family" for "messy" ribs, "great BBQ beans" and "good value."

Seattle | F | D | S | C |

Thai on Mercer | 20 | 14 | 17 | $18 |
7691 27th St. SE (77th Ave.), Mercer Island, 206-236-9990
◪ One of several such joints huddled together on the Rock, this small, tasteful eatery offers contemporary Thai cuisine that partisans pronounce "good" and "not pricey for Mercer Island"; those opposed deem the performance "Americanized" and "overrated."

That's Amore 🅂 | 18 | 13 | 17 | $19 |
1425 31st Ave. S. (S. Atlantic St.), 206-322-3677
■ "An undiscovered neighborhood jewel", this Mount Baker Italian is "a cute little family place" with a "surprising" view of the metropolis in store for the lucky ones who snag a window table; it stays "busy" with area admirers who come in to network over creative pastas and pizzas.

Theoz | 22 | 21 | 20 | $34 |
1523 Sixth Ave. (bet. Pike & Pine Sts.), 206-749-9660
◪ "New chef, new menu" has been the constant cry at this "beautiful", "modern" Downtowner, a "hot spot" that "started well" with "innovative" American cuisine that eventually evolved into country French; while it's "ideal for a business lunch", it is also a "trendy" spot that supporters tout as all-around "superb", even as foes protest an "overhyped" and "pretentious" scene.

Third Floor Fish Cafe 🅂 | 24 | 23 | 22 | $38 |
205 Lake St. S. (2nd Ave. S.), Kirkland, 425-822-3553
■ Chef Scott Staples' artfully reenvisioned menu comes as "wonderful news" for fans of this "formal but comfortable" Kirkland Med where "innovative preparations" showcasing "elegant seafood" finally do justice to the "spectacular view" of Lake Washington; the package may be "costly", but many pronounce it their "favorite Eastside" experience.

13 Coins ●🅂 | 17 | 16 | 19 | $24 |
18000 Pacific Hwy. S. (opp. Sea-Tac), 206-243-9500
125 Boren Ave. N. (bet. Denny Way & John St.), 206-682-2513
◪ This "reliable" diner-style duo caters to "all taste buds at all hours", offering "very private booths" and a counter-side "cooking show" as the chefs prepare "huge portions" of "good old" American favorites in an open kitchen; spoilers find the menu "dated", however, and one patron's "amusing retro" look can be another's "dark and seedy" setting.

Three Girls Bakery 🅂 | 20 | 8 | 15 | $9 |
Pike Place Mkt., 1514 Pike Pl. (bet. Pike & Pine Sts.), 206-622-1045
■ In a burg that "doesn't offer much good deli", this "blue-collar" lunch counter is a "Pike Place Market standout" that pulls in tourists and locals alike; there's "no atmosphere", just "big value" on "excellent soups and sandwiches" (including the "best meat loaf sandwich in town"), with "delicate pastries" to sweeten the deal.

Seattle

| F | D | S | C |

TOSONI | 27 | 15 | 25 | $34 |
14320 NE 20th St. (bet. 140th & 148th Aves.), Bellevue, 425-644-1668
■ "A slice of Europe in Bellevue?" – chef-owner Walter Walcher and his wife Wendy prove it can be done ("in a strip mall, no less"), wowing crowds at this "Eastside sleeper" with an "ambitious menu" that leans on Italy for inspiration; the fare is weighted toward "great meats", the service toward personal attention.

TOYODA SUSHI S | 26 | 14 | 19 | $24 |
12543 Lake City Way NE (125th St.), 206-367-7972
■ There's "never a dull moment" and patrons can count on "a smile from Mr. T", who slices and dices in person at this "relaxed", "crowded" Lake City "neighborhood sushi bar"; the "high standards" and "no-fuss setting" add up to "consistently fine value", making it a strong all-around contender for "best sushi in town."

Trattoria Mitchelli ●S | 15 | 15 | 15 | $19 |
84 Yesler Way (bet. Post Alley & Western Ave.), 206-623-3883
◪ "When all else fails", 'Papa' Dany Mitchelli's "loud, busy", red-gravy Italian remains a "great hangout" in a "fun location" in the heart of Pioneer Square; if the food's "nothing to write home about", at least it's "plentiful."

Triangle Lounge S | 18 | 16 | 16 | $16 |
3507 Fremont Pl. N. (35th St.), 206-632-0880
■ "All the hip kids gig" at this "funky" Fremont bistro-cum-bar, recently upgraded from a scruffy tavern ("the frat boys have moved on, so it's safe to go back"); "the new look" and an "honest", casual Mediterranean menu are winning support, but some warn it's "difficult to escape the smoke" inside (try the patio, man).

T.S. McHugh's S | 15 | 15 | 15 | $19 |
21 Mercer St. (1st Ave.), 206-282-1910
◪ This "classic pub" anchoring Queen Anne Hill is noted for serving "slabs o' beef" and other "decent Irish fare" in a "dark, noisy but welcoming" setting – as the natives say, it's "typical Tim McHugh"; those who find the eats "disappointing" and the service "questionable" are advised to "have an Irish coffee" and mellow out.

Tulio S | 24 | 22 | 21 | $32 |
Hotel Vintage Park, 1100 Fifth Ave. (Spring St.), 206-624-5500
■ A "great bistro feel" and an "intimate and crowded", "very New York" ambiance distinguish this "high-quality Italian" in the Hotel Vintage Park; with "creative and interesting" "true Med" cooking, it's "good for business lunches" or as a "pre-Downtown show" warm-up; the staff is known for professionalism tinged with "attitude."

Seattle

| | F | D | S | C |

Turkish Delight 🚬   ▽ | 19 | 8 | 14 | $9 |
Pike Place Mkt., 1930 Pike Pl. (Western Ave.), 206-443-1387
■ "You don't have to be Turkish", but it can't hurt; this lunch-only Pike Place Market entry offers "delightfully tasty" Near Eastern treats cafeteria-style; regulars arrive for a bowl of lentil soup, stay for strong coffee and sweets, and never leave without a sample of that grown-up candy known as, yes, Turkish delight.

Twenty-Two Eighteen ● | 17 | 18 | 18 | $24 |
2218 First Ave. (bet. Bell & Blanchard Sts.), 206-441-2218
◪ Providing "quite an evening of sounds, smells and tastes", this "classy" Belltown jazz venue offers a "very good" Northwestern menu (salmon au poivre is "a must") in a room enlivened by "great bands" and "genius bartenders"; doubters point to "overrated food and decor" and argue the concept is "still finding its way."

22 Fountain Court | 19 | 19 | 18 | $35 |
(fka Azaleas Fountain Court)
22 103rd Ave. NE (bet. 1st & Main Sts.), Bellevue, 425-451-0426
■ Contemporary Northwest cooking prevails on the seasonal menu at this "hidden gem" in Bellevue, where the "garden-like setting" creates a "charming atmosphere" that may be as "romantic" as the Eastside gets; the staff provides "personal attention" (though the pace can be "slow").

Twin Teepees 🚬 | 11 | 14 | 15 | $14 |
7201 Aurora Ave. (72nd St.), 206-783-9740
◪ It's "still 1940" at this "tacky" "cement teepee" roadsider in Green Lake, a three-squares-a-day "blast" from the past that gets its core support from kids and "seniors who remember" when "plain" American food and "old-fashioned martinis" were the mostest; N.B. a menu update is in the works.

Two Bells Tavern 🚬 | 19 | 14 | 16 | $13 |
2313 Fourth Ave. (bet. Battery & Bell Sts.), 206-441-3050
■ "The first and best Belltown pub" is a certified local "treasure" serving "pub fare on the urban side" in an "oh-so-friendly" atmosphere; a "favorite lunch spot", it evolves into an evening "hangout for artists and journalists", wowing the faithful with "fabulous hand-formed burgers" that merit "three napkins"; "too bad it's so smoky."

Umberto's 🚬 | 18 | 18 | 18 | $24 |
100 S. King St. (1st Ave.), 206-621-0575
◪ The "high-volume" American-style Italian fare is a "popular" success at this "Kingdome-area" trattoria where a "standard" pasta-and-pizza menu sates a crowd that swells before and after every game; still, a naysaying contingent complains of "lackluster" eating; N.B. new ownership and chef changes are not reflected in the ratings.

Seattle F | D | S | C

UNION BAY CAFE ☒ 25 | 21 | 22 | $31
3515 NE 45th St. (NE 36th Ave.), 206-527-8364
■ Laurelhurst's "wonderful little cafe" offers "casual fine dining" in the form of "primo Northwestern food and wine", and admirers say chef-owner Mark Manley's "creative combinations" "never fail to please"; achieving "surprising sophistication" in a modest setting, it's "often overlooked" but is considered the "quintessential find."

Union Square Grill ☒ 23 | 22 | 22 | $36
621 Union St. (7th Ave.), 206-224-4321
◪ "Now this is a steakhouse" say devotees of this Downtown "sister ship to the Metropolitan Grill", where the "great beef" is augmented by "excellent" seafood; it's a natural "business lunch favorite" and "the place to go pre-theater", with "professional, well-informed" service.

Vina 18 | 18 | 18 | $29
2207 First Ave. (bet. Bell & Blanchard Sts.), 206-443-1465
■ This Belltowner is foremost "a great little wine bar", but the International eats are "also good" and the "mellow atmo" makes it "easy to converse" over a glass or flight of primo vino; owner (and *P-I* wine columnist) Richard Kinssies and his partner, KIRO-TV reporter Bob Branom, offer a lesson in oenology that's "knowledgeable without pretense."

Von's Grand City Cafe ☒ 14 | 13 | 14 | $20
West Coast Roosevelt Hotel, 619 Pine St. (bet. 6th & 7th Aves.), 206-621-8667
■ Welcome to "martini central" say denizens of this American in the Roosevelt Hotel, where the "great drinks" in the "smoky" bar draw stronger support than the "marginal" meat-and-potatoes fare; proximity to the Paramount captures the concert-going crowd.

Waters ☒ 19 | 19 | 20 | $28
Woodmark Hotel, 1200 Carillon Pt. (Lake Washington Blvd.), Kirkland, 425-803-5595
■ "Great for lunch on the terrace", this Carillon Point "spot on the water" boasts a "beautiful Lake Washington view" and caters to Woodmark Hotel guests morning, noon and night; the Northwestern bistro menu appeases those who expect food that's "solid" if "nothing spectacular."

WILD GINGER ☒ 27 | 23 | 22 | $30
1400 Western Ave. (Union St.), 206-623-4450
■ "Oh the flavors, the smells, the crowds!"; the "definitive Seattle Pan-Asian" with the "chic, sparse decor" and booming satay bar remains the city's Most Popular restaurant – and possibly the noisiest; James Beard Award winner Jeem Han Lock has a "wicked way with spice" and continues to conduct "a concert of flavors without a clash of cultures"; N.B. an expansion/move (to Third and Union) is scheduled for late fall '99.

Seattle   F | D | S | C

Wolfgang Puck Cafe S   16 | 18 | 17 | $26
1221 First Ave. (University St.), 206-621-9653

For "a taste of LA in the NW", this brand-name Harbor Steps Eclectic cafe and bar hosts a "vibrant", "lively" scene, but jaded diners insist the Wolfman's rep "is not enough" to justify the "safe" but "none-too-interesting" fusion fare; it's an acknowledged "tourist attraction", though, with decor some find "playful" and others "childish."

World Class Chili ⌽   19 | 5 | 14 | $9
Pike Place Mkt., 93 Pike St. (1st Ave.), 206-623-3678

Once a humble hole-in-the-wall, Joe Canavan's "aptly named" chile joint is now ensconced in larger, less funky quarters in Pike Place Market's South Arcade; enthusiasts exult "it's great to pick" from among the versions – Cincinnati-, Texas- or Cal-style (or even vegetarian) – all guaranteed to be "hot" enough for the most peppery palate.

Yakima Grill S   20 | 18 | 16 | $25
Vance Hotel, 612 Stewart St. (bet. 6th & 7th Aves.), 206-956-0639

Theoz owners Theodora van den Beld and Gary Bocz apply their talents to the former home of Salute in Citta, transforming it into a "trendy" Nuevo Latino bistro that features "darn good tapas"; however, critics cite "boring food and nonexistent service."

Yankee Diner ●S   13 | 13 | 14 | $16
1 S. Grady Way (Hwy. 167), Renton, 425-255-8543

Yankee Grill S
5300 24th Ave. NW (Market St.), 206-783-1964
6812 Tacoma Mall Blvd. (I-5, exit 129), Tacoma, 253-475-3006

"One meal can last you all day" if it comes from one of these "huge", "kid-friendly" specialists in "good homestyle cookin'" that ranges from from "basic breakfasts" to "all-American dinners"; but though the "prices aren't bad", some suspect the "food has gone downhill."

Yanni's   18 | 12 | 15 | $18
7419 Greenwood Ave. N. (74th St.), 206-783-6945

"Cravings for skordalia and fried calamari" ("just kill me with garlic!") are assuaged with "big Greek food in Greenwood"; "traditional" fare is served in a "pleasant atmosphere" replete with faux fruit and wish-we-were-there photos of seaside villages, but some opt for takeout since the service, though "friendly", can be "terminally slow."

Yarrow Bay Beach Cafe S   18 | 20 | 18 | $24
1270 Carillon Pt. (Lake Washington Blvd.), Kirkland, 425-889-9052

The Yarrow Bay Grill's casual downstairs sibling has the same "Lake Washington backdrop", making it an ideal Carillon Point place to "watch the sunset"; supporters say it "recalls a bistro on the Mediterranean" and laud the "diverse", "interesting" NW-Eclectic menu, but skeptics contend this is only "standard" eating.

Seattle

| | F | D | S | C |

Yarrow Bay Grill S | 22 | 23 | 22 | $33 |
1270 Carillon Pt. (Lake Washington Blvd.), Kirkland,
425-889-9052
■ Chef Vicky McCaffrey's "varied menu" "keeps improving", and her "interesting, well-prepared" Northwestern dishes make this "classy" venue with a view "one of the best on the Eastside"; the "creative" cooking and "lovely atmosphere" define "fine dining on the water."

Zaina Food, Drink & Friends S ▽ | 20 | 7 | 16 | $9 |
2615 NE 65th St. (27th Ave. NE), 206-525-7747
108 Cherry St. (1st Ave.), 206-624-5687
■ The "really great falafel" and other "cheap" Middle Eastern eats are "worth queuing up for" at this Pioneer Square entry; office wonks step out of the workaday world and into a far-away place where "wonderful flavors and scents" have them wondering "where's the camel and the water pipe?"; N.B. the original on 65th Street is quieter, and the food's just as good.

Zeek's Pizza S | 20 | 11 | 15 | $12 |
6000 Phinney Ave. N. (60th St.), 206-789-0089
41 Dravus St. (Nickerson St.), 206-285-6046
419 Denny Way (5th Ave.), 206-448-6775
■ Now with three "funky" locations – near SPU, on Phinney Ridge and in the shadow of the Space Needle – this "new-style" pizza minichain specializes in "novel combinations" (e.g. the "innovative", peanut-sauced Thai-One-On or the veggie Tree Hugger), rounding out the experience with "industrial warehouse" decor and amiable service.

Indexes to Seattle Restaurants

Special Features and Appeals

Seattle Indexes

CUISINES

Afghan
Kabul Afghan

American (New)
Axis
Bick's Broadview Grill
Broadway New Amer.
Café Septieme
Chez Shea
Deluxe B&G
Gordon Biersch
Herbfarm
Longshoreman's Daughter
Restaurant, The
Rhododendron Café
Six Degrees
Stars Bar & Dining

American (Regional)
Alligator Soul
Anthony's HomePort
Anthony's Pier 66
Ark
Arnie's
Avenue One
Belltown Pub
Bistro Pleasant Beach
BluWater Bistro
Bridges B&G
Brooklyn Seafood
Cafe Nola
Canlis
Chez Shea
Christina's
Dahlia Lounge
Dash Point Lobster Shop
Delcambre's
Elliott's Oyster Hse.
Eques
Famous Pacific
5 Spot
Fullers
Georgian Room
Herbfarm
Heron Beach Inn
Hunt Club
Inn at Langley
Kaspar's
Lampreia
Oyster Bar/Chuckanut Dr.
Oyster Creek Inn
Painted Table
Palace Kitchen
Palisade
Paragon B&G
Philadelphia Fevre Steak
Place Pigalle
Queen City Grill
Restaurant, The
Rhododendron Café
Salish Lodge
Sazerac
Shoalwater
Space Needle Rest.
Spirit of Washington
Szmania's
Twenty-Two Eighteen
22 Fountain Ct.
Union Bay Cafe
Union Sq. Grill
Waters
Yarrow Bay Beach
Yarrow Bay Grill

American (Traditional)
Andy's Diner
Ark
Athenian Inn
Billy McHale's
Blue Water Diner
Broadway New Amer.
Caffè Minnie's
Charlie's B&G
Claim Jumper
Cutters Bayhouse
Daniel's Broiler
Deluxe B&G
Dish
Eggs Cetera's
El Gaucho
Emmett Watson's
14 Carrot Cafe
Frankfurter
F.X. McRory's
Gordon Biersch
Grady's Grillhouse
Green Cat Cafe
Hale's Ales
Hattie's Hat
Hidden Harbour
Hilltop Ale House
Hi-Spot Cafe
Honey Bear Bakery
icon Grill

Seattle Indexes

Kidd Valley
Kirkland Roaster
Leschi Lakecafe
Lockspot Cafe
Luna Park Cafe
Mae's Phinney Ridge
Maggie Bluffs
Maltby Cafe
Mama's Mexican
Matt's Famous
My Friends Cafe
New Jake O'Shaughnessey's
Nickerson St. Saloon
Original Pancake Hse.
Palace Kitchen
Planet Hollywood
Pyramid Alehouse
Ray's Boathouse
Red Door Alehouse
Ruth's Chris
Salmon Bay Café
Scarlet Tree
74th St. Ale Hse.
Sharp's Roaster
Streamliner Diner
13 Coins
Twin Teepees
Union Sq. Grill
Von's Grand City
World Class Chili
Yankee Diner

Asian

Asiana
Asian Wok & Grill
Ayutthaya
Blowfish Asian
Chinoise Café
Dahlia Lounge
Gordon Biersch
Heron Beach Inn
Kamon/Lake Union
Mandalay Café
Noodle Ranch
ObaChine
Pandasia
Provinces
Roy's Seattle
Shallots Asian Bistro
Wild Ginger

Bakeries

Brusseau's
Credenzia's Oven
Honey Bear Bakery
La Panzanella
Louisa's Cafe
Macrina Bakery
Three Girls Bakery

Bar-B-Q

Armadillo Barbecue
Burk's Cafe
Mac's Smokehouse
Pecos Pit BBQ
Texas Smokehouse

Cajun/Creole

Alligator Soul
Burk's Cafe
Delcambre's
New Orleans
Sazerac
Shultzy's

Caribbean

Coastal Kitchen
Paseo Caribbean

Chinese

Bamboo Garden
Black Pearl
Blowfish Asian
Chef Wang
China Gate
China Harbor
Four Seas
Honey Court
Hong's Garden
House of Hong
Hunan Garden
Louie's Cuisine
Noble Court
Ocean City
Pandasia
Sea Garden
Shanghai Cafe
Shanghai Garden
Snappy Dragon
Tai Tung

Coffeehouses/Desserts

B&O Espresso
Brusseau's
Café Dilettante
Caffe Ladro
Famous Pacific
Honey Bear Bakery
Still Life in Fremont

Seattle Indexes

Coffee Shops/Diners
Bakeman's
Caffe Ladro
CJ's Eatery
Dish
Mae's Phinney Ridge
Maltby Cafe
My Favourite Piroshky
Salmon Bay Café
Scarlet Tree
Sit & Spin
Still Life in Fremont
Streamliner Diner

Continental
Canlis
Cliff House
El Gaucho
Reiner's
Roy St. Bistro
Tosoni

Delis/Sandwich Shops
Bagel Oasis
Bakeman's
Briazz
My Friends Cafe
Plenty Cafe
Three Girls Bakery

Dim Sum
Blowfish Asian
China Gate
Four Seas
Hong's Garden
House of Hong
Noble Court
Ocean City

Eclectic/International
Axis
Bandoleone
Bay Cafe
Bell St. Diner
Bis on Main
Brasa
Bungalow Wine Bar
Cafe Flora
Cafe Starbucks
Chanterelle
Circa Neighborhood Gr.
Coastal Kitchen
Cool Hand Luke's
Crocodile Cafe
Dimitriou's Jazz Alley
Dulces Latin Bistro
Entros World Grill
Gordon Biersch
Hilltop Ale House
Jitterbug Café
Julia's of Wallingford
Kamon/Lake Union
Kirkland Roaster
L'Auberge
Maple Leaf Grill
Marco's Supperclub
Mona's Bistro
Mondo Burrito
My Friends Cafe
ObaChine
Painted Table
Pandasia
Pasta & Co.
Pasta Ya Gotcha
Pogacha
Ponti Seafood Grill
Provinces
Rhododendron Café
Rosebud Rest.
Roy's Seattle
Shultzy's
Sit & Spin
Still Life in Fremont
Swingside Cafe
Vina
Waters
Wolfgang Puck Cafe
Yarrow Bay Beach

English
Queen Mary
Roy St. Bistro

Ethiopian
Café Soleil
Kokeb

French
Bistro Provençal
Crêpe de Paris
Le Bonaparte
Le Gourmand
Rover's

French Bistro
Avenue One
Bis on Main
Bistro Lautrec
Boat St. Cafe
Cafe Campagne

Seattle Indexes

Café Septieme
Cassis
Figaro Bistro
Madison Park Cafe
Maximilien
Place Pigalle
Relais
Theoz

French (New)
Brie & Bordeaux
Campagne
Rover's
Theoz

German
Reiner's
Szmania's

Greek
Aleko's Pizzeria
Bacchus
Byzantion
Costas Greek
Costas Opa
Yanni's

Hamburgers
Deluxe B&G
Dick's Drive-In
Duke's Chowderhse.
Kidd Valley
Maggie Bluffs
Nickerson St. Saloon
Red Door Alehouse
Red Mill Burgers
Red Robin
Two Bells Tavern

Health Food
Cafe Flora
14 Carrot Cafe
Gravity Bar
Green Cat Cafe

Hot Dogs
Frankfurter
Matt's Famous
Shultzy's

Indian
Banjara
Chutneys
Chutneys Bistro
Chutneys Grille
India House
Moghul Palace
Raga
Sahib
Shamiana

Irish
Kells
T.S. McHugh's

Italian
(N=Northern; S=Southern; N&S=Includes both)
Al Boccalino (N&S)
Angelina's Trattoria (N&S)
Assaggio Rist. (N)
Bella Rosa Bistro (N&S)
Belltown Billiards (S)
Bizzarro Italian (N&S)
Botticelli Caffè (N&S)
Buca di Beppo (S)
Cafe Juanita (N)
Cafe Lago (N&S)
Cafe Nola (N&S)
Cafe Veloce (N)
Calabria Rist. (S)
Ciao Bella (N&S)
Cucina! Cucina! (N&S)
Da Vinci's Pizza (N&S)
Filiberto's (N&S)
Firenze Rist. (N&S)
Fremont Classic Pizza (N&S)
Gaspare's Rist. (S)
Grazie Ristorante (N)
Il Bacio (N)
Il Bistro (N&S)
il fiasco (N)
Il Fornaio (N&S)
Il Gambero (S)
Il Terrazzo Carmine (N)
Isabella Rist. (N&S)
Italianissimo (N)
La Buca (S)
La Fontana (S)
La Medusa (S)
La Panzanella (N&S)
LeoMelina Ristorante (S)
Lombardi's Cucina (N&S)
Lush Life (N&S)
Machiavelli (N)
Mamma Melina (S)
Olympia III Pizza (N&S)
Pasta & Co. (N&S)
Pasta Bella (N&S)

Seattle Indexes

Pasta Ya Gotcha (N&S)
Pazzo's (N&S)
Perché No (N&S)
Pink Door (N&S)
Pontevecchio (S)
Poor Italian Cafe (N&S)
Prego (N)
Ristorante Buongusto (S)
Ristorante Paradiso (S)
Ristorante Salute (S)
Saleh al Lago (N)
Salute of Bellevue (N&S)
Salvatore Rist. (N&S)
Seattle Catch (S)
Serafina (N&S)
Simpatico (N&S)
Sostanza Trattoria (N)
Stella's Trattoria (N&S)
Swingside Cafe (S)
That's Amore (N&S)
Tosoni (N)
Trattoria Mitchelli (N&S)
Tulio (N)
Umberto's (N&S)

Japanese
Aoki Japanese
Bush Garden
Eating Factory
I Love Sushi
Izumi
Kikuya
Musashi's
Nikko
Nishino
Sanmi Sushi
Shiro's Sushi
Toyoda Sushi

Kosher
Bamboo Garden

Latin American
Bandoleone
Paseo Caribbean

Lebanese
Karam's
Mediterranean Kitchen

Malaysian
Malay Satay Hut

Mediterranean
Adriatica
Andaluca
Bistro Pleasant Beach
Brasa
Cafe Langley
Capitol Club
Credenzia's Oven
El Greco
Entros World Grill
il fiasco
Karam's
L'Auberge
Neo Bistro
Palomino Euro Bistro
Pasta & Co.
Phoenecia at Alki
Shea's Lounge
Sisters European
Spazzo
Third Floor Fish
Triangle Lounge

Mexican/Tex-Mex
Azteca
Bilbo's Festivo
Burrito Loco
Cactus
Chevys Fresh Mex
Chile Pepper
Desert Fire
El Camino
El Niño Rest.
El Puerco Lloron
Galerias
Gordito's
Jalisco
Mama's Mexican
Mondo Burrito
Rosita's Mexican
Taco Del Mar

Middle Eastern
Capitol Club
Kabul Afghan
Karam's
Mediterranean Kitchen
Phoenecia at Alki
Zaina Food

Moroccan
Bella Rosa Bistro

Noodle Shops
Aoki Japanese
Fremont Noodle Hse.
Krittika Noodles
Noodle Ranch
Ocean City

Seattle Indexes

Nuevo Latino
Bandoleone
Yakima Grill

Pizza
Aleko's Pizzeria
Belltown Billiards
Big Time Pizzeria
Cafe Lago
Cafe Veloce
Ciao Italia
Coyote Creek Pizza
Cucina! Cucina!
Da Vinci's Pizza
Delfino's Pizzeria
Fremont Classic Pizza
Lush Life
Machiavelli
Mad Pizza
Neo Bistro
Olympia III Pizza
Pagliacci Pizza
Pazzo's
Pegasus Pizza
Piecora's
Romio's Pizza
Zeek's Pizza

Polynesian
Luau Polynesian

Russian
Kaleenka
My Favourite Piroshky

Seafood
Adriatica
Anthony's HomePort
Anthony's Pier 66
Ark
Arnie's
Athenian Inn
Bell St. Diner
Benjamin's/Lake Union
Brooklyn Seafood
Canlis
Chandler's Crabhse.
Chinook's/Salmon Bay
Crab Cracker
Cutters Bayhouse
Dash Point Lobster Shop
Duke's Chowderhse.
Elliott's Oyster Hse.
Emmett Watson's
Etta's Seafood
Flying Fish
Foghorn
F.X. McRory's
Hidden Harbour
Ivar's Acres
Ivar's Mukilteo
Ivar's Salmon Hse.
Jack's Fish Spot
La Palina/Duke's
LeoMelina Ristorante
Leschi Lakecafe
Lockspot Cafe
Matt's in the Mkt.
McCormick & Schmick's
McCormick & Schmick's Harbor
McCormick's Fish Hse.
Oyster Bar/Chuckanut Dr.
Oyster Creek Inn
Palisade
Pescatore
Ponti Seafood Grill
Queen City Grill
Ray's Boathouse
Salty's
Seattle Catch
Shuckers
Stanley & Seafort's
Sunfish
Third Floor Fish

Senegalese
Afrikando

South American
Copacabana Cafe

Southern/Soul
Alligator Soul
Catfish Corner
Ezell's Chicken
Kingfish Café
New Orleans
Sazerac

Southwestern
Cactus
Desert Fire
Santa Fe Cafe
Yakima Grill

Steakhouses
Benjamin's/Lake Union
Billy McHale's
Brooklyn Seafood
Canlis

Seattle Indexes

Claim Jumper
Daniel's Broiler
El Gaucho
Fullers
JaK's Grill
Lake Washington Grillhse.
Latitude 47
McCormick & Schmick's
McCormick & Schmick's Harbor
Metropolitan Grill
Ruth's Chris
Union Sq. Grill

Thai

Angel's Thai
Asiana
Ayutthaya
Bahn Thai
Bai Tong
Fremont Noodle Hse.
Krittika Noodles
Mangoes Thai
Noodle Studio
Pon Proem
Racha
Thai on Mercer

Turkish

Turkish Delight

Vegetarian

(Most Chinese, Indian and Thai restaurants)
Cafe Flora
Carmelita
Crocodile Cafe
Gravity Bar
Green Cat Cafe
Honey Bear Bakery
Plenty Cafe
Still Life in Fremont
Sunlight Cafe

Vietnamese

Café Huê
Saigon Bistro

Seattle Indexes

LOCATIONS

Bainbridge Island
Bistro Pleasant Beach
Blue Water Diner
Cafe Nola
Streamliner Diner

Ballard/Shilshole
Anthony's HomePort
Azteca
Burk's Cafe
Charlie's B&G
Dick's Drive-In
Hattie's Hat
Le Gourmand
Lockspot Cafe
Lombardi's Cucina
Louie's Cuisine
Pasta Bella
Pescatore
Ray's Boathouse
Salmon Bay Café
Yankee Diner

Beacon Hill/Seward Park
That's Amore

Bellevue
Azteca
Billy McHale's
Bis on Main
Briazz
Coyote Creek Pizza
Cucina! Cucina!
Daniel's Broiler
Duke's Chowderhse.
Eating Factory
Eques
Firenze Rist.
Frankfurter
Grazie Ristorante
Hunan Garden
I Love Sushi
Kidd Valley
Matt's Famous
Mediterranean Kitchen
Moghul Palace
My Favourite Piroshky
New Jake O'Shaughnessey's
Noble Court
Pasta & Co.
Pasta Ya Gotcha
Pogacha
Raga
Red Robin
Salute of Bellevue
Sea Garden
Shanghai Cafe
Spazzo
Taco Del Mar
Tosoni
22 Fountain Ct.

Belltown
Afrikando
Axis
Belltown Billiards
Belltown Pub
Brasa
Chef Wang
CJ's Eatery
Crocodile Cafe
El Gaucho
Flying Fish
Il Gambero
La Fontana
Lampreia
Lush Life
Macrina Bakery
Mama's Mexican
Marco's Supperclub
Mondo Burrito
Noodle Ranch
Queen City Grill
Shallots Asian Bistro
Shiro's Sushi
Sit & Spin
Twenty-Two Eighteen
Two Bells Tavern
Vina

Bothell/Kenmore
Grazie Ristorante
Jalisco
Kidd Valley
Lake Washington Grillhse.
Relais

Capitol Hill
Angel's Thai
Aoki Japanese

Seattle Indexes

Ayutthaya
Bacchus
B&O Espresso
Bistro Lautrec
Broadway New Amer.
Byzantion
Café Dilettante
Café Septieme
Caffè Minnie's
Capitol Club
Cassis
Charlie's B&G
Chutneys Grille
Coastal Kitchen
Deluxe B&G
Dick's Drive-In
El Greco
Famous Pacific
Galerias
Gravity Bar
Green Cat Cafe
Jalisco
Karam's
Kidd Valley
Kingfish Café
Kokeb
La Panzanella
Machiavelli
My Favourite Piroshky
Noodle Studio
Olympia III Pizza
Pagliacci Pizza
Pasta & Co.
Piecora's
Romio's Pizza
Rosebud Rest.
Taco Del Mar

Central District
Catfish Corner
Ezell's Chicken

Columbia City
La Medusa

Downtown
Andaluca
Assaggio Rist.
Bakeman's
Blowfish Asian
Briazz
Brooklyn Seafood
Cafe Starbucks
Crêpe de Paris
Dahlia Lounge
Desert Fire
Dimitriou's Jazz Alley
El Niño Rest.
Fullers
Gordon Biersch
icon Grill
Il Fornaio
Isabella Rist.
McCormick & Schmick's
McCormick's Fish Hse.
Metropolitan Grill
Nikko
ObaChine
Painted Table
Palace Kitchen
Palomino Euro Bistro
Pasta & Co.
Pasta Ya Gotcha
Planet Hollywood
Poor Italian Cafe
Prego
Red Robin
Restaurant, The
Roy's Seattle
Ruth's Chris
Sazerac
Shuckers
Stars Bar & Dining
Taco Del Mar
Theoz
Tulio
Union Sq. Grill
Von's Grand City
Wild Ginger
Wolfgang Puck Cafe
Yakima Grill

Edmonds/Shoreline
Anthony's HomePort
Arnie's
Brusseau's
Burrito Loco
Chanterelle
Ciao Italia
Kidd Valley
L'Auberge
Neo Bistro
Provinces
Rosita's Mexican
Sahib

Everett/Mukilteo
Alligator Soul
Anthony's HomePort

Seattle Indexes

Arnie's
Azteca
Ivar's Mukilteo
Lombardi's Cucina
Maltby Cafe

Federal Way/Seatac/Tukwila
Azteca
Bai Tong
Billy McHale's
Cucina! Cucina!
Grazie Ristorante
Mac's Smokehouse
Salty's
Sharp's Roaster
13 Coins

First Hill
Hunt Club
Mad Pizza
Reiner's

Fremont/Wallingford
Asian Wok & Grill
Bagel Oasis
Bizzarro Italian
Brie & Bordeaux
Bungalow Wine Bar
Chile Pepper
Chutneys Bistro
Costas Opa
Dick's Drive-In
Dish
Eggs Cetera's
El Camino
Fremont Classic Pizza
Fremont Noodle Hse.
Hale's Ales
Honey Bear Bakery
Jitterbug Café
Julia's of Wallingford
Kabul Afghan
Longshoreman's Daughter
Luau Polynesian
Mad Pizza
Mandalay Café
Musashi's
Nickerson St. Saloon
Olympia III Pizza
Paseo Caribbean
Pontevecchio
Ponti Seafood Grill
Red Door Alehouse

Seattle Catch
Simpatico
Still Life in Fremont
Swingside Cafe
Taco Del Mar
Triangle Lounge
Zeek's Pizza

Green Lake/Greenwood/Phinney Ridge
Alligator Soul
Bick's Broadview Grill
Carmelita
Duke's Chowderhse.
Gordito's
Kidd Valley
Krittika Noodles
Mae's Phinney Ridge
Mona's Bistro
My Friends Cafe
Red Mill Burgers
Romio's Pizza
Rosita's Mexican
Saleh al Lago
Santa Fe Cafe
74th St. Ale Hse.
Six Degrees
Twin Teepees
Yanni's
Zeek's Pizza

International District
Bush Garden
China Gate
Four Seas
Honey Court
House of Hong
Malay Satay Hut
Ocean City
Saigon Bistro
Sea Garden
Shanghai Garden
Tai Tung

Issaquah/Fall City
Cucina! Cucina!
Herbfarm
JaK's Grill
Lombardi's Cucina
Pogacha
Red Robin
Salish Lodge
Shanghai Garden

Seattle Indexes

Kent/Des Moines
Azteca
Filiberto's
Le Bonaparte

Kirkland
Anthony's HomePort
Bagel Oasis
Bistro Provençal
Cafe Juanita
Cafe Veloce
Calabria Rist.
Coyote Creek Pizza
Crab Cracker
Cucina! Cucina!
Da Vinci's Pizza
Foghorn
Izumi
Jalisco
Kidd Valley
Kirkland Roaster
Original Pancake Hse.
Pasta Ya Gotcha
Pegasus Pizza
Piecora's
Ristorante Paradiso
Shamiana
Six Degrees
Taco Del Mar
Third Floor Fish
Waters
Yarrow Bay Beach
Yarrow Bay Grill

Lake City/North Seattle
Azteca
Dick's Drive-In
Frankfurter
Gaspare's Rist.
Jalisco
Red Robin
Romio's Pizza
Toyoda Sushi

Lake Union/Eastlake
Adriatica
Arnie's
Azteca
Bandoleone
Benjamin's/Lake Union
BluWater Bistro
Bridges B&G
Chandler's Crabhse.
China Harbor
Cucina! Cucina!
Duke's Chowderhse.
Entros World Grill
14 Carrot Cafe
Hidden Harbour
I Love Sushi
Ivar's Salmon Hse.
Kamon/Lake Union
Latitude 47
Louisa's Cafe
McCormick & Schmick's Harbor
Pazzo's
Romio's Pizza
Serafina
13 Coins

Laurelhurst/Sand Point
Briazz
Kidd Valley
Pasta & Co.
Union Bay Cafe

Leschi/Madrona
Café Soleil
Cool Hand Luke's
Daniel's Broiler
Dulces Latin Bistro
Hi-Spot Cafe
Leschi Lakecafe
Plenty Cafe

Lynnwood
Billy McHale's
Buca di Beppo
Chevys Fresh Mex
Ezell's Chicken

Madison Park/Madison Valley
Cactus
Cafe Flora
Cafe Starbucks
Madison Park Cafe
Mad Pizza
Mangoes Thai
Nishino
Philadelphia Fevre Steak
Rover's
Sostanza Trattoria

Magnolia/Interbay
Chinook's/Salmon Bay
Maggie Bluffs
Palisade
Pandasia

Seattle Indexes

Red Mill Burgers
Romio's Pizza
Sanmi Sushi
Szmania's

Maple Leaf/Roosevelt
Aleko's Pizzeria
Maple Leaf Grill
Scarlet Tree
Snappy Dragon
Sunlight Cafe

Mercer Island
Pon Proem
Thai on Mercer

Montlake
Cafe Lago
Grady's Grillhouse

NW Washington
Bay Cafe
Cafe Langley
Heron Beach Inn
il fiasco
Oyster Bar/Chuckanut Dr.
Oyster Creek Inn
Rhododendron Café

Olympia
Anthony's HomePort

Pike Place Market
Athenian Inn
Avenue One
Botticelli Caffè
Cafe Campagne
Café Dilettante
Campagne
Chez Shea
Copacabana Cafe
Cutters Bayhouse
Delcambre's
El Puerco Lloron
Emmett Watson's
Etta's Seafood
Il Bistro
Jack's Fish Spot
Kaleenka
Kells
LeoMelina Ristorante
Matt's in the Mkt.
Maximilien
Pink Door
Place Pigalle

Shea's Lounge
Sisters European
Three Girls Bakery
Turkish Delight
World Class Chili

Pioneer Square/SODO
Al Boccalino
Andy's Diner
B&O Espresso
Café Huê
F.X. McRory's
Il Terrazzo Carmine
La Buca
Mac's Smokehouse
Matt's Famous
New Orleans
Pecos Pit BBQ
Pyramid Alehouse
Trattoria Mitchelli
Umberto's
Zaina Food

Queen Anne/Seattle Center
Asiana
Bahn Thai
Bamboo Garden
Banjara
Buca di Beppo
Caffe Ladro
Caffè Minnie's
Canlis
Chinoise Café
Chutneys
Credenzia's Oven
Dick's Drive-In
Famous Pacific
Figaro Bistro
5 Spot
Frankfurter
Hilltop Ale House
Jalisco
Kaspar's
Kidd Valley
La Palina/Duke's
Mediterranean Kitchen
Pagliacci Pizza
Paragon B&G
Pasta & Co.
Pasta Bella
Perché No
Racha
Ristorante Buongusto
Roy St. Bistro

Seattle Indexes

Space Needle Rest.
Taco Del Mar
T.S. McHugh's
Zeek's Pizza

Ravenna/Wedgwood
Bagel Oasis
Black Pearl
Queen Mary
Ristorante Salute
Santa Fe Cafe
Zaina Food

Redmond
Big Time Pizzeria
Billy McHale's
Claim Jumper
Cucina! Cucina!
Desert Fire
Il Bacio
Kikuya
Taco Del Mar

Renton
Billy McHale's
Hong's Garden
Kidd Valley
Pegasus Pizza
Spirit of Washington
Yankee Diner

San Juan Islands
Bilbo's Festivo
Christina's

Seattle Waterfront
Anthony's Pier 66
Bell St. Diner
Elliott's Oyster Hse.
Frankfurter
Ivar's Acres
Red Robin

South King County
Anthony's HomePort

South Seattle
Frankfurter
Jalisco

SW Washington Coast
Ark
Shoalwater

Tacoma
Anthony's HomePort
Billy McHale's
Chevys Fresh Mex
Cliff House
Cucina! Cucina!
Dash Point Lobster Shop
Stanley & Seafort's
Yankee Diner

University District/University Village
Azteca
Bella Rosa Bistro
Boat St. Cafe
Ciao Bella
Costas Greek
Delfino's Pizzeria
Georgian Room
India House
Mamma Melina
Pagliacci Pizza
Red Robin
Salvatore Rist.
Shultzy's
Stella's Trattoria

West Seattle
Angelina's Trattoria
Cafe Starbucks
Circa Neighborhood Gr.
Luna Park Cafe
Pegasus Pizza
Phoenecia at Alki
Red Robin
Salty's
Sunfish

Whidbey Island
Inn at Langley

Woodinville
Armadillo Barbecue
Italianissimo
Texas Smokehouse

Seattle Indexes

SPECIAL FEATURES AND APPEALS

Brunch
(Best of many)
Alligator Soul
Angelina's Trattoria
Anthony's HomePort
Ark
Arnie's
Bandoleone
Benjamin's/Lake Union
Blue Water Diner
Boat St. Cafe
Bridges B&G
Brie & Bordeaux
Broadway New Amer.
Cafe Campagne
Cafe Flora
Chanterelle
Circa Neighborhood Gr.
Cutters Bayhouse
El Greco
Etta's Seafood
14 Carrot Cafe
Honey Bear Bakery
Hunt Club
Ivar's Salmon Hse.
Kingfish Café
Latitude 47
Lombardi's Cucina
Longshoreman's Daughter
Madison Park Cafe
Maltby Cafe
Maximilien
Palisade
Pasta & Co.
Plenty Cafe
Ponti Seafood Grill
Queen Mary
Restaurant, The
Rhododendron Café
Rosebud Rest.
Salish Lodge
Sazerac
Seattle Catch
Space Needle Rest.
Sunlight Cafe
Waters
Yakima Grill
Yarrow Bay Grill

Buffet Served
(Check prices, days and times)
Benjamin's/Lake Union
Botticelli Caffè
Broadway New Amer.
Chutneys
Chutneys Bistro
Chutneys Grille
Dash Point Lobster Shop
Entros World Grill
Eques
Il Terrazzo Carmine
India House
Latitude 47
Le Bonaparte
Macrina Bakery
Moghul Palace
Phoenecia at Alki
Raga
Restaurant, The
Sahib
Shamiana
Texas Smokehouse
Umberto's

Business Dining
Adriatica
Al Boccalino
Andaluca
Anthony's Pier 66
Assaggio Rist.
Avenue One
Bistro Provençal
Café Huê
Cafe Juanita
Campagne
Canlis
Chutneys
Cliff House
Crêpe de Paris
Cutters Bayhouse
Daniel's Broiler
Desert Fire
El Gaucho
Elliott's Oyster Hse.
Eques
Etta's Seafood
Fullers
Georgian Room
Heron Beach Inn

109

Seattle Indexes

Hunt Club
icon Grill
Il Bistro
Il Fornaio
Il Terrazzo Carmine
Kaspar's
Lampreia
Latitude 47
LeoMelina Ristorante
McCormick & Schmick's
McCormick & Schmick's Harbor
McCormick's Fish Hse.
Metropolitan Grill
Nikko
Painted Table
Palisade
Palomino Euro Bistro
Ponti Seafood Grill
Prego
Ray's Boathouse
Reiner's
Rover's
Roy's Seattle
Ruth's Chris
Saleh al Lago
Salish Lodge
Salty's
Sazerac
Shuckers
Sostanza Trattoria
Stars Bar & Dining
Third Floor Fish
13 Coins
Tulio
22 Fountain Ct.
Union Sq. Grill
Von's Grand City
Waters
Yarrow Bay Grill

Caters
(Best of many)
Afrikando
Andaluca
Ark
Armadillo Barbecue
Bakeman's
Banjara
Bistro Pleasant Beach
Black Pearl
Brie & Bordeaux
Brusseau's
Cactus
Cafe Langley
Cafe Nola
Delfino's Pizzeria
Dulces Latin Bistro
El Gaucho
Elliott's Oyster Hse.
Four Seas
Fullers
Galerias
House of Hong
Il Fornaio
I Love Sushi
Karam's
Kaspar's
La Medusa
La Panzanella
LeoMelina Ristorante
Macrina Bakery
Madison Park Cafe
Mediterranean Kitchen
My Favourite Piroshky
Pandasia
Pasta & Co.
Provinces
Ray's Boathouse
Shallots Asian Bistro
Snappy Dragon
Szmania's
Taco Del Mar
Texas Smokehouse
That's Amore
Theoz
Tosoni
Umberto's
Union Sq. Grill
Yarrow Bay Beach
Yarrow Bay Grill

Cigar Friendly
Adriatica
Asian Wok & Grill
Avenue One
Bandoleone
BluWater Bistro
Bridges B&G
Calabria Rist.
Capitol Club
Charlie's B&G
Chevys Fresh Mex
Crab Cracker
Dulces Latin Bistro
El Gaucho
Firenze Rist.
F.X. McRory's
Gordon Biersch

Seattle Indexes

Hidden Harbour
Il Bistro
Lake Washington Grillhse.
LeoMelina Ristorante
Mac's Smokehouse
McCormick & Schmick's
McCormick & Schmick's Harbor
Metropolitan Grill
Mona's Bistro
New Orleans
Palomino Euro Bistro
Planet Hollywood
Ruth's Chris
Salute of Bellevue
Sanmi Sushi
Shallots Asian Bistro
Sharp's Roaster
Texas Smokehouse
13 Coins
Umberto's
Union Sq. Grill

Dancing/Entertainment

(Check days, times and performers for entertainment; D=dancing; best of many)
Alligator Soul (blues/jazz)
Avenue One (jazz)
Axis (jazz)
Azteca (karaoke)
Bandoleone (flamenco/jazz)
Bay Cafe (varies)
Belltown Billiards (D/jazz)
BluWater Bistro (jazz)
Bridges B&G (D/Caribbean/jazz)
Broadway New Amer. (jazz)
Bungalow Wine Bar (guitar)
Bush Garden (D/karaoke)
Calabria Rist. (varies)
Canlis (piano)
China Gate (karaoke)
China Harbor (D/band)
Ciao Italia (guitar)
Crêpe de Paris (cabaret)
Crocodile Cafe (bands)
Daniel's Broiler (jazz/piano)
Da Vinci's Pizza (DJ/karaoke)
Dimitriou's Jazz Alley (jazz)
Dulces Latin Bistro (guitar)
Eggs Cetera's (jazz)
El Camino (guitar)
El Gaucho (D/piano)
El Niño Rest. (D)
Fremont Noodle Hse. (jazz)
Galerias (guitar)
Grazie Ristorante (jazz)
Herbfarm (guitar)
Honey Bear Bakery (folk/guitar)
Hunt Club (jazz)
Isabella Rist. (jazz)
Ivar's Salmon Hse. (varies)
Kabul Afghan (varies)
Kamon/Lake Union (piano)
La Fontana (piano)
La Palina/Duke's (varies)
Latitude 47 (D)
LeoMelina Ristorante (opera)
Mamma Melina (opera)
Med. Kitchen (belly dancer)
Mona's Bistro (jazz)
New Orleans (D/bands)
Noble Court (D/bands)
ObaChine (varies)
Painted Table (jazz/piano)
Paragon B&G (jazz/R&B)
Perché No (opera/piano)
Pink Door (cabaret)
Plenty Cafe (varies)
Pontevecchio (flamenco/opera)
Provinces (bands)
Restaurant, The (piano)
Scarlet Tree (blues)
Seattle Catch (jazz)
Serafina (jazz/Latin)
Shamiana (sitar)
Sit & Spin (varies)
Six Degrees (jazz)
Stars Bar & Dining (varies)
Third Floor Fish (piano)
13 Coins (jazz/piano)
T.S. McHugh's (Irish)
Twenty-Two Eighteen (jazz)
Umberto's (jazz)
Wild Ginger (jazz)
Wolfgang Puck Cafe (jazz)

Delivers*/Takeout

(Nearly all Asians, coffee shops, delis, diners and pasta/pizzerias deliver or do takeout; here are some interesting possibilities; D=delivery, T=takeout; *call to check range and charges, if any)
Afrikando (T)
Al Boccalino (T)
Alligator Soul (T)

Seattle Indexes

Armadillo Barbecue (T)
Assaggio Rist. (T)
Athenian Inn (T)
Bagel Oasis (T)
Bakeman's (T)
B&O Espresso (T)
Bilbo's Festivo (T)
Botticelli Caffè (T)
Briazz (D,T)
Brusseau's (D,T)
Café Dilettante (T)
Cafe Nola (T)
Café Septieme (T)
Café Soleil (T)
Chanterelle (T)
Chinook's/Salmon Bay (T)
Claim Jumper (T)
Cool Hand Luke's (T)
Crêpe de Paris (T)
Cucina! Cucina! (T)
Deluxe B&G (D,T)
Duke's Chowderhse. (T)
El Puerco Lloron (T)
Ezell's Chicken (D,T)
Famous Pacific (T)
Frankfurter (D,T)
Grady's Grillhouse (T)
Gravity Bar (T)
Green Cat Cafe (T)
Hattie's Hat (T)
Hi-Spot Cafe (T)
Honey Bear Bakery (T)
Il Fornaio (T)
Jalisco (T)
La Panzanella (D,T)
Louisa's Cafe (T)
Luna Park Cafe (T)
Macrina Bakery (T)
Maggie Bluffs (T)
Maltby Cafe (T)
Mandalay Café (T)
Matt's Famous (T)
Mediterranean Kitchen (D,T)
Mondo Burrito (T)
My Favourite Piroshky (D,T)
My Friends Cafe (T)
Nickerson St. Saloon (T)
Noodle Ranch (T)
Paseo Caribbean (T)
Pasta & Co. (D,T)
Pecos Pit BBQ (T)
Philadelphia Fevre Steak (T)
Plenty Cafe (T)
Red Mill Burgers (T)
Shultzy's (T)
Sisters European (D,T)
Still Life in Fremont (T)
Streamliner Diner (T)
Sunfish (T)
Taco Del Mar (T)
Texas Smokehouse (T)
Three Girls Bakery (T)
Turkish Delight (T)
Two Bells Tavern (T)
World Class Chili (T)
Yankee Diner (D,T)
Yanni's (T)

Dessert/Ice Cream

Ark
B&O Espresso
Brusseau's
Café Dilettante
Cafe Nola
Caffe Ladro
Famous Pacific
Honey Bear Bakery
Louisa's Cafe
Queen Mary
Still Life in Fremont
Three Girls Bakery

Dining Alone

(Other than hotels, coffee shops, sushi bars and places with counter service)
Andaluca
Ayutthaya
Bai Tong
Black Pearl
Botticelli Caffè
Briazz
Brooklyn Seafood
Cafe Campagne
Cafe Flora
Café Septieme
Chinook's/Salmon Bay
Coastal Kitchen
Dick's Drive-In
Elliott's Oyster Hse.
El Puerco Lloron
Etta's Seafood
14 Carrot Cafe
Fremont Noodle Hse.
Gravity Bar
Green Cat Cafe
Il Fornaio
Jack's Fish Spot

Seattle Indexes

Jitterbug Café
Kidd Valley
Longshoreman's Daughter
Luna Park Cafe
Mac's Smokehouse
Maggie Bluffs
Maple Leaf Grill
Marco's Supperclub
Matt's Famous
Matt's in the Mkt.
McCormick & Schmick's
Mona's Bistro
Mondo Burrito
ObaChine
Palace Kitchen
Pandasia
Paseo Caribbean
Pasta & Co.
Pasta Ya Gotcha
Pecos Pit BBQ
Philadelphia Fevre Steak
Red Door Alehouse
Red Mill Burgers
Seattle Catch
74th St. Ale Hse.
Shallots Asian Bistro
Shultzy's
Sisters European
Spazzo
Sunfish
Szmania's
13 Coins
Trattoria Mitchelli
Turkish Delight
Wild Ginger

Fireplaces

Ark
Avenue One
Axis
Benjamin's/Lake Union
Bilbo's Festivo
BluWater Bistro
Bungalow Wine Bar
Cafe Juanita
Cafe Veloce
Canlis
Desert Fire
Duke's Chowderhse.
Dulces Latin Bistro
Eques
Grady's Grillhouse
Herbfarm
Heron Beach Inn

Il Fornaio
Inn at Langley
Kaspar's
LeoMelina Ristorante
Leschi Lakecafe
Lockspot Cafe
Lombardi's Cucina
Madison Park Cafe
Mandalay Café
McCormick & Schmick's Harbor
Neo Bistro
Oyster Bar/Chuckanut Dr.
Paragon B&G
Pasta Bella
Pogacha
Ponti Seafood Grill
Relais
Restaurant, The
Salish Lodge
Salute of Bellevue
Sostanza Trattoria
Stars Bar & Dining
Szmania's
T.S. McHugh's
22 Fountain Ct.
Yarrow Bay Grill

Game in Season

Asian Wok & Grill
Axis
Bandoleone
Bella Rosa Bistro
Bistro Pleasant Beach
BluWater Bistro
Bridges B&G
Campagne
Cassis
Christina's
Crêpe de Paris
Dimitriou's Jazz Alley
El Gaucho
Filiberto's
Fullers
Georgian Room
Grazie Ristorante
Herbfarm
Hunt Club
icon Grill
Il Fornaio
Le Gourmand
LeoMelina Ristorante
Maximilien
Raga
Reiner's

Seattle Indexes

Relais
Rover's
74th St. Ale Hse.
Stars Bar & Dining
Szmania's
Union Bay Cafe
Yarrow Bay Grill

Historic Interest
(Year opened; *building)
1896 Shoalwater*
1906 Georgian Room*
1906 Shuckers
1909 Athenian Inn
1909 Hunt Club*
1912 Chanterelle
1912 Three Girls Bakery
1914 Avenue One*
1916 Salish Lodge
1917 Lockspot Cafe
1921 Provinces*
1922 Noodle Studio
1922 Oyster Creek Inn
1925 Cliff House
1930 Christina's*
1930 Dash Point Lobster Shop*
1930 Oyster Bar/Chuckanut Dr.
1934 Maltby Cafe*
1935 Tai Tung
1937 Twin Teepees*
1938 Ivar's Acres
1948 Blue Water Diner*
1950 Ark
1950 Canlis*

Hotel Dining
Alexis Hotel
   Painted Table
Four Seasons Olympic
   Georgian Room
   Shuckers
Heron Beach Inn
   Heron Beach Inn
Hotel Edgewater
   Restaurant, The
Hotel Monaco
   Sazerac
Hotel Vintage Park
   Tulio
Hyatt Regency Hotel
   Eques
Inn at Langley
   Inn at Langley
Madison Renaissance
   Prego
Mayflower Park Hotel
   Andaluca
Paramount Hotel
   Blowfish Asian
Salish Lodge & Spa
   Salish Lodge
Shelburne Inn
   Shoalwater
Sheraton Hotel & Towers
   Fullers
Sorrento Hotel
   Hunt Club
Vance Hotel
   Yakima Grill
West Coast Roosevelt
   Von's Grand City
Westin Hotel
   Nikko
   Roy's Seattle
Woodmark Hotel
   Waters

"In" Places
Axis
Bandoleone
Cactus
Cafe Campagne
Cafe Lago
Dahlia Lounge
El Camino
El Gaucho
Etta's Seafood
Flying Fish
Il Fornaio
Kingfish Café
La Medusa
Marco's Supperclub
Palace Kitchen
Palomino Euro Bistro
Paragon B&G
Pink Door
Rosebud Rest.
Sazerac
Seattle Catch
Shea's Lounge
Six Degrees
Stars Bar & Dining
Trattoria Mitchelli
Triangle Lounge
Tulio
Two Bells Tavern

Seattle Indexes

Late Late – After 12:30
(All hours are AM)
Belltown Billiards (1)
Blowfish Asian (1)
Broadway New Amer. (1:30)
Caffè Minnie's (24 hrs.)
Charlie's B&G (2)
China Gate (1:30)
Deluxe B&G (2)
Dick's Drive-In (2)
El Gaucho (1)
Flying Fish (1)
Honey Court (2)
Palace Kitchen (1)
Sea Garden (2)
Stella's Trattoria (24 hrs.)
13 Coins (24 hrs.)
Trattoria Mitchelli (4)

Meet for a Drink
(Most top hotels and the following standouts)
Adriatica
Avenue One
Axis
Bandoleone
Belltown Billiards
BluWater Bistro
Brasa
Brooklyn Seafood
Cafe Campagne
Campagne
Capitol Club
Cassis
Chandler's Crabhse.
Cucina! Cucina!
Cutters Bayhouse
Daniel's Broiler
El Camino
El Gaucho
Elliott's Oyster Hse.
El Niño Rest.
Etta's Seafood
5 Spot
Flying Fish
F.X. McRory's
icon Grill
Il Bistro
Il Fornaio
Kaspar's
LeoMelina Ristorante
Leschi Lakecafe
Luau Polynesian
Marco's Supperclub
McCormick & Schmick's
McCormick & Schmick's Harbor
McCormick's Fish Hse.
Metropolitan Grill
Mona's Bistro
ObaChine
Palace Kitchen
Palisade
Palomino Euro Bistro
Paragon B&G
Pescatore
Pink Door
Place Pigalle
Ray's Boathouse
Rosebud Rest.
Ruth's Chris
Salty's
Serafina
Shea's Lounge
Sostanza Trattoria
Spazzo
Stars Bar & Dining
Theoz
Third Floor Fish
Triangle Lounge
Twenty-Two Eighteen
Umberto's
Union Sq. Grill
Vina
Wild Ginger
Wolfgang Puck Cafe
Yarrow Bay Beach
Yarrow Bay Grill

Noteworthy Newcomers (42)
Afrikando
Alligator Soul
Asian Wok & Grill
Avenue One
Axis
Banjara
Blowfish Asian
Brasa
Brie & Bordeaux
Buca di Beppo
Carmelita
Cassis
Chef Wang
Chinoise Café
El Niño Rest.
Figaro Bistro
Gordon Biersch

Seattle Indexes

icon Grill
Il Fornaio
Il Gambero
Kingfish Café
Krittika Noodles
La Fontana
La Medusa
Luau Polynesian
Lush Life
Matt's in the Mkt.
Neo Bistro
Noodle Ranch
ObaChine
Original Pancake Hse.
Pontevecchio
Racha
Roy's Seattle
Roy St. Bistro
Sahib
Sazerac
Seattle Catch
Shallots Asian Bistro
Six Degrees
Stars Bar & Dining
Yakima Grill

Noteworthy Closings (26)
Asia Grille
Boca
Bombore
Cafe Counter Intelligence
Cafe Illiterati
Cafe Los Gatos
Cafe Sophie
Casa U-Betcha
Domani
du jour
Il Paesano
Julia's Park Place
Kamalco
Kitto Japanese Noodle House
Labuznik
Macheezmo Mouse
Manca's
Moe's Mo'Roc'N Cafe
New Mikado
Quintana Roo
Rattler's Grill
Salute in Citta
Surrogate Hostess
TestaRossa
Ventana
Virazon

Offbeat
Afrikando
Alligator Soul
Armadillo Barbecue
Bandoleone
Bizzarro Italian
Buca di Beppo
Café Septieme
Capitol Club
Coastal Kitchen
Crocodile Cafe
Entros World Grill
Gravity Bar
Green Cat Cafe
Jitterbug Café
Kingfish Café
Luau Polynesian
Luna Park Cafe
Mae's Phinney Ridge
Mama's Mexican
Matt's in the Mkt.
Mona's Bistro
Mondo Burrito
Paseo Caribbean
Pink Door
Plenty Cafe
Pontevecchio
Rhododendron Café
Shea's Lounge
Shultzy's
Sit & Spin
Still Life in Fremont
Swingside Cafe
Triangle Lounge
Twenty-Two Eighteen
Twin Teepees

Outdoor Dining
(G=garden; P=patio;
S=sidewalk; T=terrace;
best of many)
Anthony's HomePort (P,W)
Anthony's Pier 66 (P,W)
Arnie's (P,W)
Avenue One (P,S)
Axis (P,S)
Bell St. Diner (P,W)
Belltown Pub (P,S)
Benjamin's/Lake Union (P,W)
Bick's Broadview Grill (P)
Bilbo's Festivo (P)
Bis on Main (P)
Bistro Pleasant Beach (T)
BluWater Bistro (P,W)

Seattle Indexes

Botticelli Caffè (S)
Bridges B&G (P,W)
Broadway New Amer. (P)
Brooklyn Seafood (S)
Brusseau's (G)
Bungalow Wine Bar (P,T)
Cafe Flora (P)
Cafe Juanita (P)
Cafe Nola (P)
Cafe Veloce (P)
Campagne (P)
Capitol Club (T)
Chandler's Crabhse. (P,W)
Chinook's/Salmon Bay (T)
Christina's (T,W)
Ciao Bella (P)
Claim Jumper (P)
Cool Hand Luke's (P)
Copacabana Cafe (T)
Cucina! Cucina! (P,W)
Daniel's Broiler (P,W)
Dash Point Lobster Shop (P,W)
Da Vinci's Pizza (P,W)
Desert Fire (P)
Duke's Chowderhse. (P,W)
El Camino (P)
Elliott's Oyster Hse. (P)
Emmett Watson's (P)
Firenze Rist. (P)
Hidden Harbour (P,W)
Hi-Spot Cafe (P)
I Love Sushi (P,W)
Il Terrazzo Carmine (T)
Ivar's Mukilteo (P)
Ivar's Salmon Hse. (P)
Kamon/Lake Union (P,W)
Kells (P)
Kirkland Roaster (P)
La Fontana (P)
Lake Washington Grillhse. (P,W)
Latitude 47 (P,W)
LeoMelina Ristorante (P,W)
Leschi Lakecafe (P,W)
Lush Life (P)
Madison Park Cafe (P)
Maggie Bluffs (P,W)
Mama's Mexican (P)
Mandalay Café (P)
Marco's Supperclub (P,S)
Mondo Burrito (P)
New Jake O'Shaughnessey's (P)
New Orleans (P)
Nickerson St. Saloon (P)
Oyster Bar/Chuckanut Dr. (W)
Oyster Creek Inn (W)
Palisade (T)
Pecos Pit BBQ (G,P,T)
Pescatore (P,T,W)
Pink Door (G,P,W)
Place Pigalle (P)
Ponti Seafood Grill (P,W)
Ray's Boathouse (P,W)
Red Door Alehouse (P)
Relais (P)
Restaurant, The (W)
Rhododendron Café (T)
Ristorante Buongusto (P)
Rosebud Rest. (P)
Rover's (P)
Serafina (G)
Simpatico (P)
Sisters European (G,T)
Sostanza Trattoria (P)
Stars Bar & Dining (T)
Still Life in Fremont (S)
Sunfish (P,W)
Triangle Lounge (P)
22 Fountain Ct. (T)
Union Bay Cafe (T)
Waters (T,W)
Yarrow Bay Beach (P,W)
Yarrow Bay Grill (P,W)

Oyster Bars

Brooklyn Seafood
Chandler's Crabhse.
Daniel's Broiler
Emmett Watson's
F.X. McRory's
Izumi
Jack's Fish Spot
McCormick & Schmick's
McCormick's Fish Hse.
Wolfgang Puck Cafe

Parking/Valet

(L=parking lot;
V=valet parking;
*=validated parking)

Adriatica (L)
Alligator Soul (L)
Andaluca (V)*
Anthony's HomePort (L,V)
Anthony's Pier 66 (V)*
Aoki Japanese*
Ark (L)
Armadillo Barbecue (L)
Arnie's (L)

Seattle Indexes

Asian Wok & Grill (L)
Assaggio Rist. (V)
Avenue One (V)
Axis (V)
Azteca (L,V)
Bahn Thai (L)
Bai Tong (L)
Bamboo Garden (L)
Bandoleone*
Bay Cafe (L)
Bell St. Diner (V)*
Benjamin's/Lake Union (V)*
Bick's Broadview Grill (L)
Big Time Pizzeria (L)
Bilbo's Festivo (L)
Billy McHale's (L)
Bis on Main (L)
Bistro Pleasant Beach (L)
Black Pearl (L)
Blue Water Diner (L)
BluWater Bistro (L,V)*
Botticelli Caffè (L)
Briazz (L)
Bridges B&G (L)
Brooklyn Seafood (V)
Brusseau's (L)
Buca di Beppo (L)
Burrito Loco (L)
Bush Garden (L)
Cafe Campagne*
Cafe Flora (L)
Cafe Juanita (L)
Cafe Veloce (L)
Calabria Rist. (L)
Campagne*
Canlis (V)
Cassis (L)
Chandler's Crabhse. (L,V)*
Charlie's B&G (L)
Chevys Fresh Mex (L)
Chez Shea (V)*
China Harbor (L)
Chinook's/Salmon Bay (L)
Chutneys Bistro (L)
Chutneys Grille (L)
Ciao Italia (L)
Circa Neighborhood Gr. (L)
Claim Jumper (L)
Cliff House (L)
Costas Greek (L)
Coyote Creek Pizza (L)
Crab Cracker (L)
Crêpe de Paris*
Cucina! Cucina! (L,V)*
Cutters Bayhouse*
Dahlia Lounge*
Daniel's Broiler (L,V)*
Dash Point Lobster Shop (L)
Da Vinci's Pizza (L)
Delfino's Pizzeria (L)
Deluxe B&G*
Desert Fire (L,V)
Dimitriou's Jazz Alley (L)
Dish (L)
Duke's Chowderhse. (L,V)*
Eating Factory (L)
El Gaucho (V)*
Elliott's Oyster Hse.*
Eques*
Ezell's Chicken (L)
Filiberto's (L)
Foghorn (L)
Four Seas (L)
Fullers (V)*
Galerias (L)
Georgian Room (V)*
Gordon Biersch (V)
Gravity Bar*
Grazie Ristorante (L)
Hattie's Hat (L)
Herbfarm (L)
Heron Beach Inn (L)
Hidden Harbour (L)
Hong's Garden (L)
House of Hong (L)
Hunan Garden (L)
Hunt Club*
icon Grill (V)
Il Bistro (V)
il fiasco*
Il Fornaio (L)
I Love Sushi (L)
Il Terrazzo Carmine (V)*
India House (L)
Inn at Langley (L)
Isabella Rist. (V)
Italianissimo (L)
Ivar's Mukilteo (L)
Ivar's Salmon Hse. (L)
Izumi (L)
JaK's Grill (L)
Julia's of Wallingford (L)
Kamon/Lake Union (L)
Kaspar's (L,V)*
Kikuya (L)
Kirkland Roaster (L)
Kokeb (L)
Lake Washington Grillhse. (L,V)

Seattle Indexes

La Panzanella (L)
Latitude 47 (L,V)
Le Bonaparte (L)
LeoMelina Ristorante*
Leschi Lakecafe (L)
Lockspot Cafe (L)
Lombardi's Cucina (L)
Louie's Cuisine (L)
Louisa's Cafe (L)
Luna Park Cafe (L)
Machiavelli (L)
Mac's Smokehouse (L)
Mad Pizza (L)
Mae's Phinney Ridge (L)
Maggie Bluffs (L)
Maltby Cafe (L)
Maple Leaf Grill (L)
Matt's Famous (L)
Maximilien (V)*
McCormick's Fish Hse. (L)
Mediterranean Kitchen (L)
Metropolitan Grill (V)
Moghul Palace (L)
Mondo Burrito (L)
My Favourite Piroshky (L)
New Jake O'Shaughnessey's (L)
Nikko (V)*
Nishino (L)
Noble Court (L)
Ocean City (L)
Olympia III Pizza (L)
Original Pancake Hse. (L)
Oyster Bar/Chuckanut Dr. (L)
Oyster Creek Inn (L)
Painted Table (V)
Palisade (V)
Palomino Euro Bistro (L)
Pandasia (L)
Pasta & Co. (L)
Pasta Bella (L)*
Pecos Pit BBQ (L)
Perché No (V)
Pescatore (V)
Piecora's (L)
Place Pigalle (V)
Pogacha (L)
Pon Proem (L)
Ponti Seafood Grill (V)
Prego (V)*
Provinces (L)
Pyramid Alehouse (L)
Raga (L)*
Ray's Boathouse (V)
Red Mill Burgers (L)
Reiner's*
Relais (L)
Restaurant, The (L,V)*
Rhododendron Café (L)
Ristorante Buongusto (L)
Ristorante Paradiso (L)
Rosita's Mexican (L)
Roy's Seattle (L,V)*
Ruth's Chris (V)
Saigon Bistro*
Saleh al Lago (L)
Salish Lodge (L,V)*
Salmon Bay Café (L)
Sanmi Sushi (L)
Sazerac (V)*
Scarlet Tree (L)
Sea Garden (L)
Seattle Catch (L)
Serafina (L)
Shamiana (L)
Shanghai Cafe (L)
Shanghai Garden (L)
Sharp's Roaster (L)
Shea's Lounge (V)*
Shoalwater (L)
Shuckers (V)
Simpatico (L)
Six Degrees (L)
Space Needle Rest. (V)
Spazzo (L)*
Spirit of Washington (L)
Stars Bar & Dining (L,V)
Streamliner Diner (L)
Szmania's (L)
Taco Del Mar (L)
Tai Tung (L)
Texas Smokehouse (L)
Third Floor Fish (L)
13 Coins (L)
Tosoni (L)
Toyoda Sushi (L)
T.S. McHugh's (L)
Tulio (L,V)*
Union Sq. Grill (V)*
Waters (L,V)*
Yankee Diner (L)
Yarrow Bay Beach (L,V)
Yarrow Bay Grill (L,V)
Zeek's Pizza (L)

Seattle Indexes

Parties & Private Rooms
(Any nightclub or restaurant charges less at off-times; * indicates private rooms available; best of many)

Adriatica*
Afrikando
Al Boccalino*
Alligator Soul*
Andaluca*
Anthony's HomePort*
Anthony's Pier 66
Ark
Armadillo Barbecue
Assaggio Rist.*
Avenue One*
Axis*
Belltown Billiards
Benjamin's/Lake Union*
Bis on Main
Bistro Pleasant Beach
Bistro Provençal*
Blowfish Asian*
BluWater Bistro*
Broadway New Amer.
Brooklyn Seafood
Bush Garden*
Cafe Flora
Cafe Juanita*
Calabria Rist.*
Canlis*
Carmelita
Chandler's Crabhse.
Chez Shea
Christina's*
Cliff House*
Cutters Bayhouse*
Dahlia Lounge*
Daniel's Broiler*
Dash Point Lobster Shop*
Dulces Latin Bistro*
El Gaucho*
Elliott's Oyster Hse.
Entros World Grill
Eques*
Filiberto's*
5 Spot*
Flying Fish*
Four Seas*
Fullers*
F.X. McRory's*
Georgian Room*
Gordon Biersch*
Herbfarm*
Heron Beach Inn*
Hidden Harbour*
icon Grill*
Il Fornaio*
Ivar's Acres*
Ivar's Salmon Hse.*
Kamon/Lake Union*
Kaspar's*
La Buca*
La Fontana*
Le Gourmand
LeoMelina Ristorante*
Madison Park Cafe*
Maximilien*
McCormick & Schmick's
McCormick & Schmick's Harbor
Metropolitan Grill*
Mona's Bistro*
Nikko*
Ocean City
Oyster Bar/Chuckanut Dr.*
Oyster Creek Inn*
Painted Table*
Palace Kitchen*
Palisade*
Pandasia*
Perché No*
Pescatore
Planet Hollywood*
Pogacha*
Pontevecchio
Ponti Seafood Grill*
Queen Mary
Raga*
Ray's Boathouse*
Reiner's
Relais*
Restaurant, The
Ristorante Buongusto*
Rover's*
Roy's Seattle
Roy St. Bistro
Ruth's Chris*
Salty's
Santa Fe Cafe
Sazerac*
Sea Garden*
Shallots Asian Bistro*
Shiro's Sushi*
Shoalwater*
Sostanza Trattoria*
Spazzo*
Spirit of Washington

Seattle Indexes

Stars Bar & Dining*
Szmania's*
Theoz*
Third Floor Fish*
13 Coins*
T.S. McHugh's*
Tulio*
Twenty-Two Eighteen*
22 Fountain Ct.*
Umberto's*
Union Sq. Grill
Wild Ginger*
Yankee Diner
Yarrow Bay Beach*
Yarrow Bay Grill*

People-Watching
Assaggio Rist.
Avenue One
Axis
B&O Espresso
Bell St. Diner
Belltown Billiards
Broadway New Amer.
Cafe Campagne
Café Septieme
Caffè Minnie's
Carmelita
Coastal Kitchen
Copacabana Cafe
Cucina! Cucina!
Cutters Bayhouse
Deluxe B&G
El Gaucho
Entros World Grill
Etta's Seafood
Flying Fish
Gordon Biersch
Gravity Bar
Il Fornaio
Jack's Fish Spot
Kingfish Café
Longshoreman's Daughter
Macrina Bakery
Marco's Supperclub
McCormick & Schmick's
New Jake O'Shaughnessey's
Palace Kitchen
Palomino Euro Bistro
Pescatore
Ray's Boathouse
Red Door Alehouse
Sazerac
Sisters European

Sostanza Trattoria
Spazzo
Stars Bar & Dining
Third Floor Fish
Triangle Lounge
Tulio
Union Sq. Grill
Wild Ginger
Wolfgang Puck Cafe

Power Scenes
Benjamin's/Lake Union
Brooklyn Seafood
Campagne
Canlis
Daniel's Broiler
El Gaucho
Georgian Room
Il Terrazzo Carmine
McCormick & Schmick's
Metropolitan Grill
Palomino Euro Bistro
Rover's
Saleh al Lago
Sazerac
Shuckers
Stars Bar & Dining
Tulio

Pubs/Bars/ Microbreweries
Belltown Pub
Bick's Broadview
Billy McHale's
Circa Neighborhood Gr.
Eggs Cetera's
F.X. McRory's
Gordon Biersch
Grady's Grillhouse
Hale's Ales
Hilltop Ale House
Kells
Kirkland Roaster
Leschi Lakecafe
Maple Leaf Grill
Nickerson St. Saloon
Pyramid Alehouse
Red Door Alehouse
74th St. Ale Hse.
Two Bells Tavern

Quiet Conversation
Adriatica
Al Boccalino

Seattle Indexes

Andaluca
Ark
Avenue One
Brie & Bordeaux
Bungalow Wine Bar
Cafe Juanita
Café Soleil
Campagne
Canlis
Chez Shea
Christina's
Chutneys
Chutneys Bistro
Daniel's Broiler
Dulces Latin Bistro
Eques
Etta's Seafood
Fullers
Georgian Room
Herbfarm
Heron Beach Inn
Hunt Club
Il Bistro
il fiasco
Il Gambero
Il Terrazzo Carmine
Inn at Langley
Isabella Rist.
Kaspar's
La Fontana
Lampreia
Le Bonaparte
Le Gourmand
LeoMelina Ristorante
Lush Life
Madison Park Cafe
Painted Table
Ponti Seafood Grill
Prego
Queen Mary
Reiner's
Relais
Restaurant, The
Rover's
Roy St. Bistro
Saleh al Lago
Salish Lodge
Shea's Lounge
Shoalwater
Sostanza Trattoria
22 Fountain Ct.
Union Bay Cafe

Romantic Spots

Adriatica
Al Boccalino
Andaluca
Assaggio Rist.
Avenue One
Bandoleone
Bella Rosa Bistro
Bistro Lautrec
Bistro Provençal
Brasa
Brie & Bordeaux
Cafe Campagne
Cafe Juanita
Campagne
Canlis
Chez Shea
Christina's
Dahlia Lounge
Dulces Latin Bistro
El Gaucho
Georgian Room
Herbfarm
Hunt Club
Il Bistro
Il Gambero
Il Terrazzo Carmine
Isabella Rist.
Kaspar's
La Buca
La Fontana
Lampreia
Le Gourmand
LeoMelina Ristorante
Lush Life
Marco's Supperclub
Matt's in the Mkt.
Mona's Bistro
Pink Door
Place Pigalle
Pontevecchio
Ponti Seafood Grill
Queen City Grill
Reiner's
Relais
Rover's
Salish Lodge
Salvatore Rist.
Sazerac
Serafina
Shea's Lounge
Shoalwater
Sostanza Trattoria
Spirit of Washington

Seattle Indexes

Stars Bar & Dining
Szmania's

Saturday – Best Bets
(B=brunch; L=lunch;
best of many)
Andaluca (L)
Anthony's HomePort (L)
B&O Espresso (B,L)
Bandoleone (B)
Bell St. Diner (L)
Belltown Pub (L)
Benjamin's/Lake Union (L)
Bilbo's Festivo (L)
Bistro Pleasant Beach (L)
Blowfish Asian (B,L)
BluWater Bistro (L)
Brie & Bordeaux (B)
Broadway New Amer. (B,L)
Brusseau's (L)
Cactus (L)
Cafe Campagne (L)
Café Dilettante (L)
Cafe Flora (B)
Cafe Nola (L)
Café Septieme (L)
Café Soleil (L)
Caffe Ladro (L)
Chinook's/Salmon Bay (L)
Chutneys (L)
Circa Neighborhood Gr. (B)
CJ's Eatery (L)
Cliff House (L)
Coastal Kitchen (L)
Copacabana Cafe (L)
Crocodile Cafe (L)
Cucina! Cucina! (L)
Cutters Bayhouse (L)
Da Vinci's Pizza (L)
Deluxe B&G (L)
Desert Fire (L)
Duke's Chowderhse. (L)
Eggs Cetera's (L)
El Greco (B)
Elliott's Oyster Hse. (L)
El Puerco Lloron (L)
Emmett Watson's (L)
Eques (L)
Etta's Seafood (B,L)
5 Spot (L)
Four Seas (L)
Fremont Noodle Hse. (L)
F.X. McRory's (L)
Galerias (L)
Gordon Biersch (L)
Grady's Grillhouse (L)
Gravity Bar (L)
Green Cat Cafe (L)
Hale's Ales (L)
Honey Bear Bakery (B,L)
Honey Court (L)
Hong's Garden (L)
House of Hong (L)
Hunt Club (B,L)
icon Grill (L)
Il Fornaio (L)
India House (L)
Ivar's Salmon Hse. (L)
Jitterbug Café (L)
Julia's of Wallingford (L)
Kaleenka (L)
Kells (L)
LeoMelina Ristorante (L)
Leschi Lakecafe (L)
Longshoreman's Daughter (B,L)
Louisa's Cafe (L)
Luna Park Cafe (L)
Macrina Bakery (B,L)
Maggie Bluffs (L)
Mama's Mexican (L)
Mangoes Thai (L)
Matt's in the Mkt. (L)
Maximilien (L)
Nickerson St. Saloon (L)
Noodle Ranch (L)
ObaChine (L)
Ocean City (L)
Original Pancake Hse. (L)
Oyster Creek Inn (L)
Palisade (L)
Palomino Euro Bistro (L)
Paragon B&G (L)
Pescatore (L)
Pink Door (L)
Plenty Cafe (B,L)
Pyramid Alehouse (L)
Racha (L)
Ray's Boathouse (L)
Red Door Alehouse (L)
Red Mill Burgers (L)
Restaurant, The (L)
Rhododendron Café (B,L)
Roy's Seattle (L)
Ruth's Chris (L)
Salish Lodge (L)
Salmon Bay Café (L)
Salty's (L)
Santa Fe Cafe (L)

Seattle Indexes

Sazerac (L)
Sea Garden (L)
74th St. Ale Hse. (L)
Shanghai Cafe (L)
Shanghai Garden (L)
Shoalwater (L)
Shuckers (L)
Sisters European (L)
Six Degrees (L)
Snappy Dragon (L)
Spirit of Washington (L)
Stars Bar & Dining (L)
Still Life in Fremont (L)
Streamliner Diner (L)
Sunfish (L)
Theoz (L)
13 Coins (L)
Triangle Lounge (L)
Tulio (L)
Two Bells Tavern (L)
Waters (B)
Wild Ginger (L)
Wolfgang Puck Cafe (L)
Yakima Grill (B,L)
Yarrow Bay Beach (L)

Sunday – Best Bets

(B=brunch; L=lunch; D=dinner; plus all hotels and most Asians)
Afrikando (L,D)
Anthony's HomePort (B,L,D)
Armadillo Barbecue (L,D)
Bell St. Diner (L,D)
Benjamin's/Lake Union (B,D)
Bistro Pleasant Beach (L,D)
BluWater Bistro (L,D)
Brie & Bordeaux (B)
Brusseau's (L)
Cafe Campagne (B)
Cafe Flora (B,D)
Cafe Nola (L)
Chandler's Crabhse. (B,L,D)
Chinook's/Salmon Bay (L,D)
CJ's Eatery (L)
Cliff House (L,D)
Coastal Kitchen (L,D)
Copacabana Cafe (L,D)
Cutters Bayhouse (B,L,D)
Dash Point Lobster Shop (B,D)
El Greco (B)
Elliott's Oyster Hse. (L,D)
El Puerco Lloron (L,D)
Emmett Watson's (L)
Etta's Seafood (B,L,D)
5 Spot (L,D)
Hale's Ales (L,D)
Hilltop Ale House (L,D)
Honey Bear Bakery (B,L,D)
Il Fornaio (L,D)
India House (L,D)
Jitterbug Café (L,D)
Kingfish Café (B)
LeoMelina Ristorante (L,D)
Leschi Lakecafe (L,D)
Longshoreman's (B,L,D)
Luna Park Cafe (L,D)
Macrina Bakery (B,L)
Maggie Bluffs (L,D)
Maximilien (B)
Original Pancake Hse. (L)
Oyster Creek Inn (L,D)
Palisade (B,L,D)
Palomino Euro Bistro (L,D)
Planet Hollywood (L,D)
Plenty Cafe (B,L,D)
Ponti Seafood Grill (B,D)
Pyramid Alehouse (L,D)
Ray's Boathouse (L,D)
Red Door Alehouse (L,D)
Red Mill Burgers (L,D)
Rhododendron Café (B,L,D)
Salmon Bay Café (L)
Seattle Catch (B,D)
74th St. Ale Hse. (L,D)
Six Degrees (L,D)
Space Needle Rest. (B,L,D)
Spirit of Washington (L,D)
Stars Bar & Dining (L,D)
Still Life in Fremont (L,D)
Streamliner Diner (L)
Sunfish (L,D)
Sunlight Cafe (B,L,D)
13 Coins (L,D)
Twin Teepees (L,D)
Yarrow Bay Beach (B,L,D)
Yarrow Bay Grill (B,D)

Senior Appeal

Andy's Diner
Ark
Arnie's
Bistro Provençal
Chanterelle
Cliff House
Dash Point Lobster Shop
Foghorn
Fremont Classic Pizza

Seattle Indexes

McCormick & Schmick's Harbor
Original Pancake Hse.
Provinces
Queen Mary
Ray's Boathouse
Reiner's
Relais
Salish Lodge
Salmon Bay Café
Shoalwater
Space Needle Rest.
Spirit of Washington
Streamliner Diner
Thai on Mercer
13 Coins
Three Girls Bakery
Twin Teepees
Umberto's
Yankee Diner

Singles Scenes

Avenue One
BluWater Bistro
Broadway New Amer.
Caffè Minnie's
Capitol Club
Coastal Kitchen
Crocodile Cafe
Cucina! Cucina!
Da Vinci's Pizza
Deluxe B&G
Duke's Chowderhse.
Eggs Cetera's
El Niño Rest.
Entros World Grill
Gravity Bar
Hattie's Hat
Julia's of Wallingford
Kirkland Roaster
Leschi Lakecafe
Machiavelli
Mama's Mexican
Marco's Supperclub
Mondo Burrito
New Orleans
Palace Kitchen
Paragon B&G
Pink Door
Queen City Grill
Rosebud Rest.
Sazerac
Scarlet Tree
Serafina
Sit & Spin

Six Degrees
Still Life in Fremont
Trattoria Mitchelli
Triangle Lounge
Wild Ginger

Sleepers

(Good to excellent food, but little known)
Aleko's Pizzeria
Café Soleil
Chanterelle
Christina's
Ciao Italia
Circa Neighborhood Gr.
Dish
Heron Beach Inn
Izumi
Jack's Fish Spot
Karam's
Kikuya
Le Bonaparte
Louisa's Cafe
Oyster Bar/Chuckanut Dr.
Paseo Caribbean
Philadelphia Fevre Steak
Pon Proem
Provinces
Sahib
Saigon Bistro
Sunfish
Zaina Food

Teflons

(Get lots of business, despite so-so food, i.e. they have other attractions that prevent criticism from sticking)
Azteca
Billy McHale's
Briazz
Buca di Beppo
Planet Hollywood
Space Needle Rest.
Yankee Diner

Teenagers & Other Youthful Spirits

Armadillo Barbecue
Billy McHale's
Bizzarro Italian
Blowfish Asian
Blue Water Diner
Buca di Beppo

Seattle Indexes

Cafe Veloce
Chevys Fresh Mex
Claim Jumper
Coyote Creek Pizza
Cucina! Cucina!
Da Vinci's Pizza
Desert Fire
Dick's Drive-In
Duke's Chowderhse.
Entros World Grill
Frankfurter
Gravity Bar
Ivar's Salmon Hse.
Jalisco
Jitterbug Café
Julia's of Wallingford
Kidd Valley
Kirkland Roaster
Luna Park Cafe
Mad Pizza
Mama's Mexican
New Jake O'Shaughnessey's
Pagliacci Pizza
Pasta Ya Gotcha
Pazzo's
Pegasus Pizza
Planet Hollywood
Pyramid Alehouse
Red Mill Burgers
Romio's Pizza
Shultzy's
Sit & Spin
Spazzo
Still Life in Fremont
Streamliner Diner
Sunfish
Sunlight Cafe
Trattoria Mitchelli
Umberto's
Wolfgang Puck Cafe
Yankee Diner
Zeek's Pizza

Theme Restaurants

Blue Water Diner
Buca di Beppo
Cafe Veloce
Claim Jumper
Cucina! Cucina!
Desert Fire
Entros World Grill
Planet Hollywood

Visitors on Expense Accounts

Anthony's Pier 66
Brooklyn Seafood
Campagne
Canlis
Cliff House
Daniel's Broiler
El Gaucho
Fullers
Georgian Room
Herbfarm
Heron Beach Inn
Hunt Club
Il Fornaio
Il Terrazzo Carmine
Kaspar's
McCormick & Schmick's
Metropolitan Grill
Painted Table
Palisade
Palomino Euro Bistro
Prego
Ray's Boathouse
Relais
Rover's
Roy's Seattle
Ruth's Chris
Salish Lodge
Sazerac
Shoalwater
Shuckers
Space Needle Rest.
Stars Bar & Dining
Theoz
13 Coins
Tulio
Union Sq. Grill
Waters
Yakima Grill

Wheelchair Access

(Most places now have wheelchair access; call in advance to check)

Wine/Beer Only

Al Boccalino
Alligator Soul
Aoki Japanese
Armadillo Barbecue
Ayutthaya
Bacchus
Bahn Thai

Seattle Indexes

- Bai Tong
- Banjara
- Bella Rosa Bistro
- Bis on Main
- Bistro Lautrec
- Bistro Pleasant Beach
- Bizzarro Italian
- Black Pearl
- Blue Water Diner
- Boat St. Cafe
- Briazz
- Brie & Bordeaux
- Bungalow Wine Bar
- Burk's Cafe
- Burrito Loco
- Byzantion
- Café Dilettante
- Cafe Flora
- Café Huê
- Cafe Lago
- Cafe Langley
- Cafe Nola
- Café Soleil
- Cafe Starbucks
- Cafe Veloce
- Caffè Minnie's
- Carmelita
- Chanterelle
- Chinoise Café
- Ciao Bella
- Ciao Italia
- Circa Neighborhood Gr.
- CJ's Eatery
- Cool Hand Luke's
- Copacabana Cafe
- Costas Greek
- Coyote Creek Pizza
- Credenzia's Oven
- Delcambre's
- Delfino's Pizzeria
- Eating Factory
- Eggs Cetera's
- El Greco
- El Puerco Lloron
- Emmett Watson's
- 14 Carrot Cafe
- Fremont Classic Pizza
- Fremont Noodle Hse.
- Gaspare's Rist.
- Gordito's
- Grazie Ristorante
- Green Cat Cafe
- Hale's Ales
- Herbfarm
- Hilltop Ale House
- Hi-Spot Cafe
- Honey Court
- Il Bacio
- Il Gambero
- Inn at Langley
- Izumi
- Julia's of Wallingford
- Kabul Afghan
- Kaleenka
- Karam's
- Kingfish Café
- Kokeb
- La Fontana
- La Medusa
- L'Auberge
- Le Gourmand
- Longshoreman's Daughter
- Luna Park Cafe
- Macrina Bakery
- Madison Park Cafe
- Mad Pizza
- Maltby Cafe
- Mamma Melina
- Mandalay Café
- Mangoes Thai
- Maple Leaf Grill
- Matt's in the Mkt.
- Mediterranean Kitchen
- Mondo Burrito
- Musashi's
- Noodle Ranch
- Noodle Studio
- Olympia III Pizza
- Oyster Bar/Chuckanut Dr.
- Oyster Creek Inn
- Pagliacci Pizza
- Pandasia
- Pasta Bella
- Pegasus Pizza
- Perché No
- Philadelphia Fevre Steak
- Phoenecia at Alki
- Plenty Cafe
- Pogacha
- Pon Proem
- Pontevecchio
- Pyramid Alehouse
- Queen Mary
- Racha
- Red Door Alehouse
- Rhododendron Café
- Ristorante Paradiso
- Romio's Pizza

Seattle Indexes

Saigon Bistro
Salmon Bay Café
Salvatore Rist.
74th St. Ale Hse.
Shallots Asian Bistro
Shamiana
Shanghai Cafe
Sit & Spin
Still Life in Fremont
Sunlight Cafe
Taco Del Mar
Texas Smokehouse
Thai on Mercer
That's Amore
Tosoni
Toyoda Sushi
Two Bells Tavern
Union Bay Cafe
Vina
World Class Chili
Yanni's
Zeek's Pizza

Winning Wine Lists

Adriatica
Ark
Avenue One
Axis
Brie & Bordeaux
Brooklyn Seafood
Bungalow Wine Bar
Cafe Campagne
Cafe Juanita
Cafe Lago
Campagne
Canlis
Christina's
Cutters Bayhouse
Dahlia Lounge
Elliott's Oyster Hse.
Etta's Seafood
Fullers
Georgian Room
Heron Beach Inn
Hunt Club
Il Bistro
Il Terrazzo Carmine
Inn at Langley
Kaspar's
Lampreia
Le Gourmand
Palace Kitchen
Place Pigalle
Queen City Grill
Ray's Boathouse
Relais
Rover's
Saleh al Lago
Salish Lodge
Shoalwater
Stars Bar & Dining
Wild Ginger

Worth a Trip

Bothell
  Relais
Bow
  Oyster Bar/Chuckanut Dr.
  Oyster Creek Inn
  Rhododendron Café
Eastsound, Orcas Island
  Christina's
Fall City
  Herbfarm
Kirkland
  Cafe Juanita
Langley, Whidbey Island
  Inn at Langley
Maltby
  Maltby Cafe
Nahcotta
  Ark
Renton
  Spirit of Washington
Seaview
  Shoalwater
Snoqualmie
  Salish Lodge

Young Children

(Besides the normal fast-food places; * indicates children's menu available)
Azteca*
Bell St. Diner*
Benjamin's/Lake Union*
Billy McHale's*
Blue Water Diner*
Brusseau's*
Buca di Beppo
Chevys Fresh Mex*
Claim Jumper*
Coastal Kitchen*
Cool Hand Luke's*
Cucina! Cucina!*
Da Vinci's Pizza*
Desert Fire*
Dick's Drive-In

Seattle Indexes

Dish*
Ezell's Chicken*
5 Spot*
Frankfurter*
Fremont Classic Pizza*
Ivar's Acres*
Ivar's Mukilteo*
Ivar's Salmon Hse.*
Jalisco*
Julia's of Wallingford*
La Medusa*
Leschi Lakecafe*
Lombardi's Cucina*
Luna Park Cafe*
Maggie Bluffs*
Maltby Cafe*
Olympia II Pizza*
Olympia III Pizza*
Original Pancake Hse.*
Pagliacci Pizza
Pasta Ya Gotcha
Pazzo's*
Pescatore*
Piecora's*
Planet Hollywood*
Pogacha*
Red Mill Burgers
Restaurant, The*
Rhododendron Café*
Rosita's Mexican*
Sharp's Roaster*
Simpatico*
Space Needle Rest.*
Spirit of Washington*
Sunfish
Sunlight Cafe*
Taco Del Mar*
Texas Smokehouse*
That's Amore*
Twin Teepees*
Wolfgang Puck Cafe*
Yankee Diner*
Yarrow Bay Beach*

Portland

Portland's Most Popular

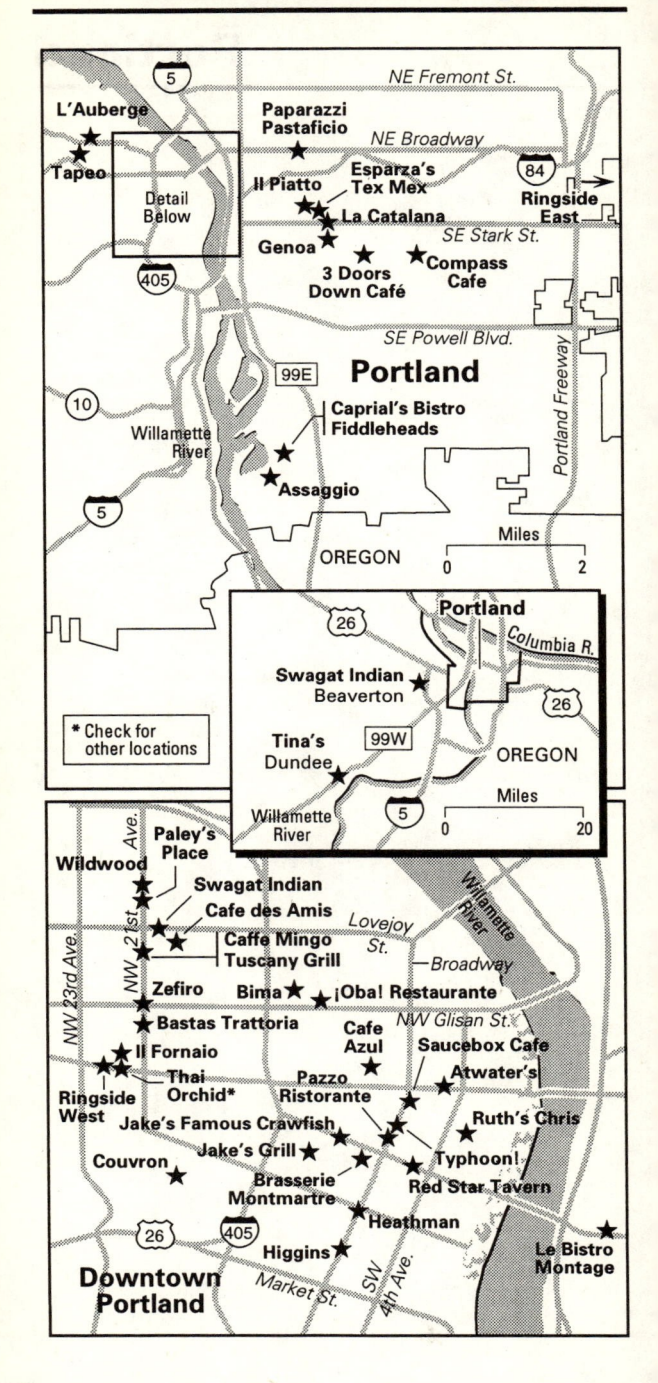

Portland's Most Popular Restaurants

Each of our reviewers has been asked to name his or her five favorite restaurants. The 40 spots most frequently named, in order of their popularity, are:

1. Genoa
2. Higgins
3. Paley's Place
4. Wildwood
5. Cafe des Amis
6. Zefiro
7. Assaggio
8. Heathman
9. 3 Doors Down Café
10. Caffe Mingo
11. Caprial's Bistro
12. Pazzo Ristorante
13. Il Piatto
14. Jake's Famous Crawfish
15. Il Fornaio
16. Couvron
17. Atwater's
18. Saucebox Cafe
19. Fiddleheads
20. Typhoon!*
21. Compass Cafe
22. Esparza's Tex Mex
23. Tina's*
24. Red Star Tavern
25. Jake's Grill
26. L'Auberge*
27. ¡Oba! Restaurante*
28. Cafe Azul
29. Le Bistro Montage*
30. Ruth's Chris*
31. Thai Orchid
32. Tuscany Grill*
33. La Catalana
34. Ringside*
35. Bastas Trattoria
36. Paparazzi Pastaficio*
37. Bima
38. Brasserie Montmartre*
39. Swagat Indian*
40. Tapeo

It's obvious that many of the restaurants on the above list are among the most expensive, but Portland diners also love a bargain. Were popularity calibrated to price, we suspect that a number of other restaurants would join the above ranks. Thus, we have listed over 80 Best Buys on pages 139–140.

---

* Tied with the restaurant listed directly above it.

Top Ratings*

Top 40 Food Ranking

- **29** Genoa
- **28** Paley's Place
- **27** Couvron
  Pearl Bakery
  Heathman
  Tina's
- **26** Caprial's Bistro
  Restaurant Murata
  3 Doors Down Café
  Cafe des Amis
  Wildwood
  Nick's Italian Cafe
  Bugatti's Ristorante
- **25** Lemongrass Thai
  Zefiro
  Higgins
  Typhoon!
  Caffe Mingo
  Paparazzi Pastaficio
  Compass Cafe

  Tapeo
  Cafe Azul
- **24** L'Auberge
  Il Piatto
  Nicholas'
  Atwater's
  Couch St. Seafood
  Lucy's Table
  Hands on Café
  Papa Haydn
  Winterborne
  London Grill
- **23** Campbell's Bar-B-Q
  Assaggio
  Pazzo Ristorante
  Swagat Indian
  Grand Central Bakery
  Ruth's Chris
  Jake's Famous Crawfish
  Thai Orchid

Top Spots by Cuisine

American (New)
- **24** Atwater's
  Lucy's Table
- **21** Besaw's Cafe
- **19** Veritable Quandry
  Paragon

American (Northwest)
- **28** Paley's Place
- **27** Tina's
- **26** Caprial's Bistro
  Wildwood
- **25** Compass Cafe

American (Traditional)
- **24** Couch St. Seafood
- **23** Ruth's Chris
  Jake's Famous Crawfish
  Jake's Grill
- **21** Red Star Tavern

Bakeries
- **27** Pearl Bakery
- **23** Grand Central Bakery
- **21** Pazzoria
- **20** Il Fornaio
- **–** Marsee Baking

Breakfast**
- **23** Original Pancake Hse.
  Zell's
- **22** Bijou Cafe
- **21** Besaw's Cafe
  Marco's Cafe

Brunch
- **26** Wildwood
- **25** Compass Cafe
- **24** Hands on Café
  Papa Haydn
  London Grill

---

* Excluding restaurants with low voting.
** Other than hotels.

Top Food

Burger/Sandwich
- **21** Besaw's Cafe
  Little Wing Cafe
- **20** Stanich's
  Bread & Ink Cafe
- **19** Kornblatt's Deli

Chinese
- **22** Legin
- **21** Fong Chong
- **19** Hunan
- **18** FuJin

Dessert
- **28** Paley's Place
- **27** Heathman
- **26** Wildwood
- **25** Zefiro
- **24** Papa Haydn

Eclectic/International
- **25** Zefiro
  Higgins
  Compass Cafe
- **24** Lucy's Table
  Hands on Café

French
- **27** Couvron
  Heathman
- **26** Cafe des Amis
- **24** L'Auberge
- **19** Brasserie Montmartre

Hotel Dining
- **27** Heathman
  Heathman Hotel
- **25** Typhoon! on Broadway
  Imperial Hotel
- **24** London Grill
  Benson Hotel
- **23** Pazzo Ristorante
  Hotel Vintage Plaza
- **21** Esplanade
  River Place Hotel

Indian
- **23** Swagat Indian
  Bombay Cricket Club
- **22** Indigine
- **21** Plainfields' Mayur
  India House

Italian
- **29** Genoa
- **26** 3 Doors Down Café
  Nick's Italian Cafe
  Bugatti's Ristorante
- **25** Caffe Mingo

Japanese
- **26** Restaurant Murata
- **22** Koji Osakaya
- **20** Obi Japanese
- **19** Takahashi
  Kento Bento

Mediterranean
- **25** Tapeo
- **23** La Catalana
- **22** Alexis
- **20** Fernando's Hideaway
  Berbati

Mexican/Tex-Mex
- **25** Cafe Azul
- **22** ¡Oba! Restaurante
- **21** Esparza's Tex Mex
- **20** El Burrito Loco
- **18** Chez Jose

Middle Eastern
- **24** Nicholas'
- **21** Al-Amir
  Abou Karim
- **17** Garbonzos

Newcomers/Rated
- **25** Cafe Azul
- **24** Lucy's Table
- **22** Tao of Tea
- **21** Portland Steak
- **19** Southpark Seafood

Top Food

Newcomers/Unrated
- Bernie's Southern Bistro
- Fratelli
- John Street Cafe
- Le Bouchon
- Saburo's Sushi House

Offbeat
- 22 Wild Abandon
- 21 Esparza's Tex Mex
- 19 Le Bistro Montage
- 18 Caswell
- 17 Brazen Bean

People-Watching
- 22 Saucebox Cafe
- ¡Oba! Restaurante
- 19 Bima
- Le Bistro Montage
- Paragon

Pizza
- 23 Pizzicato
- 22 Accuardi's
- 21 Pazzoria
- Escape from NY Pizza
- 19 Hot Lips Pizza

Seafood
- 24 Couch St. Seafood
- Winterborne
- 23 Jake's Famous Crawfish
- 22 Waterzooies
- McCormick & Schmick's

Southern/Soul/BBQ
- 23 Campbell's Bar-B-Q
- 22 Tennessee Red's
- 21 Delta Cafe
- 20 Doris' Cafe
- 19 Le Bistro Montage

Steakhouses
- 23 Ruth's Chris
- 22 Ringside
- 21 Portland Steak
- 20 Opus Too
- 19 Sayler's Old Country

Thai/Vietnamese
- 25 Lemongrass Thai
- Typhoon!
- 23 Thai Orchid
- 22 Pho Van
- 20 Saigon Kitchen

Upscale Pubs
- 20 Black Rabbit
- 19 Widmer Gasthaus
- 17 BridgePort Ale Hse.
- 16 BridgePort Brewpub
- 15 Alameda Brewhouse

Wild Card
- 24 London Grill (Continental)
- 22 Tao of Tea (Teahouse)
- Saucebox Cafe (Pan-Asian)
- 19 Bima (Gulf Coast)
- 17 Chez Grill (Southwestern)

Worth a Trip
- 27 Tina's
  - Dundee
- 26 Nick's Italian Cafe
  - McMinnville
- Bugatti's Ristorante
  - West Linn
- Joel Palmer House*
  - Dayton
- 23 Red Hills Provincial*
  - Dundee

---

* Low votes.

Top 40 Decor Ranking

26 Tao of Tea
Atwater's
Avalon
25 ¡Oba! Restaurante
Paley's Place
24 London Grill
Cafe des Amis
Esplanade
Heathman
Zefiro
Brazen Bean
Marrakesh
Genoa
23 Higgins
Southpark Seafood
Wildwood
Pazzo Ristorante
L'Auberge
Couch St. Seafood
Il Piatto
Harborside
Couvron
Cafe Azul
Tapeo
22 Brasserie Montmartre
Fiddleheads
Lucy's Table
Jo Bar & Rotisserie
Il Fornaio
Black Rabbit
3 Doors Down Café
Bima
Red Star Tavern
Assaggio
Casablanca
Esparza's Tex Mex
21 Plainfields' Mayur
Jake's Famous Crawfish
Beaches
Pearl Bakery

Outdoor

Beaches
Compass Cafe
Hall Street Grill
Hands on Café
Harborside
Riccardo's
Sammy's
Trio

Romantic

Assaggio
Brazen Bean
Cafe des Amis
Couvron
Genoa
Il Piatto
Marrakesh
Paley's Place
Tao of Tea
Tapeo

Rooms

Bima
Cafe Azul
Fiddleheads
Heathman
Higgins
Il Fornaio
¡Oba! Restaurante
Southpark Seafood
Wildwood
Zefiro

Views

Alexander's
Atwater's
Avalon
Beaches
Esplanade
Harborside

Top 40 Service Ranking

- **28** Genoa
- **27** Cafe des Amis
- **26** Paley's Place
  - Heathman
- **25** Atwater's
  - Tina's
  - London Grill
  - Couvron
  - Couch St. Seafood
- **24** Higgins
  - Winterborne
  - Compass Cafe
  - Nick's Italian Cafe
  - 3 Doors Down Café
- **23** Lucy's Table
  - Zefiro
  - Cafe Azul
  - Bugatti's Ristorante
  - Paparazzi Pastaficio
  - Wildwood
  - L'Auberge
  - Esplanade
  - Ruth's Chris
  - Wild Abandon
- **22** Marrakesh
  - Tapeo
  - Pazzo Ristorante
  - Caprial's Bistro
  - Caffe Mingo
  - Jake's Famous Crawfish
  - Ringside
  - Alexis
- **21** Il Piatto
  - Riccardo's Ristorante
  - Cassidy's
  - McCormick's Fish House
  - Avalon
  - Tuscany Grill
  - Three Square Grill
  - Jake's Grill

Best Buys

60 Top Bangs For The Buck

This list reflects the best dining values in our *Survey*. It is produced by dividing the cost of a meal into the combined ratings for food, decor and service.

1. Tao of Tea
2. Pearl Bakery
3. Good Dog/Bad Dog
4. Escape from NY Pizza
5. Anne Hughes Kit. Table
6. El Burrito Loco
7. Pazzoria
8. Hungry Dog Burrito
9. Little Wing Cafe
10. Grand Central Bakery
11. Kento Bento
12. Hot Lips Pizza
13. Taco del Mar
14. Pasta Veloce
15. Pho Van Vietnamese
16. Hands on Café
17. Nicholas'
18. Bijou Cafe
19. Delta Cafe
20. Original Pancake Hse.
21. Fat City Cafe
22. Macheezmo Mouse
23. Garbonzos
24. Zell's
25. Pizzicato
26. Produce Row Cafe
27. Foothill Broiler
28. Stanich's
29. BridgePort Brewpub
30. Kornblatt's Deli
31. La Buca
32. Maya's Taqueria
33. Tennessee Red's
34. Misohapi
35. Alameda Brewhouse
36. Esparza's Tex Mex
37. Gustav's Bier Stube
38. Marco's Cafe
39. Brazen Bean
40. Widmer Gasthaus
41. Paparazzi Pastaficio
42. Campbell's Bar-B-Q
43. Vista Spring Cafe
44. Saigon Kitchen
45. Besaw's Cafe
46. FuJin
47. Thai Orchid
48. Swagat Indian
49. Three Square Grill
50. Caswell
51. Old Wives' Tales
52. Santa Fe Taqueria
53. Thanh Thao
54. Chez Jose
55. Le Bistro Montage
56. Abou Karim
57. Casablanca Moroccan
58. Tabor Hill Cafe
59. Al-Amir
60. Doris' Cafe

Additional Good Values
(A bit more expensive, but worth every penny)

- Alexis
- Beaches
- Berbati
- Bombay Cricket Club
- Bread & Ink Cafe
- Chevy's
- Chez Grill
- Fong Chong
- Fusion
- Gino's
- Jarra's Ethiopian
- John Street Cafe
- Ken's Home Plate
- Khun Pic's Bahn Thai
- Legin
- Noho's Hawaiian Cafe
- Obi Sushi Bar
- Red Electric Cafe
- Saburo's Sushi House
- Salvador Molly's
- Stickers
- Sweetwater's Jam House
- Takahashi
- Tara Thai House
- Typhoon!
- Yen Ha

Alphabetical Directory of Portland Restaurants

Portland

| F | D | S | C |

Abou Karim   21 | 14 | 18 | $16
221 SW Pine St. (bet. 2nd & 3rd Aves.), 503-223-5058
■ Surveyors swoon over the "high variety" meze plate at this Downtown Middle Eastern where there's always "a good basic lunch", but too much of a "cafeteria feel" at dinner; though a few call it "Mideast by NW standards", the general word is that this "little bit of heaven" is "solid."

Accuardi's Old Town Pizza ●S   22 | 18 | 15 | $13
226 NW Davis St. (bet. 2nd & 3rd Aves.), 503-222-9999
■ Parents who were taken to this Old Town pizzeria as kids now bring their own children to keep the tradition alive; it's nothing fancy and bucks the trend toward gourmet concoctions, but the pies are reliably "good" and the old-fashioned parlor evokes all the right memories of yesteryear.

Alameda Brewhouse S   15 | 20 | 16 | $14
4765 NE Fremont St. (47th Ave.), 503-460-9025
■ This "friendly" Beaumont New American earns high marks for its "industrial tech" decor in a redone warehouse; some say the "food plays second fiddle" to the "nice" ambiance, but if you "stick with the standards" ("huge onion rings", "killer grilled portobellos"), "you can't go wrong."

Al-Amir S   21 | 18 | 20 | $18
223 SW Stark St. (bet. 2nd & 3rd Aves.), 503-274-0010
■ "The baba ghanoush sets the standard" at this "real deal" Lebanese where "warm" and "attentive service" "makes you feel like family"; a "dark and mysterious" dining room, set in the "beautiful", historic Bishop's House, supplies the "exotic" ambiance at this "undiscovered gem" Downtown.

Alexander's S   19 | 18 | 20 | $26
Portland Hilton, 921 SW Sixth Ave. (bet. Salmon & Taylor Sts.), 503-226-1611
■ While the food's "good", it's the "fabulous view" of the surrounding city that draws folks to this Northwestern atop Downtown's Hilton; though some come simply for "drinks and appetizers", a "great staff" and a pianist also lure locals; N.B. a new chef's arrival is not yet reflected in the ratings.

Alexis S   22 | 18 | 22 | $19
215 W. Burnside St. (bet. 2nd & 3rd Aves.), 503-224-8577
■ For "good solid Greek" cooking, this "reasonable" Old Town taverna dishes out "amazing lemon soup" and "exciting saganaki"; granted, it's "not in a great location", but those who "love belly dancers" wink it's "worth the trip."

Portland

| | F | D | S | C |

Anne Hughes Kitchen Table ⊄   18 | 16 | 15 | $8
400 SE 12th Ave. (Oak St.), 503-230-6977

■ Eastsiders like this "cozy, neighborhood" American "soup kitchen" for its "solid, homestyle" cooking ("good soup", "yummy cornbread", "superb pies") in "cheerful, well-lit" surroundings; though nothing fancy, it's "warm, sincere and simple."

ASSAGGIO   23 | 22 | 21 | $24
7742 SE 13th Ave. (Lambert St.), 503-232-6151

◪ "Outstanding" Italian fare and a "great wine bar" bring crowds to this "hip and stylish" Sellwood spot where the "pasta sampler is a good bet" (*assàggio* translates as 'little taste'); foes fuss it's "noisy" and "overpriced", and even devotees concur that the "major drawback" is the "no-reservations" policy that results in "long waits."

ATWATER'S RESTAURANT & BAR S   24 | 26 | 25 | $40
US Bancorp Tower, 111 SW Fifth Ave., 30th fl. (W. Burnside St.), 503-275-3600

◪ "Every plate is a party" at this New American "dress-up treat" on the 30th floor of the Downtown US Bancorp Tower, offering "the best view in town"; though a few hedge that "altitude isn't everything" and say the "food doesn't live up to the setting", the majority finds the "monthly-changing menu" to be "terrific", and the "great jazz in the lounge" (Tuesday–Saturday) pleases imbibers.

AVALON S   21 | 26 | 21 | $33
4630 SW Macadam Ave. (Hamilton Ct.), 503-227-4630

◪ A "sumptuously appointed space" sets the "high-tech" tone at this Downtown riverside French/Asian where "otherworldly" cuisine excites "esoteric" palates; more pedestrian types say it's "trying too hard to be trendy" and becoming "too quirky" and "really pricey" in the process, but all allow the splendid water view makes you "feel like you're aboard an ocean liner."

Bamboos S   ∇ 21 | 13 | 21 | $14
103 NW 21st Ave. (Davis St.), 503-241-8122

◪ Few surveyors are aware of this "acceptable" Chinese in the NW District, but those who have visited tout its "tasty appetizers", including some hard-to-find "East Coast favorites"; though the decor eschews the standard "pink and red" color scheme, it still strikes some as "weird."

Bangkok Kitchen ⊄   20 | 9 | 14 | $14
2534 SE Belmont St. (26th Ave.), 503-236-7349

◪ Stalwarts remain steadfast to this Southeast Belmont Thai where the "very spicy" fare is among the "best in town"; too bad it's a "dive" with a "mediocre environment" and "slow service", yet first-timers are still dazzled by the "surprisingly good" cooking.

Bastas Trattoria [S] 19 | 17 | 17 | $20

410 NW 21st Ave. (Flanders St.), 503-274-1572

◪ "If you're looking for carboloading" at "very honest prices", try this Northwest trattoria housed in "former fast-food" digs; admirers adore its "tasty", "truly Italian" fare, even if the unconvinced mutter "tired", "average" and "overrated"; your call.

Beaches Restaurant & Bar [S] 18 | 21 | 18 | $19

1919 SE Columbia River Dr. (south of Hwy. 14), Vancouver, WA, 360-699-1592

■ The "fabulous view of the Columbia River" makes for a "fun dining environment" at this casual Vancouver American, particularly when weather permits eating alfresco; still, the "best happy-hour prices around" keep the bar hopping no matter what the climate with a "young crowd" of "LA wanna-bes."

Beaterville Cafe [S]≠ – | – | – | I

2201 N. Killingsworth St. (bet. Gay & Omaha Aves.), 503-735-4652

"Another hip cafe" comes to North Portland, this one a favorite among slackers who like the funky hubcap decor and "great [American] food", especially the "green eggs and ham"; "breakfast is tops", but locals also linger here over lunch.

Berbati 20 | 15 | 17 | $17

19 SW Second Ave. (bet. Ankeny & Burnside Sts.), 503-226-2122

◪ This family-run Downtown Greek has a dual personality: there's "imaginative" Hellenic fare (including "excellent vegetarian pastitsio and moussaka") in the front room and live performances in the rear boîte, Berbati's Pan; some say "food quality has gone down since more attention now goes toward the club", but bacchanalians "go there to dance, not to eat."

Berlin Inn Restaurant & Bakery [S] ▽ 21 | 16 | 19 | $17

3131 SE 12th Ave. (Powell Blvd.), 503-236-6761

■ "Delicious", "homey" fare can be expected at this Southeast Deutschlander, and überfans pipe up "don't pass up the [attached] bakery"; 'heart smart' and vegetarian entrees lure the healthy, while a varied selection of German beers and wines thrill the devil-may-care crowd.

Bernie's Southern Bistro – | – | – | M

2904 NE Alberta St. (29th Ave.), 503-282-9864

A newcomer to the Northeast Alberta Street neighborhood, an area of town that's taking off in restaurant popularity, this Southern bistro with a Cajun accent is the place to sup on blackened catfish, buttermilk fried chicken and fried green tomatoes; the casual dining room befits the comfort food menu.

Besaw's Cafe [S] 21 | 17 | 19 | $16

2301 NW Savier St. (23rd Ave.), 503-228-2619

■ Known for its "awesome" breakfasts, this NW District Contemporary American old-timer (since 1903) also turns out "excellent lunches" and "homey" bistro dinners, including some of "the best steak and garlic mashed potatoes" around; regulars recommend you "get there early" since "it's very tiny" and there's "always a line at peak hours."

Big Dan's West Coast Bento ⊘ ▽ 20 | 7 | 13 | $9

2346 NW Westover Rd. (23rd Pl.), 503-227-1779

◪ A man behind the counter and a line outside the door comprise this bento box in Northwest that's popular at lunch because of the "good prices" and quick, if limited, service; if you don't expect anything more than tasty meat on a stick, rice and a soda pop chaser, you won't be disappointed.

Bijou Cafe [S]⊘ 22 | 17 | 20 | $13

132 SW Third Ave. (Pine St.), 503-222-3187

■ "Wholesome, full-bodied breakfasts" are the signature of this "popular" Downtown Eclectic that's famed for its "dynamite snapper hash", "homemade sausages" and "veteran waiters"; but "don't go if you can't wait", as there can be "long lines", particularly on weekends; N.B. dinner is now being served.

Bima ◐ 19 | 22 | 17 | $23

1338 NW Hoyt St. (bet. 13th & 14th Aves.), 503-241-3465

◪ "Too cool for words", this "très chic" Regional American is set in a "dark, stark and very metropolitan" "converted warehouse" in the Pearl District that "feels like SoHo" to its "hip singles" crowd; though probably more renowned as a "cruise bar" than a place to eat, some speak up for the "sassy flavors" on its Gulf Coast menu; P.S. don't forget to "dress in black."

Bistro 921 [S] 16 | 16 | 17 | $18

Portland Hilton, 921 SW Sixth Ave. (Taylor St.), 503-220-2685

◪ Better known to those in transit than locals, this street-level Regional Northwestern in the Downtown Hilton puts forth straightforward "business-style food for business travelers"; though some yawn it's "pedestrian", those on the go rate it "excellent" for "fast service."

Black Rabbit [S] 20 | 22 | 20 | $23

McMenamins Edgefield, 2126 SW Halsey St. (bet. 238th & 256th Sts.), Troutdale, 503-492-3086

■ A "local microbrewery chain meets fine dining" at this former poor farm in Troutdale that's been transformed into a "campus" comprised of a restaurant, theater, B&B, brewery, winery and distillery; this "great date spot" is a "fun place to explore", and the "good pub food" with a Northwest bent earns kudos as well.

Bombay Cricket Club [S] 23 | 17 | 21 | $19

1925 SE Hawthorne Blvd. (bet. 19th & 20th Aves.), 503-231-0740

◪ There's a lot to "tempt the palate" at this Hawthorne Indian sleeper, most notably the mango margaritas and prawns masala; owners Karim and Sherri Ahmad infuse warmth into more than the vindaloo with their kind service, making this "small place" a "smashing success", but regulars rely on staff recommendations to avoid a "hit-or-miss" meal.

Brasserie Montmartre ◐ [S] 19 | 22 | 18 | $21

626 SW Park Ave. (bet. Alder & Morrison Sts.), 503-224-5552

◪ "Great for late-night dining", this "smoky" Downtown French bistro offers "a magician doing card tricks", "live jazz" and "inconsistent", "ok food" – though a "new chef" has begun making "cautious changes to the menu" (and "so far, so good"); though the bored bray it's "better to sit at the bar for a drink", Europhiles describe this "interesting" "touch of Paris" as amusing and "fun."

Brazen Bean ◐ 17 | 24 | 16 | $16

2075 NW Glisan St. (NW 21st Ave.), 503-294-0636

■ Velvet couches and "lots of candles" set a seductive mood at this clandestine NW Eclectic, the "ultimate in romantic dessert places"; "it's a kick if you like martinis, chocolates and cigars" say the "young, hip" types who populate this "nice hideaway."

Bread & Ink Cafe [S] 20 | 18 | 18 | $19

3610 SE Hawthorne Blvd. (36th Ave.), 503-239-4756

■ Sunday's "Yiddish Brunch is the best" at this "always reliable" Hawthorne Eclectic where the kitchen, though "innovative", is famed for its "great burgers"; a spacious dining room with floor-to-ceiling windows makes for an "upscale" yet "cozy" "place to hang", and though service is generally "friendly", sometimes it can be "indifferent."

BridgePort Ale House [S] 17 | 19 | 17 | $14

(fka Hawthorne St. Ale House)

3632 SE Hawthorne Blvd. (bet. 36th & 37th Aves.), 503-233-6540

◪ Hawthorne's "classy" New American pub inspires debate about its ambiance ("comfortable" vs. "cold") as well as its cooking ("superb" vs. "so-so"), but its "nice big beers" and "creative ales" provoke the most toasts.

BridgePort Brewpub [S] 16 | 16 | 14 | $11

1313 NW Marshall St. (bet. 13th & 14th Sts.), 503-241-7179

■ "Beer and pizza reign" at this "cavernous" pub, Oregon's oldest craft brewery, that's "housed in a warehouse" in the Pearl District; the "loud, young crowd" at this "local hangout" "keeps going back" for its "family" feeling.

Portland | F | D | S | C |

BUGATTI'S RISTORANTE S | 26 | 20 | 23 | $26 |
18740 Willamette Dr. (Fairview Way), West Linn, 503-636-9555
■ Savor "carefully made Italian dishes", "excellent fresh pasta" and "heavenly desserts" at this West Linn trattoria where the decor is plain but pleasing, and partisans sing the praises of the "short but diverse menu."

Bush Garden S | 18 | 18 | 18 | $22 |
900 SW Morrison St. (9th Ave.), 503-226-7181
8290 SW Nyberg St. (Tualatin-Sherwood Rd.), Tualatin, 503-691-9744
■ "Classic Japanese cuisine" draws the faithful to this Asian duo for some of the "best sushi in Portland" or a visit to their "charming tatami rooms"; naysayers neigh they're "all business, no class" and snort that the "high prices don't match the fast-food atmosphere."

Buster's Texas-Style Barbecue S | – | – | – | I |
1355 NE Burnside St. (Division St.), Gresham, 503-667-4811
17883 SE McLoughlin Blvd. (bet. Boardman & Jennings Aves.), Milwaukee, 503-652-1076
11419 SW Pacific Hwy. (65th Ave.), Tigard, 503-452-8384
1118 NE 78th St. (13th Ave.), Vancouver, WA, 360-546-2439
"Locals love" the "great tasting" wood-pit 'cue – especially the eponymous Texas-style stuff – at this local minichain; "large portions" provide diners a sweet-and-spicy bang for the buck.

Cadillac Cafe S | – | – | – | I |
914 NE Broadway (9th Ave.), 503-287-4750
"Fun, funky", pink stucco Northeaster diner where "delicious breakfasts" are the draw; since there's "always a line out front" on weekends, insiders advise: "bring the Sunday paper"; N.B. breakfast and lunch only.

CAFE AZUL | 25 | 23 | 23 | $30 |
112 NW Ninth Ave. (bet. Couch & Davis Sts.), 503-525-4422
◪ There's "no compromising" at this "sophisticated" Pearl District Mexican where the kitchen turns out "creative cuisine and sauces" ("the best mole on earth") and "lots of organics"; critics' main carp is that it's "extraordinarily overpriced" "for what you get", but otherwise many call it close to "perfect."

CAFE DES AMIS | 26 | 24 | 27 | $35 |
1987 NW Kearney St. (20th Ave.), 503-295-6487
■ "From pâté to dessert", everything's "fabulous, darling" at this "classy" NW District French bistro that's particularly distinguished for its extraordinary service (voted No. 2 in Portland); loyalists love the intimate setting at this "great romantic spot" and are amazed by its "consistency" – "this good for this long is astonishing!"

Portland   F | D | S | C

CAFFE MINGO ⓢ   25 | 20 | 22 | $24
807 NW 21st Ave. (bet. Kearney & Johnson Sts.), 503-226-4646
■ "Delicious, simple fare" is the forte of this "excellent" NW District Italian trattoria that also offers a "relaxed atmosphere", "knowledgeable waiters" and "reasonable prices"; it's no surprise that this "small, intimate space" can get "too crowded" and it's "irritating" there are "no rezzies" for parties less than six, but even though fans "wish it weren't so tough to get a table", they "keep coming back."

Campbell's Bar-B-Q   23 | 11 | 18 | $14
8701 SE Powell Blvd. (bet. 87th & 88th Aves.), 503-777-9795
■ "Good, messy, tasty" BBQ in "huge portions" comes to you 'Texas-style' at this Southeast 'cue parlor on the outskirts of town; "if you're meek and mild", be warned that the "hot sauce is actually hot", so "don't choose medium" ("it's got fire"); P.S. "leave room for the cobbler" and the "decadent" sweet potato pie.

CAPRIAL'S BISTRO & WINE   26 | 19 | 22 | $27
7015 SE Milwaukie Ave. (Bybee Blvd.), 503-236-6457
■ "Local celebrity" Caprial Pence – author and cooking show host – might "greet you at the door" of her Pacific Northwest bistro in Westmoreland; "inspired meals" that are a "feast for the eyes" thrill enthusiasts, while "low wine prices" win the hearts of penny-pinching oenophiles; N.B. a recent expansion has doubled the dining area and added an open kitchen.

Casablanca Moroccan ⓢ   19 | 22 | 18 | $18
2221 SW Hawthorne Blvd. (22nd Ave.), 503-233-4400
◪ The "truly Moroccan atmosphere" – a baffled fabric ceiling, brass tables and cushioned banquettes – "transports you to another era" at this unassuming North African in Hawthorne; though the "fine food" (particularly the signature seafood couscous) pleases most, it clearly plays second fiddle to the "fabulous decor."

Cassidy's ◐ⓢ   18 | 16 | 21 | $19
1331 SW Washington St. (bet. 13th & 14th Aves.), 503-223-0054
■ Although best known for its "great bar" and "late-night" allure, this Downtown New American also draws applause for its Caesar salad and one of the "best veggie burgers" around; while party poopers call the food "iffy", slick types appreciate its "close-to-the-freeway" locale that makes "quick getaways" easy.

Caswell ◐ⓢ   18 | 19 | 17 | $16
533 SE Grand Ave. (Washington St.), 503-232-6512
■ Eastsiders "treasure" this "best value" Eclectic that shows "what happens when Gen Xers open a restaurant"; the young and the pierced say the "gumbo is to die for" and appreciate the kitchen's willingness to "whip up something fun" that's not on the menu.

Celadon [S]

	F	D	S	C
▽	22	20	21	$21

1203 NW 23rd Ave. (Northrup St.), 503-464-9222

■ This "undiscovered treat" in a Northwest neighborhood offers "authentic" Japanese fare with Korean influences; an "amazing wine list" and complete sushi bar are also available at this "out-of-the-way" spot; dinner only.

Chevy's [S]

F	D	S	C
16	15	16	$15

8400 SE Nimbus Ave. (Hall Blvd.), Beaverton, 503-626-7667
12520 SE 93rd Ave. (Sunnyside Rd.), Clackamas, 503-654-1333
1951 NW 185th Ave. (Cornell Rd.), Hillsboro, 503-690-4524
14991 SW Bangy Rd. (Meadows Rd.), Lake Oswego, 503-620-7700
4315 SE Thurston Way (500 Hwy.), Vancouver, WA, 360-256-6922

◪ "As far as generic Mexican food goes", this "above-average chain" is "dependable" and "inexpensive" according to amigos, even if nonbelievers call it "typical", "dumbed-down" fare that's "mediocre but filling"; 'El Machino', the tortilla-making machine, saves the day by providing the "cheapest children's entertainment" around.

Chez Grill [S]

F	D	S	C
17	20	17	$18

2229 SE Hawthorne Blvd. (bet. 22nd & 23rd Aves.), 503-239-4002

■ It always feels like a party at this colorful Hawthorne Southwestern, the "upscale" offspring from the Chez Jose folks, where "fabulous tamales" and "warm gorditas" are washed down with fresh-squeezed lime margaritas; though some say the "dinners are disappointing" vis-à-vis the bar menu, at least the "cool-looking food goes with the decor."

Chez Jose East [S]

F	D	S	C
18	15	17	$15

2200 NE Broadway (22nd Ave.), 503-280-9888

Chez Jose West [S]

8502 SW Terwilliger Blvd. (Taylors Ferry Rd.), 503-244-0007

■ An "excellent squash enchilada" is one of the many "good vegetarian dishes" available at this Mexican duo where the "wonderful" staff delights "high maintenance" types; tykes like them for being "fun and noisy", and at the East Side outpost youngsters under the age of six eat "free from 5–7 PM."

Cindy's Helvetia Cafe [S]⊘

F	D	S	C
–	–	–	I

(fka Shakers)

1212 NW Glisan St. (12th St.), 503-221-0011

Formerly Shakers, this campy Pearl District diner packs 'em in on weekends for griddle cakes and home fries; gone are the vintage salt and pepper shakers, but you can still swivel your stool at the counter while waiting for tasty burgers, fries and shakes.

Portland | F | D | S | C |

COMPASS CAFE S | 25 | 20 | 24 | $24 |
4741 SE Hawthorne Blvd. (48th Ave.), 503-231-4840
■ Every month the compass points to a new direction and cuisine at this "very small" Hawthorne Pacific Northwest 'world bistro'; insiders insist this "great surprise" is "consistently good and imaginative" and hint that the monthly "wine dinners" shouldn't be missed; P.S. weather permitting, there's "marvelous seating" in the "best backyard garden in town."

COUCH STREET SEAFOOD & FINE STEAKS | 24 | 23 | 25 | $39 |
105 NW Third Ave. (bet. Couch & Davis Sts.), 503-223-6173
■ "Always perfect, beautifully presented" seafood is the forte of this "classy" Old Town "gourmet" fish house, which garners particularly high marks for its "professional", tuxedo-clad staff that serves from silver trays; carpers complain it's "stuffy" and "overpriced", catering to an "expense-account crowd", yet overall, most call it "excellent"; dinner only.

COUVRON | 27 | 23 | 25 | $53 |
1126 SW 18th Ave. (Madison St.), 503-225-1844
■ "World-class ambitions" inform everything about this "upscale" West Side Contemporary French that offers "unusual presentations" of "outstanding" cuisine along with "very attentive" service that's "perfect for a special occasion"; though the "too-small space" and "spendy" tabs leave some gasping for air, most take a deep breath and declare "it's worth saving up for."

Cozze S | 20 | 15 | 20 | $23 |
1205 SE Morrison St. (12th Ave.), 503-232-3275
■ "Famous for its [occasional] *Big Night* dinner", which "starts with mussels and ends with a conga line", this Italian-Asian in Southeast is known for its "imaginative renditions of standard dishes"; though the "banal atmosphere" draws some jeers, the "well-crafted" cuisine keeps adherents sticking by it.

Cup & Saucer Cafe S | – | – | – | I |
3566 SE Hawthorne Blvd. (bet. 35th & 36th Aves.), 503-236-6001
"Breakfasts [that are] worth waiting for" are served until the 9 PM closing at this sunny Hawthorne American cafe; in addition to "simple, healthy, cheap" lunch and dinner fare like soups, salads and sandwiches, there are extensive vegetarian options.

Dan & Louis' Oyster Bar S | – | – | – | I |
208 SW Ankeny St. (bet. 2nd & 3rd Aves.), 503-227-5906
Plenty of people "pop in and slurp up a half dozen or so oysters" at this old-time, Old Town seafood "institution" (since 1907); reasonable prices and kitschy nautical knickknacks make it a popular place for families.

Portland | F | D | S | C |

Delta Cafe 🆂⌀ | 21 | 14 | 16 | $11 |
4607 SE Woodstock Blvd. (46th Ave.), 503-771-3101
■ Look for "Soul Food done right" at this "funky" Woodstock Cajun-Southerner where the beads-and-Formica ambiance strikes some as "circa 1974"; Reedies think everything here is "yummy" and "wish they would expand their menu."

Dog House, The 🆂⌀ | – | – | – | I |
2845 E. Burnside St. (bet. 28th & 29th Aves.), 503-239-3647
Not much larger than a real canine abode, this Northeaster hut plunked in the middle of a parking lot is "the place for a dog"; in addition to the classic American version, this "friendly, inexpensive" spot also serves up kielbasa and bratwurst; since an open deck provides the only seating, you may want to rest your dogs and use the drive-through.

Doris' Cafe 🆂 | 20 | 14 | 16 | $15 |
325 NE Russell St. (MLK Jr. Blvd.), 503-287-9249
◼ Soul Food stalwarts think they've died and gone to "cholesterol heaven" at this "wonderful" Southern cafe in Northeast; though a few skinny-minnies gripe about "all that fat" and grouse that the grub's "extremely overrated", finger lickin' types "go there often" for the "lovely fried chicken."

Dot's Cafe ◐🆂⌀ | – | – | – | I |
2521 SE Clinton St. (bet. 25th & 26th Aves.), 503-235-0203
Southeast's "basic hipster lounge" has "cool", kitschy decor (check out the "sock monkeys") and cheap, plentiful Eclectic eats – beer, burgers, burritos and "spicy fries to die for."

El Burrito Loco 🆂⌀ | 20 | 8 | 15 | $7 |
1942 N. Portland Blvd. (Denver Ave.), 503-735-9505
3126 NE 82nd Ave. (Siskiyou St.), 503-252-1343
18238 SE Division St. (182nd St.), Gresham, 503-669-1253
■ "Three words: 'chile rellenos burritos'" sum up the appeal of these "hole-in-the-wall" Mexicans known for "no atmosphere whatsoever", just "cheap", "mouthwatering" eats; regulars add their own two words of advice: "take out."

Escape From N.Y. Pizza 🆂⌀ | 21 | 12 | 15 | $8 |
622 NW 23rd Ave. (bet. Hoyt & Irving Sts.), 503-227-5423
◼ "Who cares if service is laid-back and the place looks like it could stand a real cleaning?" ask partisans of this Northwest pizzeria who "wouldn't want it any other way"; though a few pie purists proclaim "there's better to be had", many cite it as the source for the "best slice in town."

ESPARZA'S TEX MEX CAFE | 21 | 22 | 18 | $17 |
2725 SE Ankeny St. (28th Ave.), 503-234-7909
■ "Lots of Roy Rogers memorabilia", "the best jukebox in town" and a "hip", "fiesta atmosphere" make this Southeast Tex-Mex nothing less than "a hoot", though fans point out there's also "serious good food" that's a "treat for the adventurous"; the only drawback is "no reservations", which results in "mob scenes", especially on weekends.

Portland | F | D | S | C |

ESPLANADE 🆂 | 21 | 24 | 23 | $33 |
River Place Hotel, 1510 SW Harbor Way (bet. Clay & Montgomery Sts.), 503-295-6166
■ The "dreamy water view" of the Willamette marina and a "creative chef" contribute to the "special meal" ambiance of this Downtown Regional Northwestern that's "the epitome of expensive hotel restaurants"; though often overlooked by locals, it's treasured by out-of-towners, who dig the jazz in the bar Tuesday–Saturday.

Fat City Cafe 🆂 | 18 | 13 | 18 | $11 |
7820 SW Capitol Hwy. (35th Ave.), 503-245-5457
■ A blast from the past when burgers and shakes stood for a more innocent America, this Multnomah diner is a "place to return to again and again", whether for a "great breakfast" or a "quick" lunch (they're not open for dinner); regulars recommend you "try the cinnamon rolls."

Fernando's Hideaway 🆂 | 20 | 20 | 20 | $23 |
824 SW First Ave. (bet. Taylor & Yamhill Sts.), 503-248-4709
■ Though many have "only been there for dancing and drinks", this bilevel Iberian also offers "yummy tapas" and exclusively Spanish vintages in its downstairs dining room; though some hedge it's "smoky" and "noisy", most call it just plain "fun" and are happy it has just expanded with a wine bar next door.

FIDDLEHEADS 🆂 | 23 | 22 | 21 | $29 |
6716 SE Milwaukie Ave. (Bybee Blvd.), 503-233-1547
◪ Anticipate "the most interesting and daring menu in Portland" at this Westmoreland Eclectic that incorporates dishes from Alaska to South America and all points in between; though stay-at-homes sniff it "can be erratic", "precious" and "too expensive to do very often", the majority finds the fare "original and delicious" and says it "deserves all the fuss."

Fong Chong 🆂 | 21 | 11 | 14 | $14 |
301 NW Fourth Ave. (Everett St.), 503-220-0235
■ Zero in on this Chinatown Cantonese for "dependable", "bargain" dim sum that just might be "the best between San Francisco and British Columbia"; though its "somewhat depressed surroundings" and "lousy service" turn off a few, many more laud the "great selection" at this "always wonderful" spot.

Foothill Broiler ⇎ | 17 | 10 | 12 | $10 |
Uptown Shopping Ctr., 33 NW 23rd Pl. (W. Burnside St.), 503-223-0287
■ Some of the "cheapest burgers in town" draw the penny-wise to this cafeteria-style American that's a "Northwest landmark"; true, it's not much on looks, but when it comes to "good fast food", this "hamburger joint" cuts the mustard.

Fratelli [S] – | – | – | M
1230 NW Hoyt St. (bet. 12th & 13th Aves.), 503-241-8800
Italian newcomer to the Pearl District that combines boisterous Uptown ambiance with down-home warmth – exposed beams, rustic farm tables and candelabra; while some of the family-style plates are quite successful, others are just so-so – hopefully, time will bring greater consistency to the food, as well as the service.

FuJin 18 | 9 | 18 | $13
3549 SE Hawthorne Blvd. (bet. 35th & 36th Aves.), 503-231-3753
■ "Don't go for the decor" at this "no-nonsense" Hawthorne Chinese – go for the "yummy crispy eggplant" or some of the other "great dishes" on the "huge menu"; and if a dish isn't listed, "they'll cook to order any request."

Fuller's Coffee Shop 🚫 ▽ 18 | 16 | 19 | $9
136 NW Ninth Ave. (Davis St.), 503-222-5608
■ If "breakfast all day" suits your lifestyle, this longtime American diner with a "'50s feel" (down to the "authentic fraying at the edges") is "the place to go"; expect everyone from hardware store clerks to starving artists at this Pearl District icon, but don't expect dinner, as they close at 4 PM.

Fusion [S] – | – | – | I
4100 SE Division St. (41st Ave.), 503-233-6950
What's fused at this Southeast cafe makes for "a new kind of experience" – i.e. vintage collectibles meet modern eats; choose from an Eclectic menu offering "novel but delicious" salads, sandwiches and light meals with Asian and Mediterranean accents, then cast an eye on the "comfy and inviting" surroundings where most everything, excluding the tables and chairs, is for sale.

Garbonzos [S] 17 | 11 | 14 | $10
922 NW 21st Ave. (Lovejoy St.), 503-227-4196 ◐
3433 SE Hawthorne Blvd. (34th Ave.), 503-239-6087 ◐
6341 SW Capitol Hwy. (Sunset Blvd.), 503-293-7335
■ For a "solid lunch" or a midnight falafel, these Middle Eastern cafes fill the need with "quick", "cheap" and "healthy" chow; their Gen X following tolerates the nothing-special decor and "lousy service" because of their high ranking "on the too-small list of late-night" options.

GENOA 29 | 24 | 28 | $55
2832 SE Belmont St. (29th Ave.), 503-238-1464
■ Rated No. 1 for Food and Service, this Italian "treasure" in Southeast has also garnered the title of Portland's Most Popular restaurant, and stalwarts say "everything is impeccable", from the "inspired", seven-course prix fixe menu to the "intimate atmosphere" and "unsurpassed" staff; though a minority moans it's "too dark" and "very spendy", the majority agrees that "quality has never faltered" at this "still special experience."

Portland

F | D | S | C

Gino's Restaurant & Bar S
▽ 21 | 16 | 19 | $18
8051 SE 13th Ave. (Spokane St.), 503-233-4613
■ Though this "solid" Sellwood Italian might not garner as much press as its famed neighbor Assaggio, boosters aver that its "very friendly" service and "neighborhood" charm more than compensate for the lower profile; "good, plain food at reasonable prices" is the cornerstone of its appeal.

Good Day Restaurant S
– | – | – | I
312 NW Couch St. (bet. 3rd & 4th Aves.), 503-223-1393
Only a few voters are hip to this Chinatown Cantonese, but those in the know laud its "many outstanding dishes" ("great crispy-skin chicken") and "fast service"; good value here means few entrees exceed $8.

Good Dog/Bad Dog S
21 | 13 | 16 | $8
708 SW Alder St. (Broadway), 503-222-3410
■ "Kiss your diet goodbye" at this "funky" Downtown "sausage lovers' dream" where the theme is "NY-style" "dogs 'n' suds"; though it could "use more seating", well-wishers say it's just right for a "quick, unusual lunch" and also nominate it for "best-named" restaurant in town.

Grand Central Bakery & Cafe S
23 | 16 | 16 | $10
1444 NE Weidler St. (15th Ave.), 503-288-1614
■ "Yummy smells" entice initiates into this Broadway bakery/cafe that offers "exotic breads", "jammers and cinnamon rolls to die for"; a "great place" for "reading the paper on Saturday morning" or for a take-out "sack lunch", its only shortcoming seems to be "slow service."

Gustav's Bier Stube S
20 | 20 | 19 | $16
5035 NE Sandy Blvd. (bet. 50th & 51st Aves.), 503-288-5503
12605 SE 97th Ave. (west of 132rd Ave.), Clackamas, 503-653-1391
■ There's "nothing fancy" going on at these German pubs, just "first-class, hearty fare" and an "outstanding selection of beer"; fans are fond of the "authentic" Bavarian decor.

Hall Street Grill S
21 | 20 | 19 | $23
3775 SW Hall Blvd. (Center St.), Beaverton, 503-641-6161
☒ The "menu changes with the seasons" at this Beaverton Regional Northwestern where some of the "best prime rib" around joins forces with "great scotch and cigars"; though cons find it "disappointing" and "overpriced", others tout the "very professional service" and "good business lunches."

HANDS ON CAFÉ S⌀
24 | 18 | 18 | $13
Oregon College of Art & Craft, 8215 SW Barnes Rd. (Leahy Rd.), 503-297-1480
■ A "delicious oasis" smack-dab in the middle of the Oregon College of Art & Craft, this "flavorful" Eclectic "gathering spot" draws droves almost as large as the student body; though the "unique food combinations" might not be for everyone ("don't take picky eaters"), most find the fare "as artful as the restaurant's setting."

Portland   F | D | S | C

Harborside Restaurant S   21 | 23 | 20 | $25
309 SW Montgomery St. (Harbor Blvd.), 503-220-1865
◪ "Fish and seafood done to perfection" are no match for the "great view of the Willamette" that brings folks to this Northwestern on Riverside Marina; while wet blankets deride the "noisy environment" and "iffy service", the besotted rhapsodize about the "wonderful outside dining."

HEATHMAN, THE S   27 | 24 | 26 | $36
Heathman Hotel, 1001 SW Broadway (Salmon St.), 503-241-4100
■ Chef Philippe Boulot unveils "superb" French-NW cuisine at this "sublime" Downtown hotel dining room that's "class all the way"; a "top-notch wine list", "casual but sharp" service and a "sophisticated" setting gladden its "gourmet guests", and despite a few who mumble "overrated", the majority considers this a "truly adult experience"; N.B. a gradual remodeling should be completed in early 2000.

HIGGINS RESTAURANT & BAR S   25 | 23 | 24 | $34
1239 SW Broadway (Jefferson St.), 503-222-9070
■ "Greg Higgins is the man", for his Eclectic with a pronounced French accent elates acolytes with "fresh, smart" dishes that make for a "premier food experience"; though faultfinders fuss there's "sometimes too much happening on one plate", most call it "absolute perfection", especially "Portland's art elite", who make the bar their own after the theater lets out.

Horn of Africa   ▽ 21 | 5 | 19 | $10
3939 NE MLK Jr. Blvd. (bet. Failing & Shaver Sts.), 503-331-9844
■ "Bring an appetite" to this "family-run", "very friendly" African, an "authentic adventure" that's an "ethnic treat", though admittedly not much to look at; low votes most likely reflect its newcomer status (open just over a year) and its "hard [Northeast] neighborhood" location.

Hot Lips Pizza S   19 | 11 | 14 | $8
1909 SW Sixth Ave. (bet. College & Hall Sts.), 503-224-0311
Raleigh Hills Fred Meyer Shopping Ctr., 4825 SW 76th Ave. (Hillsdale Hwy.), Beaverton, 503-297-8424
■ Look for "great" pies, made from scratch, along with organic salads and fresh juices at this pizzeria duo; the Sixth Avenue branch caters to the PSU crowd, who drop by for an "after-class" slice or opt for the "good delivery service."

Huber's Cafe ●   19 | 21 | 19 | $19
411 SW Third Ave. (bet. Stark & Washington Sts.), 503-228-5686
■ Portland's oldest restaurant (in various locations since 1879), this Downtown Traditional American is renowned for its "great Spanish coffee", as well as its "flawless turkey dishes" that hit the spot when you're "hankering for a Thanksgiving meal"; the "deep, dark decor" – a melding of mahogany, brass and terrazzo – supplies the "historical" charm at this "old-time" "institution."

Hudson's Bar & Grill [S] ▽ 20 22 18 $26

7805 NE Greenwood Dr. (bet. 41st St. & Parkway Dr.), Vancouver, WA, 360-816-6100

■ Vancouverites have taken to this relatively new Regional Northwestern, a "great addition to town" thanks to its "beautiful building" and "fabulous interior"; a pianist keeps things rhythmic Tuesday–Friday, and on Sundays a jazz duo takes over.

Hunan [S] 19 12 14 $15

Morgan's Alley, 515 SW Broadway (Park Ave.), 503-224-8063

■ "Dynamite kung pao chicken" and some of the "best sesame beef in town" are up for grabs at this Chinese in Morgan's Alley that's a popular lunch choice for Downtowners; "slow service" irks some, but all is forgiven when the "good deal weekly specials" arrive.

Hungry Dog Burrito [S] 17 11 16 $8

2310 NW Everett St. (23rd Ave.), 503-226-1978

■ "A college student's ideal", this NW District Mexican excites scholars with "huge", "tasty" burritos that are "authentic" and "well seasoned"; though spoilsports bark the fare's "generic" and deride the "industrial atmosphere", most applaud it for being "cheap and fast."

IL FORNAIO [S] 20 22 19 $25

115 NW 22nd Ave. (Burnside St.), 503-248-9400

◪ The "regional menus are a blast" at this California-based Italian chain link in Northwest, where "terrific bread" and "tasty sauces" add to the dining pleasure; though "service can be bad" ("like pulling teeth to get our dinner") and some sum up the experience as "fake everything", others find it "surprisingly good" and "nice for large groups."

IL PIATTO [S] 24 23 21 $24

2348 SE Ankeny St. (24th Ave.), 503-236-4997

◪ "Inventive but not trendy" fare fills out the menu at this "charming little neighborhood" trattoria in the residential Southeast; while doubters declare the chef can be "too ambitious" and advise "stick with the specials", loyalists salute the "fine wine list" at this "haven for homemade gnocchi" and suggest they "should play opera" to complete the mood.

India House [S] 21 14 17 $17

1038 SW Morrison St. (11th Ave.), 503-274-1017

◪ For "the most delicious Indian food outside of India", check out this Downtown "favorite" that's "especially good on a cold, wet night"; though nitpickers dismiss the "regular" fare and "boring decor", midday diners speak highly of the daily lunch buffet that can be had at a very "reasonable" price.

Indigine [S] 22 | 15 | 19 | $26

3725 SE Division St. (37th Ave.), 503-238-1470

■ "Arrive famished" to appreciate chef Millie Howe's "wild menu", an "indescribable but delicious" International Mix with an accent on Indian dishes; though a few quibble about "odd" service, most feel everything's "outstanding" at this intimate Southeast District spot that's been wowing fans since 1973; N.B. don't miss the Saturday night prix fixe feast.

JAKE'S FAMOUS CRAWFISH [S] 23 | 21 | 22 | $29

401 SW 12th Ave. (Stark St.), 503-226-1419

◪ Some dub this "timeless" Downtown seafooder "old faithful" as it's been serving "consistently excellent" fin fare since 1892, and the hooked "love the crawfish dishes" and "super gumbo"; dissenters hedge "when it's good, it's great, but it's good only half the time" and add that the "tired" scene could use "a breath of fresh air."

JAKE'S GRILL [S] 23 | 21 | 21 | $26

Governor Hotel, 611 SW 10th Ave. (Alder St.), 503-220-1850

◪ Relax with a "steak, a stogie, and a scotch" at this Downtown surf 'n' turfer that's favored by both singles and suits for its "quaint" "men's club atmosphere"; though skeptics shrug it's "just so-so" and "too expensive", fans adore the "beautiful old bar" and say you "can't beat it" at "happy hour" when "good values" abound.

Jarra's Ethiopian Restaurant 18 | 10 | 17 | $18

1435 SE Hawthorne Blvd. (14th Ave.), 503-230-8990

◪ "Tingle your taste buds" at this family-run Hawthorne Ethiopian where the service is as "warm" as the spicy cuisine; neat freaks take exception to the "messy", eat-with-your-fingers approach to dining, but the faithful say it's "underrated", "inexpensive" and just "what you'd expect."

Jo Bar & Rotisserie [S] 21 | 22 | 19 | $24

715 NW 23rd Ave. (bet. Irving & Johnson Sts.), 503-222-0048

■ "Hip" and "happening", this Regional Northwestern is a "fun" "neighborhood drop-in" spot that's perfect for "people-watching" thanks to "windows facing 23rd Avenue" ('trendy-third' in local parlance); while a few are "disappointed" with the food, there are no complaints about the "luscious desserts" brought in from adjacent parent Papa Haydn.

Joel Palmer House ▽ 26 | 25 | 25 | $37

600 Ferry St. (6th St.), Dayton, 503-864-2995

■ "Wonderful mushroom dishes" inform the menu at this self-billed 'Northwest Freestyle' in Dayton; it's a "true destination restaurant" for those willing to undertake the long drive from Portland – its "only drawback" – and intrepid types say if "you have the dough", it's worth it to be "waited on hand and foot."

Portland F | D | S | C

John Street Cafe S — | — | — | I
8338 N. Lombard St. (John St.), 503-247-1066
Run by the former owner of Tabor Hill Cafe on Hawthorne, this "small" St. Johns American is, for many, "the old cafe with a new location and new name"; but here, breakfast and lunch only translate as "awesome omelets", terrific seasonal pancakes and tasty sandwiches.

Ken's Home Plate ▽ 22 | 15 | 24 | $14
1852 SE Hawthorne Blvd. (19th Ave.), 503-236-9520
◪ Local chef Ken Gordon prepares a wide range of "excellent" 'foods-to-go' at this Hawthorne Eclectic takeout, which consists of a service counter, deli cases and eight tables; skeptics call it "pricey" and "not conducive for dining in", but few refute the quality.

Kento Bento ⌽ 19 | 10 | 15 | $9
212 NE 164th Ave. (1st St.), Vancouver, WA, 360-260-8826
■ "Do as the locals do and eat bento" at this Vancouver Japanese, which a few rate as "excellent"; others advise "plan to take out" since "there's not much to look at" here in the way of decor.

Khun Pic's Bahn Thai S⌽ — | — | — | M
3429 SE Belmont St. (bet. 34th & 35th Aves.), 503-235-1610
"Exquisite", "marvelous flavors" set the tone at this "romantic" Thai, located in a colorfully restored Victorian house on Belmont; service at this newcomer, however, lacks speed and polish.

Koji Osakaya S 22 | 15 | 16 | $21
7007 SW Macadam Ave. (Texas St.), 503-293-1066
606 SW Broadway (bet. Alder & Morrison Sts.), 503-294-1169
11995 SW Beaverton-Hillsdale Hwy. (Lombard Ave.), Hillsdale, 503-646-5697
1502 NE Weidler St. (15th Ave.), 503-280-0992
■ "Big screen TVs" featuring "sumo wrestling" provide the chuckles at this "dependable" Japanese quartet where "reliably excellent sushi" and other "authentic" treats draw fans; "painfully slow service" doesn't keep them from "filling up at lunch", so "get there early" or show up "after 1 PM"; N.B. the Weidler location is new and unrated.

Kornblatt's Delicatessen S 19 | 13 | 15 | $12
628 NW 23rd Ave. (bet. Hoyt & Irving Sts.), 503-242-0055
◪ This Jewish deli in the Northwest evokes some very contradictory responses: those opposed sigh "it ain't NY" because of the "not great food" and "rude service", while equally vocal enthusiasts advise "don't miss" the "good ethnic" eats and "sassy servers" "with humor" who will "match NY expectations"; your call.

La Buca [S] — 20 | 14 | 19 | $13

2309 NW Kearney St. (23rd Ave.), 503-279-8040

■ This "small, modest" Northwest Italian is "good to go" to when it comes to "cheap eats"; "inventive pasta dishes" that "taste like someone's grandmother had you over for dinner" also elate enthusiasts who deem it "outstanding for what it is."

La Catalana [S] — 23 | 19 | 20 | $25

2821 SE Stark St. (28th Ave.), 503-232-0948

◪ "Order lots of tapas" and a pitcher of "great sangria" at this "romantic" Catalan in Southeast that's "recently expanded" and "still fabulous"; though a few killjoys dis the "bad service" and "uneven" cooking, there's consensus that it's "fun for a group" or "for a splurge"; dinner only.

La Cruda [S] — – | – | – | I

2500 SE Clinton St. (25th Ave.), 503-233-0745

"Big portions" and "cheap" prices make this Clinton Street Mexican popular with locals who also like the "laid-back", "funky" cantina atmosphere; some question its authenticity, but the fresh salsa bar with five flavors has its fans.

Lamthong — 22 | 12 | 17 | $17

213 SW Broadway (Ankeny St.), 503-223-4214
12406 SW Broadway (Hall Blvd.), Beaverton, 503-646-3350 [S]
1503 SE Tualatin Valley Hwy. (bet. 13th & 18th Aves.), Hillsboro, 503-693-9222 [S]

■ One of Oregon's first Thais has expanded to three metropolitan outposts, building its reputation on "supreme food" and "service with a smile"; though these old-time Asians might get lost in the shuffle, loyalists remain steadfast.

Laslow's Broadway Bistro [S] — – | – | – | M

3135 NE Broadway (32nd Ave.), 503-281-8337

Expect well-executed NW fare fused with French bistro cooking at this Northeaster run by husband-and-wife team Eric Laslow and Connie De Silva; set in a converted house, the atmosphere is sophisticated and the service personable.

L'AUBERGE [S] — 24 | 23 | 23 | $36

2601 NW Vaughn St. (bet. 26th & 27th Aves.), 503-223-3302

◪ "Visual and olfactory ecstasy" is yours at this "elegant" but "spendy" Contemporary French in Northwest, where "dramatic presentations" of "seasonal regional menus" have been drawing fans since 1969; though aesthetes moan the "space feels dated", Francophiles say "fantastique!"

LE BISTRO MONTAGE ◐ [S] ≠ — 19 | 19 | 17 | $16

301 SE Morrison St. (3rd Ave.), 503-234-1324

■ A "trendy", "twentysomething" crowd warns: "be prepared to be jolted when they cry 'oyster shooter'" at this infectiously energetic, "always crowded" Cajun-Eclectic in Southeast with "great late-night hours", boardinghouse-style seating and "spicy" mac 'n' cheese ("at last").

Portland | F | D | S | C |

Le Bouchon S | – | – | – | M |
517 NW 14th Ave. (bet. Everett & Hoyt Sts.), 503-248-2193
Gallic newcomer located on the edge of the Pearl District that combines the "charm of French-speaking waiters" with "very good" bistro basics such as boeuf bourguignon, escargot and tarte Tatin; another plus is that the price is right.

Legin ●S | 22 | 11 | 17 | $16 |
8001 SE Division St. (82nd Ave.), 503-777-2828
◪ Look for the crustacean and fish tanks upon entering this Chinese in Southeast, the "dim sum capital of Portland" and home to such signature seafood dishes as a ginger-and-onion lobster and shrimp with honey-glazed walnuts; with a huge menu, 1,300 seats and a "festive" atmosphere that includes karaoke nightly, it's naturally "good for a large party."

LEMONGRASS THAI S⊄ | 25 | 18 | 16 | $20 |
1705 NE Couch St. (bet. E. Burnside St. & Sandy Blvd.), 503-231-5780
◪ "Your mouth will enjoy the spicy Thai ride of its life" say adoring reviewers of this top-rated Asian tucked into a residential Northeast neighborhood; while it's possible to "make a good meal" out of the "wonderful" soups and starters, hungry, impatient types warn of "small portions" and "long waits when busy."

Little Wing Cafe | 21 | 13 | 14 | $9 |
529 NW 13th Ave. (bet. Glisan & Hoyt Sts.), 503-228-3101
■ Local artwork on the walls adds to the charming alleyway ambiance of this Pearl District bakery/deli serving "delicious soups" and "great sandwiches" ("amazing PB&J") at "excellent prices"; N.B. dinner is now served.

LONDON GRILL S | 24 | 24 | 25 | $37 |
Benson Hotel, 309 Broadway (bet. Oak & Stark Sts.), 503-295-4110
■ Now celebrating its 50th anniversary, and with the same chef for the last 27 years, this Downtown Northwest-Continental keeps on pleasing with "wonderful service" ("attentive sommelier"), "classic decor" and that perfect "special occasion" ambiance, including a harpist nightly; while hipsters gibe "great if you're going to the prom or over 55", the overwhelming majority calls it a "Portland institution"; P.S. don't miss the "best champagne brunch."

LUCY'S TABLE | 24 | 22 | 23 | $31 |
706 NW 21st Ave. (Irving St.), 503-226-6126
◪ This dimly lit, "delightful" "new kid" (on a Northwest block that could be renamed 'Restaurant Row') features a "creative", "well-conceived menu" loaded with "interesting flavors", and service that's "almost too good"; only the cautious say "too soon to tell."

Portland

| | F | D | S | C |

Macheezmo Mouse S | 14 | 11 | 13 | $9 |

Portland Int'l Airport, 7000 NE Airport Way, 2nd fl., 503-280-2208
1200 NE Broadway (Weidler St.), 503-249-0002
811 NW 23rd Ave. (bet. Johnson & Kearney Sts.), 503-274-0500
Pioneer Pl., 700 SW Fifth Ave. (Taylor St.), 503-248-0917
723 SW Salmon St. (bet. Broadway & Park Ave.), 503-228-3491
6141 SW Macadam Ave. (California St.), 503-245-1617
10719 SW Beaverton-Hillsdale Hwy. (107th Ave.),
Beaverton, 503-646-6000
8870 SE Sunnyside Rd. (bet. 84th & 93rd Aves.),
Clackamas, 503-659-4400
1435 NE 185th Ave. (Walker St.), Hillsboro, 503-629-5049
Washington Sq. Mall, 9585 Washington Sq. Rd., Tigard,
503-639-2379

■ "When you need a quick plate of beans" or are looking for a "change from burgers", some surveyors say these "healthy" Mexican fast-food venues in industrial-swank cafeterias will do; bashers, noting a decline, say "what happened to a great idea?"

Manila's Best S | – | – | – | I |

4811 SE Powell Blvd. (bet. 48th & 49th Aves.), 503-788-6454
Pansip bijon (noodles with vegetables and meat) and *chicken adobo* are some of the "different" offerings at what is ostensibly Portland's only Filipino, "a gem" worth seeking out despite an "easy to overlook" Southeast location and "small", slightly divey surroundings.

Marco's Cafe & Espresso Bar S | 21 | 16 | 21 | $16 |

7910 SW 35th Ave. (Multnomah Blvd.), 503-245-0199

■ "Popular for breakfast" as a "neighborhood gathering place" where parents sip "great coffee" while taking a break from supervising their kids, this three-meals-a-day Multnomah Eclectic can be counted on to serve "reliably good" food, including "great sandwiches" and lots of healthy offerings, in "always-fast" time.

Marrakesh S | 22 | 24 | 22 | $22 |

1201 NW 21st Ave. (Northrup St.), 503-248-9442

■ Tapestries, low lights and cushions in the place of chairs set the scene at this Moroccan in Northwest, where the evening begins with a ceremonial hand washing; in addition to exotic atmosphere, there's one of the least expensive ($16.50) five-course meals in town, consisting of "authentic, excellent food" ideal for sharing with "a group"; overall, "a nice change of pace."

Marsee Baking S | – | – | – | I |

Portland Int'l Airport, 7000 NE Airport Way, 503-281-7000
519 SW Sixth Ave. (Alder St.), 503-973-5000
1221 SW Fourth Ave. (bet. Jefferson & Madison Sts.),
503-294-6000
845 SW Fourth Ave. (bet. Taylor & Yamhill Sts.), 503-226-9000
(Continues)

Portland | F | D | S | C |

Marsee Baking (Cont.)
1625 SE Bybee Blvd. (16th Ave.), 503-952-5000
935 NE Broadway (10th St.), 503-280-8800
1323 NW 23rd Ave. (Overton St.), 503-295-5900
104 Eighth St. (Kenala St.), Lake Oswego, 503-697-5600
16064 SW Tualatin-Sherwood Rd. (Hwy. 99), Sherwood, 503-625-6400

A rapid rate of expansion in a short amount of time has put a Marsee bakery into almost every Portland nabe; they're known for "great bread" and pastries (especially the oat scones), as well as pizza, soup and sandwiches.

Maya's Taqueria S | 17 | 11 | 12 | $10 |
1000 SW Morrison St. (10th Ave.), 503-226-1946
■ "Big portions" and "cheap prices" explain the lunchtime lines at this no-frills Downtown taqueria, with a "large selection" of Mexican favorites – tacos and burritos, as well as thirst-quenching aguas frescas and margaritas.

McCormick & Schmick's S | 22 | 20 | 21 | $26 |
235 SW First Ave. (Oak St.), 503-224-7522
■ For "consistently" "high-class cuisine of the sea" and "above-board service", reel in a "great private booth" or snare a seat at the "cozy, San Francisco"–like bar at this popular "fuddy-duddy, white guy hangout" Downtown.

McCormick's Fish House S | 22 | 18 | 21 | $26 |
9945 SW Beaverton-Hillsdale Hwy. (99th Ave.), Beaverton, 503-643-1322
■ Enthusiasts say "try the cedar-plank salmon" and "best popcorn shrimp" at this Beaverton seafood chain link, with 30 varieties of fish and the same overall "winning" formula as its more stylish, less casual sibling.

Misohapi | 19 | 15 | 16 | $13 |
1123 NW 23rd Ave. (Northrup St.), 503-796-2012
■ Concrete floors and black accents add elemental notes to the spare dining area of this Northwest Thai-Vietnamese that does a brisk bargain bento box business at noon and prepares a generally "flavorful variety of Asian foods."

Morton's of Chicago S | – | – | – | E |
213 SW Clay St. (bet. 2nd & 3rd Aves.), 503-248-2100
Traditional American steakhouse fare – shrimp cocktail, slabs of beef and NY cheesecake – is the name of the game at this Downtown outpost of the national chain; expect high-quality food and corresponding prices.

New York Richie's ⌻ | ∇ 18 | 7 | 14 | $9 |
8086 E. Mill Plain Blvd. (Garrison Sq.), Vancouver, WA, 360-696-4001
■ While Richie's no longer around, this Vancouver strip mall deli/pizzeria still gets a few votes from Big Apple transplants for "the best hero sandwiches outside of New York", especially the much-vaunted Philly cheese steak.

Portland

	F	D	S	C

NICHOLAS' RESTAURANT 🅂⊄   24 | 7 | 17 | $10
381 SE Grand Ave. (bet. Oak & Pine Sts.), 503-235-5123
■ Personifying the adage: "when the food is great people will come", is this Middle Eastern in Southeast, "a total dive" with "gritty" atmosphere that packs in a clientele ranging from the "pin-striped to the pierced"; sure, "if they'd spruce up the place" it would be more appealing, but considering it may serve the "best cheap meal in the city" ("superb tabbouleh"), it's hard to be ungrateful.

NICK'S ITALIAN CAFE 🅂   26 | 19 | 24 | $37
521 NE Third St. (bet. Evans & Ford Sts.), McMinnville, 503-434-4471
■ "An old favorite in the middle of the Wine Country", this Northern Italian has a "hearty" menu featuring "large servings" of "excellent minestrone", "fabulous pasta" and "not-to-miss" crème brûlée; factor in an "extensive NW wine list" at a "low markup", and it's no surprise many say it's "worth the trip."

Noho's Hawaiian Cafe   – | – | – | I
2525 SE Clinton St. (bet. 25th & 26th Aves.), 503-233-5301 🅂
515 SW Carolina (Virginia Ave.), 503-977-2771
A local Clinton neighborhood crowd frequents the original Hawaiian with a "homey atmosphere" for "great grilled chicken, ribs and fruit drinks", though a few take exception to its "no alcohol" policy; however, the new Johns Landing location offers wine and beer in a more polished setting.

¡OBA! RESTAURANTE 🅂   22 | 25 | 20 | $25
555 NW 12th Ave. (Hoyt St.), 503-228-6161
◪ The "dramatic, high-style" "colorful decor" of this Nuevo Latino in a converted Pearl District warehouse sets the mood for coolly "checking people out" while sipping "sophisticated drinks" or downing the "to-die-for" ahi tuna or "incredible chocolate [volcano] dessert"; while "not super expensive", it's not for those who use phrases such as "poor value."

Obi Japanese Sushi Bar   20 | 11 | 17 | $20
101 NW Second Ave. (Couch St.), 503-226-3826
◪ This small and lively Old Town Japanese has a cult-like following with Gen Xers who go for "quality sushi" in an unpretentious but amusing setting – a dining room with a sushi bar on one side and a TV on another.

Old Wives' Tales 🅂   18 | 12 | 16 | $14
1300 E. Burnside St. (SE 13th Ave.), 503-238-0470
◪ "Portland's best place to take" "rambunctious" tots thanks to a "wonderful playroom", this Eclectic Southeaster is also known for its "something-for-everyone" menu that includes a "solid, vegetarian focus" ("great salad bar"), chicken and seafood dishes and options for people with food allergies and special diets.

Portland | F | D | S | C |

Opus Too ◐ S | 20 | 18 | 19 | $25 |
33 NW Second Ave. (Couch St.), 503-222-6077
■ "How can you say 'no' to mesquite-grilled prime rib?" ask converts to this "dark", "lively" seafooder/steakhouse in Old Town, where chef groupies "sit at the counter and watch 'em cook" and music buffs snag a cozy booth in the lounge for nightly jazz.

Original Pancake House S ⊅ | 23 | 14 | 18 | $12 |
8601 SW 24th Ave. (Barbur Blvd.), 503-246-9007
☑ "Everyone's got to go once" to this "original" Southwest breakfast stop (there are now 80 franchises) prized for delicious Dutch Babies and "apple pancakes to die for"; P.S. the "long wait" on weekends means more time to ponder the "funky, old decor."

PALEY'S PLACE | 28 | 25 | 26 | $36 |
1204 NW 21st Ave. (Northrup St.), 503-243-2403
☑ "Outstanding", "refined" Northwest Regional cuisine using local and organic ingredients awaits diners at Vitaly and Kimberly Paley's "intimate" bistro in a turn-of-the-century NW home; expect some of the "most personal service in town" and more spacious and stylish digs, thanks to a nifty redo that added "cozy banquettes", a "charming" bar, "great vintage posters" and five points to the decor rating; N.B. the sweetbreads and crème brûlée are a must.

PAPA HAYDN EAST S | 24 | 18 | 20 | $21 |
5829 SE Milwaukie St. (SE Knight St.), 503-232-9440
PAPA HAYDN WEST
701 NW 23rd Ave. (bet. Irving & Johnson Sts.), 503-228-7317
☑ It's sweet purgatory at these Northwest Regional cafes where "sinful desserts" are worth the "almost eternal wait"; with time to take in the surroundings, surveyors note that a "table by the fireplace" and a "cool location" on 23rd Avenue make the Westside eatery more Uptown, while the East Side branch has a more casual, neighborly feel.

PAPARAZZI PASTAFICIO S | 25 | 19 | 23 | $19 |
2015 NE Broadway (21st Ave.), 503-281-7701
■ "Where we always wind up when we want comfort food", this NE Broadway neighborhood Italian features a "fabulous variety" of "reliably good" homemade pasta, some of the "best ravioli in Portland" and serious risotto; a "small" but "comfortable" setting bedecked with black-and-white photos of Italian film stars furthers its appeal.

Paragon Restaurant & Bar ◐ S | 19 | 20 | 19 | $25 |
1309 NW Hoyt St. (13th Ave.), 503-833-5060
☑ Attracting a "young, preppy" crowd, especially "after 9 PM" when it becomes a "brash" "meet market", this Pearl District American also wins votes for its "wonderful bar and booths"; while the "diverse" menu doesn't get much notice, a few think it "has improved" under a new chef.

Portland | F | D | S | C |

Pasta Veloce | 22 | 17 | 17 | $11 |
1022 SW Morrison St. (bet. 10th & 11th Aves.), 503-916-4388
■ "Yummy" made-to-order pastas served with bruschetta, "very quick" service and "cheap" prices have quickly made this Downtown Italian a "perfect spot for lunch", especially when the sun is out ("sidewalk seating"); those working late take solace in an identical menu and prices at dinner.

Pazzoria | 21 | 19 | 18 | $10 |
625 SW Washington St. (bet. 5th & 6th Aves.), 503-228-1695
■ Pizza by the slice, "good soup" and panini sandwiches are the attraction at this casual Italian bakery (adjoining Pazzo Ristorante), a nice place for "quick eats at lunch" or for a leisurely pastry and one of the "beautiful coffee drinks."

PAZZO RISTORANTE S | 23 | 23 | 22 | $27 |
Hotel Vintage Plaza, 627 SW Washington St. (Broadway), 503-228-1515
◪ "Grab a barstool" at the counter – "the best seat in the house" – for "great theater" and "free cooking lessons" provided by the open kitchen of this "warm" Downtown Italian, a "favorite" place "to entertain" or conduct a "business lunch"; while many praise the "great, garlicky food", a few observers note that it's only now "recovering" from the "ups and downs" of a chef change.

PEARL BAKERY ⌀ | 27 | 21 | 20 | $10 |
102 NW Ninth Ave. (Couch St.), 503-827-0910
■ "Could it be more beautiful or perfect?" ask acolytes of this "charming", light-filled Pearl District bakery, the source of "fig and anise panini that will make you melt", "mmm"-good olive bread and awesome almond croissants; while there are "few places to sit" and you'd better "get there early or you'll be sorry", these are minor inconveniences for what's easily "Portland's best bakery."

Pho Van Vietnamese Noodle Soups & Grill S | 22 | 13 | 18 | $11 |
1919 SE 82nd Ave. (bet. Division & Stark Sts.), 503-788-5244
■ A "class act" Vietnamese in a "lovely", "spacious" setting of slate floors and wooden booths, this Southeast sleeper is "a must" for pho soup, delicious chargrilled skewers of meat and exotic smoothies made from jackfruit or avocado; the "friendly" service and "inexpensive" tab only add to its charm; N.B. the decor rating does not reflect the new digs.

Piatti on Broadway ☻S | 20 | 20 | 20 | $23 |
Benson Hotel, 319 SW Broadway (Stark St.), 503-525-0945
■ Located on the street level of the Benson Hotel, this Downtown Italian combines "very good food" with "elegant" trattoria surroundings and "friendly service" to produce a popular place for "business lunches"; happy-hour food specials and "expert" drink makers entice insiders to advise "avoid the wait, eat in the bar."

Pizzicato [S] | 23 | 14 | 16 | $13 |
1630 SE Bybee Blvd. (Milwaukie Ave.), 503-736-0174
705 SW Alder St. (Broadway), 503-226-1007
505 NW 23rd Ave. (Glisan St.), 503-242-0023
2811 E. Burnside St. (NE 28th Ave.), 503-236-6045
Hillsdale Shopping Ctr., 6358 SW Capitol Hwy. (Beaverton-Hillsdale Hwy.), 503-452-7166
1749 SW Skyline Blvd. (Hwy. 26, Sylvan exit), 503-221-8784
530 NW 23rd Ave. (bet. Glisan & Hoyt Sts.), 503-274-8855
Oak Hills Shopping Ctr., 14740 NW Cornell Rd. (143rd Ave.), 503-531-8989
Robin Wood Shopping Ctr., 19098 Willamette Dr. (Cedar Oak Dr.), West Linn, 503-697-1877
■ "Outstanding", "gourmet" pies with "fabulous" crusts and "delicious", "unusual" toppings – "not [just] your standard tomato sauce and pepperoni" – are produced at these "trendy" "pizza boutiques", No. 1 in the *Survey* for their category; salad mavens say the Caesar is sublime.

Plainfields' Mayur [S] | 21 | 21 | 19 | $29 |
852 SW 21st Ave. (Taylor St.), 503-223-2995
◪ "Surround yourself with exotic flavors and art" at this "elegant", "upscale Indian" located in a West Side Victorian house; despite plugs for the "good wine list" and strong scores across the board, surveyors are split on whether it's worth the "splurge."

Portland Steak & Chophouse [S] | 21 | 21 | 21 | $28 |
Embassy Suites Hotel, 121 SW Third Ave. (bet. Ash & Pine Sts.), 503-223-6200
■ Leather booths, martinis and "big pieces of meat with no hassle" make this Downtown hotel steakhouse a "home run" for those in need of "an antidote to too much healthy food"; signature dishes include crab cakes and New York pepper steak; N.B. open for breakfast on weekends.

Portofino [S] | 20 | 17 | 18 | $22 |
8075 SE 13th Ave. (Tacoma Ave.), 503-234-8259
■ The lights are no longer momentarily dimmed to allow for 'a little kissy, kissy', but this small, cozy Sellwood Italian cafe still offers predictable, unpretentious fare, including daily specials and a six-course dinner ideal for hungry big spenders.

Produce Row Cafe ◐ [S] 🚭 | 15 | 13 | 14 | $10 |
204 SE Oak St. (2nd Ave.), 503-232-8355
◪ Post-college slackers mingle with a blue-collar crowd at this East Side pub known for its mammoth beer menu (28 on tap, 150 in the bottle) that leans heavily toward international and microbrew labels; other draws include a "great backyard deck", an eclectic rotation of bands and "sloppy", "inexpensive sandwiches."

Portland

| | F | D | S | C |

Red Coach ◐⌀
▽ | 16 | 11 | 20 | $9

615 SW Broadway (bet. Alder & Morrison Sts.), 503-227-4840

■ Downtowners in need of a "quick weekday lunch" appreciate the "all-American" menu – burgers, fries, BLTs, milk shakes – and "excellent service" at this throwback to the '50s hamburger joint tucked into the old Berg building.

Red Electric Cafe S
▽ | 17 | 16 | 16 | $16

6440 SW Capitol Hwy. (Bertha Blvd.), 503-293-1266

◪ Offering three meals a day, this cozy, roadside cafe in Hillsdale specializes in upgrading American classics with fresh, homemade ingredients, which translates into tasty sandwiches and homey soups for a bustling lunch crowd, and meat loaf, turkey breast and lots of salmon at dinner.

Red Hills Provincial Dining S
▽ | 23 | 21 | 23 | $28

276 Hwy. 99 W. (3rd St.), Dundee, 503-538-8224

■ This provincial Wine Country bistro combines Northwest ingredients with traditional European techniques to produce "well-crafted, imaginative food" complemented by a noteworthy international vino list; set in a converted house, the "nice feel" extends to warm summer evenings, when patrons take in the breeze from the open-casement windows or sit on the patio out back.

RED STAR TAVERN & ROAST HOUSE S
21 | 22 | 19 | $25

Fifth Avenue Suites Hotel, 503 SW Alder St. (5th Ave.), 503-222-0005

◪ The wood grill and rotisserie perfume the upscale cowboy decor at this Traditional American Downtowner, where "business diners" and out-of-towners saddle up for tasty "comfort food"; longtime observers quibble over "increased prices and decreased portions", but are more than content to "simply enjoy" the "great" bar.

RESTAURANT MURATA
26 | 18 | 21 | $27

200 SW Market St. (bet. 2nd & 3rd Aves.), 503-227-3653

■ Surveyors report "huge slices" of "beautifully presented", "excellent sushi" from master chef Ryoshiro Murata at this Downtown Japanese in a "traditional" setting (i.e. a "bit formal"); to get a sense of how "unusual and authentic" his offerings are, call 48 hours in advance for the *kaiseki ryori*, a multicourse dinner whose price you set ($45 minimum).

Riccardo's Ristorante
22 | 18 | 21 | $26

16035 SW Boones Ferry Rd. (Bryant Rd.), Lake Oswego, 503-636-4104

■ Unexpected pleasures – "excellent food, service" and a praiseworthy wine list – await those who seek out this Italian that's just outside of Lake Oswego; take a shot at the "fun" bocce courts, and consider the outside terrace, a charming place to dine alfresco when it's not *a freddo* (cold out).

Portland | F | D | S | C |

Ringside ⓢ | 22 | 18 | 22 | $31 |
2165 W. Burnside St. (22nd Ave.), 503-223-1513 ☽
14021 NE Glisan St. (140th Ave.), 503-255-0750
◪ Though national brand-name steakhouses continue to land in Portland, for many these local institutions are "still the only places for steak and onion rings"; fans also like the "dark, clubby" surroundings and "superb service", while those less loyal beef at "dark", "'70s decor" and "good ol' boy" ambiance.

Rustica ⓢ | 19 | 20 | 18 | $19 |
1700 NE Broadway (17th Ave.), 503-288-0990
◪ "Good, basic pasta" and an "extensive pizza menu" make this NE Broadway neighborhood Italian "our local" for both couples and families; a complimentary "soup or salad with the meal", cute street-scene mural and "relaxing" ambiance help quiet the minority who thinks "it should be better."

RUTH'S CHRIS STEAK HOUSE ⓢ | 23 | 21 | 23 | $42 |
309 SW Third Ave. (Oak St.), 503-221-4518
◪ It's "about time Portland got a quality steakhouse" huff carnivores pleased that this "top-dog" chain has opened a "clubby" Downtown location; expect the usual "great martinis", "excellent steaks" and "super sides" ("try the au gratin potatoes"), but be warned, if you're used to a Ringside tab you might find this outfit "overpriced."

Saburo's Sushi House ⓢ | – | – | – | M |
1667 SE Bybee Blvd. (bet. 16th & 17th Aves.),
503-236-4237
"Customers come back" to this "authentic and eclectic" Westmoreland Japanese for what some call the "cheapest, most generous" sushi in town; with such "great word of mouth", it's no wonder it's often "too packed to get in."

Saigon Kitchen ⓢ | 20 | 10 | 17 | $13 |
835 NE Broadway (Weller St.), 503-281-3669
3829 SE Division St. (39th Ave.), 503-236-2312
■ Having decided they're "not cooking tonight", surveyors' minds quickly turn to these two Thai-Vietnamese specialists for "basic but consistently good" dishes, such as an invigorating hot and sour soup and tasty spring rolls; the nothing-special decor also makes them "a take-out favorite."

Salvador Molly's | 18 | 16 | 14 | $15 |
1523 SW Sunset Blvd. (Capitol Hwy.), 503-293-1790
◪ "Hot, hot, hot" scream the chile heads who enjoy "throwing peanuts on the floor" of this Hillsdale Caribbean-Eclectic as much as they like the "spicy, flavorful" "huge portions" and "tropical drinks"; a few grumble that the kitchen can be "erratic", but the "fun, fun, fun" atmosphere triumphs in the end.

Portland

| | F | D | S | C |

Sammy's Restaurant & Bar S | 18 | 18 | 19 | $22 |
333 NW 23rd Ave. (bet. Everett & Flanders Sts.), 503-222-3123

■ There's "something for everyone" on the "always good" weekend brunch menu of this Northwest International Mix that's known for "gigantic portions" and "reasonable prices"; the atmospherically attuned add that inside is a "quiet" "place to wind down" at dinner and that "sidewalk seating" is "excellent for people-watching."

Santa Fe Taqueria S | 15 | 12 | 11 | $11 |
831 NW 23rd Ave. (Kearney St.), 503-220-0406

■ "Sit outside" and sip the "great" punch bowl–sized margaritas advise "twentysomethings" commenting on this Northwest Mexican, a "value" stop with ethnic standards and cafeteria-style, "assembly line" service.

Satay House S   ∇ | 17 | 21 | 21 | $25 |
8601 SW Terwilliger Blvd. (Taylors Ferry Rd.), 503-452-3636

◪ "Indonesian elegance" in the way of linens and potted palms, and an unfamiliar menu with authentic *rijsttafel*, lure fans to this Southwester; however, a few who've been to Jakarta find this place "pretentious" and "pricey."

SAUCEBOX CAFE & BAR | 22 | 21 | 19 | $22 |
214 SW Broadway (Burnside St.), 503-241-3393

■ "Very chic", "dark" and "narrow", this Downtown Pan-Asian appeals to both the "beautiful people" who "drip coolness" while sipping cocktails and "hip" foodies who appreciate the "assortment of fresh fish and noodle dishes", especially the "fantastic Javanese salmon"; those who don't fit in find it "too trendy."

Sayler's Old Country Kitchen S | 19 | 16 | 20 | $22 |
10519 SE Stark St. (105th Ave.), 503-252-4171
4655 SW Griffith Dr. (Beaverton-Hillsdale Hwy.), Beaverton, 503-644-1492

■ Loyal followers of these long-standing surf 'n' turfers with "coffee shop atmospheres" find them "trusted friends" for "good meals"; "darn, that's a big steak!" alludes to the 72-ounce top sirloin, a permanent fixture on the tried-and-true menu, which comes complimentary to any carnivore who can eat it in an hour.

Southpark Seafood Grill & Wine Bar S | 19 | 23 | 20 | $29 |
901 SW Salmon St. (Park Ave.), 503-326-1300

◪ Fans praise the "drop-dead sophisticated decor", "first-rate bar" and "inventive", "well-crafted" seafood dishes at this Downtown Mediterranean; but nostalgics, who miss the former B. Moloch/Heathman Bakery & Pub that resided in the same space, call this new endeavor "way too hip for itself."

Portland | F | D | S | C |

Stanich's ⌀ | 20 | 12 | 16 | $12 |
5627 SW Kelly Ave. (Flower St.), 503-246-5040
4915 NE Fremont St. (49th Ave.), 503-281-2322
◪ "If you like eating in bars" or are "hungover" and "need a fix" of the "best greasy burger in town", consider these "old-style" hamburger joints; bashers say "I beg to differ" about the patty's reputation and find the decor wanting.

Stickers S | – | – | – | I |
6808 SE Milwaukie Ave. (SE Bybee Blvd.), 503-239-8739
Potstickers, "awesome pad Thai" and reasonable prices lure dumpling devotees and wallet-watchers alike to this "super cute" Westmoreland Pan-Asian; happy hour from 5 PM–7 PM every evening is the time for 'Double Happiness' – six potstickers and a well drink for $4.50.

Swagat Indian Cuisine S | 23 | 14 | 16 | $16 |
2074 NW Lovejoy St. (21st Ave.), 503-227-4300
4325 SW 109th Ave. (bet. Beaverton-Hillside Hwy. & Canyon Rd.), Beaverton, 503-626-3000
■ "Now that's a buffet" declare impressed reviewers of the "bargain" midday meal at these top-rated Indians with such impressively spiced choices as *masala dosa* and *palak paneer*; since the Beaverton original has "plain", "very modest" decor, some aesthetes think the "NW location is much nicer."

Sweetwater's Jam House ●S | 17 | 18 | 16 | $17 |
3350 SE Morrison St. (34th Ave.), 503-233-0333
■ "Where else can you eat gator", "curried goat" and "killer coconut shrimp" than at this Belmont Caribbean with "some of the hottest hot sauces" in town?; while service can be "slow", this colorful "slacker paradise" is "always fun" and upbeat, perhaps because it also offers what management claims to be the largest rum selection in the state.

Tabor Hill Cafe S | 15 | 13 | 16 | $13 |
3766 SE Hawthorne Blvd. (38th Ave.), 503-230-1231
◪ A "small, tight" American cafe on Hawthorne that's seen its ratings and popularity wane since an ownership change; those just discovering it give their stamp of approval to the "$7 steak and $2 wine."

Taco del Mar S⌀ | 15 | 10 | 13 | $8 |
923 SW Oak St. (9th Ave.), 503-827-3041
3106 SE Hawthorne Blvd. (31st Ave.), 503-232-7763
437 SW Fourth Ave. (Washington St.), 503-226-2362
438 SE MLK Jr. Blvd. (Stark St.), 503-232-7695
736 SW Taylor St. (Park Ave.), 503-232-7695
◪ These Mission-style Mexicans scattered around town receive mixed reviews from the masses: supporters primarily point to "cheap" prices, with a few lonely votes for tasty burritos and "fish tacos with style"; the scornful roll their eyes, then calmly and diplomatically say "so-so."

Portland | F | D | S | C |

Takahashi, The S | 19 | 17 | 18 | $16 |
10324 SE Holgate Blvd. (104th Ave.), 503-760-8135
24 NW Broadway (Burnside St.), 503-224-3417
■ "Sushi sale nights" and "too, too fabulous" kitschy decor make this twosome Portland's most "wacky" Japanese; for those keeping score, self-service at the Downtown location means pulling raw fish–filled plates off a train that rides along the counter; at the Southeast location the caboose runs just below the ceiling, without conveying food.

TAO OF TEA, THE S | 22 | 26 | 18 | $10 |
3430 SE Belmont St. (bet. 34th & 35th Aves.), 503-736-0119
■ Tables fashioned from wooden tea boxes and water trickling from a rock fountain supply the charm at this "serene" Belmont teahouse, the "most creative [and top-rated] interior in Portland", and also voted No. 1 Bang for the Buck; look for world travelers sipping "great" tea and nibbling on a small selection of Asian- and Indian-themed treats, highlighted by delicious flat breads.

TAPEO | 25 | 23 | 22 | $24 |
2764 NW Thurman St. (28th Ave.), 503-226-0409
◪ The closest thing to an "authentic" tapas bar in the metro area, this Northwest Iberian gets heaps of praise from those who "love" to fashion a "fantastic" meal out of "a little bit of everything" and sip on one of the innumerable sherries from the "great Spanish wine list"; a "wonderful" chef-owner who "makes you feel at home" and a "lovely", "intimate" dining room further its appeal.

Taqueria Chavez S ⊘ | ▽ 23 | 8 | 14 | $8 |
5703 SE 82nd Ave. (Reedway St.), 503-777-2282
◪ "Don't be scared" of the "grungy-looking building" that houses this taqueria, set in a part of Southeast that's better known for car lots than homemade tamales; the reason: inside, the Chavez family whips up "great down-home Mexican", including what is "perhaps Portland's best taco."

Tara Thai House S | 20 | 14 | 16 | $16 |
1310 NW 23rd Ave. (Overton St.), 503-222-7840
◪ Differing from its competitors in offering Northern Thai and Laotian dishes on its menu, this "solid" Northwest venue achieves its fresh flavors by procuring high-quality fixings; those trying to kick the Sunday morning pancake-and-waffle habit should consider trying brunch here.

Tennessee Red's Barbecue Co. S | 22 | 12 | 13 | $12 |
2133 SE 11th Ave. (Grant St.), 503-231-1710
■ "Yee haw" hoot voters excited by the "great BBQ" and winning cornbread at this Southeast smokehouse where it's best to "go early" and "wear old clothes" due to "limited seating" and lots of "messy" fingerlickin'; those doing takeout like "driving those 20 miles with the intoxicating aroma" of Red's ribs beside them.

Portland	F	D	S	C

Thai Kitchen S | – | – | – | I |
2840 SW Cedar Hills Blvd. (Walker Rd.), 503-626-7150
This "not well-known" Beaverton Thai earns praise for the "authentic flavors" found in such dishes as the "wonderful chicken with sweet basil" and the "best pad Thai"; service is "friendly" and, overall, there's "excellent value" here.

Thai Orchid S | 23 | 15 | 19 | $17 |
2231 W. Burnside St. (bet. 22nd & 23rd Aves.), 503-226-4542
10075 SW Barbur Blvd. (Capitol Hwy.), 503-452-2544
10004 Washington St. (Evergreen St.), Vancouver, WA, 360-695-7786
18740 Willamette Dr. (Fairview Way), West Linn, 503-699-4195
■ An "affordable" menu of "reliable", "well-prepared" Thai dishes awaits visitors to this awesome foursome that gets the "authentic" stamp of approval from fans; voters are especially grateful to the "knowledgeable", "sweet" servers who help decode the "huge" menu.

Thai Touch S | ∇ 18 | 8 | 18 | $11 |
4806 SE Stark St. (48th Ave.), 503-230-2875
■ With a single-digit decor rating that's probably attributable to the fluorescent glare, it's no surprise this Southeast Thai is delicately described as a "neighborhood take-out" choice; that said, your phone order should definitely include the standout "drunken noodles and hot basil chicken."

Thai Villa S | ∇ 22 | 12 | 19 | $15 |
340 N. First St. (A Ave.), Lake Oswego, 503-635-6164
■ "The menu never changes" at this family-run Thai in Lake Oswego; while considered a "solid performer", delicate palates note that it has a reputation for off-the-chart spices.

Thanh Thao S | 20 | 8 | 16 | $13 |
4005 SE Hawthorne Blvd. (40th Ave.), 503-238-6232
■ Expect "a wait to get in" at this "very popular" Hawthorne Thai-Vietnamese with "wonderful soups" and "extensive vegetarian dishes"; an "inexpensive" tab and a large number of choices help neutralize the unimpressive decor.

Thien Hong ●S | ∇ 24 | 11 | 21 | $12 |
6749 NE Sandy Blvd. (bet. 67th & 68th Aves.), 503-281-1247
■ "Busy" and "bright", this Chinese in Northeast is a "favorite" for "above-average, consistent food", whether it's lunch on the run or a family dinner; those in the know always order the salt-and-pepper shrimp.

3 DOORS DOWN CAFÉ | 26 | 22 | 24 | $25 |
1429 SE 37th Ave. (Hawthorne Blvd.), 503-236-6886
■ Acolytes gush "three thumbs up" for the "perfectly cooked pasta", "intimate" setting ("very flattering" lighting) and "informed" "servers who are glad to see you" at this Hawthorne Italian; sure, there's "always a line to get in" and "no reservations", but the price is a "value" and to some it's "consistently the best meal in town."

Three Square Grill [S] 21 | 15 | 21 | $17

Hillsdale Shopping Ctr., 6320 SW Capitol Hwy. (bet. Bertha & Sunset Blvds.), 503-244-4467

■ This Hillsdale strip mall cafe serving Regional American fare with a Southern accent is a much more "comfortable", "friendly" place than its location portends; regulars praise the "delicious, homestyle cooking" and "diverse menu" that ranges from the signature black-eyed pea stew topped with a grilled fillet to homemade preserves and pickles.

TINA'S [S] 27 | 21 | 25 | $30

760 Hwy. 99 W. (opp. fire station), Dundee, 503-538-8880

■ The big news at this French-accented Northwestern in the Wine Country is the renovation that has doubled the size of the dining area and added a fireplace and "cute little bar"; while the atmosphere's "clearly better", the kitchen has always turned out "superb", "creative" dishes and the "outstanding staff" deftly knows its way around the vino list, which is heavily weighted toward local pinot noir treasures.

Trianon ▽ 19 | 19 | 20 | $27

9225 SW Allen Blvd. (Scholls Ferry Rd.), Beaverton, 503-245-2775

◪ Adventurous diners say "the pickle soup is wild" at this Beaverton Continental that takes great pride in its signature Wiener schnitzel and tableside steak Diane; a piano lounge helps keep atmosphere buffs attuned.

Trio Restaurant & Bar ▽ 23 | 23 | 22 | $29

4627 NE Fremont St. (46th Ave.), 503-249-3247

■ "Don't tell anyone" but the "lovely, romantic garden" out back makes this dinner-only Northwestern with French accents in Beaumont a "summertime" favorite of alfresco freaks; atmospherics aside, the food rating is nothing to sniff at ("great pork roast") and it's only minutes from the airport.

Tuscany Grill [S] 22 | 21 | 21 | $26

811 NW 21st Ave. (bet. Johnson & Kearney Sts.), 503-243-2757

◪ While regulars say the "calamari salad brings me back" and appreciate the "friendly, energetic" staff at this "warm" "taste of Tuscany" in Northwest, critics find it "too loud" with a menu that's "not too daring"; N.B. the 120-label, all-Italian wine list should keep you occupied for a while.

TYPHOON! [S] 25 | 19 | 20 | $21

2310 NW Everett St. (23rd Ave.), 503-243-7557

TYPHOON! ON BROADWAY [S]

Imperial Hotel, 400 SW Broadway (Stark St.), 503-224-8285

■ "The most creative", "gorgeous" Thai food in Portland, served on "cool plates", can be found at this top-rated "yuppie haven" that's opened a new branch in the Imperial Hotel; while portions can be "small" and prices "high", this "amazing experience" is "breaking new ground", and the Broadway location reputedly has the largest tea selection (150 choices) of any restaurant in the country.

Portland | F | D | S | C |

Umenoki ▽ | 19 | 14 | 15 | $22 |
2330 NW Thurman St. (bet. 23rd & 24th Aves.), 503-242-6404
■ "Above-average" Japanese food, including popular *yakiniku* (barbecued) beef and chicken *katsu* (cutlets), is the draw behind this "low-key" spot in Northwest; despite an unspectacular decor score, the rice paper screens in the dining room are a nice touch.

Uogashi ▽ | 20 | 19 | 16 | $18 |
107 NW Couch St. (1st Ave.), 503-242-1848
■ Bargain hunters give the nod to the "fresh and divine lunchtime sushi special that comes with miso soup" at this Old Town Japanese, whose chef prides himself on using organically grown products; understated in decor, and usually "not too busy", it especially appeals to precocious, hamachi-nibbling five-year-olds and their parents.

Veritable Quandry S | 19 | 20 | 17 | $20 |
1220 SW Front Ave. (Jefferson St.), 503-227-7342
◪ Though the post-college crowd comes to this Downtown American-Eclectic because it's "a great place to drink too much" (especially on the "nice patio") and has a series of rooms that "give the impression of intimacy", others find solace in the solid menu, highlighted by the signature osso buco.

Vista Spring Cafe S | 18 | 18 | 17 | $15 |
2440 SW Vista St. (Spring St.), 503-222-2811
■ This "cute", "corner" pizzeria in Portland Heights is the kind of "neighborhood" place everyone wishes they had close to home; look for some of the "best" pies in town, "generally very good salads" and a "friendly" feel enhanced by the warm, worn decor of window booths and wood floors.

Waterzoies | 22 | 20 | 21 | $26 |
2574 NW Thurman St. (bet. 25th & 26th Aves.), 503-225-0641
■ Emu (ask for it), venison and other exotica, as well as plenty of seafood dishes, contribute to the "lively" Northwest menu at this converted house in NW; the "good people" who work there, including a friendly chef, "always make you want to go back."

Widmer Gasthaus S | 19 | 20 | 19 | $16 |
955 N. Russell St. (I-5), 503-281-3333
■ "The place" to hash out a conversation over a "fine beer" brewed on the premises and some German food with a Northwest twist – "imagine a vegetarian Reuben" – this attractive upscale pub located under the Fremont bridge near the train tracks also works for teetotalers hankering for a housemade root beer float.

Portland

| | F | D | S | C |

Wild Abandon ❖   22 | 18 | 23 | $23
2411 SE Belmont St. (bet. 25th & 26th Aves.), 503-232-4458
◼ "Bacchus would be proud" of this hedonistic Eclectic on Belmont that pairs "wildly good", "innovative cuisine" and "cheap wine" with a "quirky" decor that makes you feel like you're "in a play"; other "charming, hidden pleasures" include its suitability for first dates.

WILDWOOD ❖   26 | 23 | 23 | $34
1221 NW 21st Ave. (Overton St.), 503-248-9663
◼ "Like a San Francisco restaurant" is the big city compliment respondents pay to this "trendy" "exponent of Northwest" cuisine, known for chef-owner Cory Shreiber's "bold" seasonal food, "snappy service" and "avant-garde" decor; the "cramped seating" and "noisy" room annoy a few of the "pretty people", but overall it's still a top-five "favorite."

Winterborne   24 | 19 | 24 | $29
3520 NE 42nd Ave. (Fremont St.), 503-249-8486
◼ There's no meat on the French-influenced Northwest menu but plenty of "fish, fish, fish", "the way it should be" ("simple" and "treated with joy"), at this "tiny" (10 tables) dining room in NE; reservations are required.

Yen Ha ☾❖   20 | 8 | 15 | $15
6820 NE Sandy Blvd. (68th Ave.), 503-287-3698
◼ Voters are of mixed minds about this Vietnamese in Northeast: "cheap" and "authentic" with an "excellent selection" vs. "unremarkable" ("maybe I went on an off-night"); while decor ratings are unimpressive, there's a full bar and karaoke in the adjoining lounge, which means weekends can be lively.

Yoko's ❖   – | – | – | I
2878 SE Gladstone St. (bet. 28th & 29th Aves.), 503-736-9228
"Imaginative sushi rolls with a NW accent", "terrific appetizers and small meals" are the draws at this "little" sushi house in Southeast Portland, which is also praised for its "excellent service."

ZEFIRO   25 | 24 | 23 | $35
500 NW 21st Ave. (Glisan St.), 503-226-3394
◼ For many surveyors, this Eclectic in Northwest "still sets the standard", with "beautiful", "cutting-edge" food – look for the signature rare-seared ahi tuna – inspired by the cuisines of the Mediterranean and Asia; the "gorgeous room" draws a "hip and beautiful" crowd of "slick yups", though the less glamorous contend it's "a bit pretentious" and "still too noisy"; N.B. the menu changes every three weeks.

Portland | F | D | S | C |

Zell's S | 23 | 18 | 19 | $14 |
1300 SE Morrison St. (13th Ave.), 503-239-0196
■ In addition to being "popular" with the neighbors, Westsiders also "hop over the river" to this American cafe in Southeast, where an "excellent breakfast" begins with complimentary "outstanding scones", then moves on to exemplary eggs Benedict and German pancakes; a few who haven't had their morning coffee carp about "long waits", but otherwise this is clearly "another good one."

Zen S | ▽ 16 | 16 | 13 | $22 |
910 SW Salmon St. (Park Ave.), 503-222-3056
■ Uninviting from the street, and not well known by surveyors even though it's been around for 27 years, this Downtown Japanese is suitable for a quiet conversation in one of the "very authentic rooms"; regulars favor it "for lunch" over dinner.

Indexes to Portland Restaurants

Special Features and Appeals

Portland Indexes

CUISINES

African
Horn of Africa

American (New)
Alameda Brewhse.
Atwater's
Besaw's Cafe
BridgePort Ale Hse.
Cassidy's
Caswell
Lucy's Table
Paragon Rest.
Red Electric Cafe
Veritable Quandry

American (Regional)
Alexander's
Bijou Cafe
Bima
Bistro 921
Black Rabbit
Caprial's Bistro
Compass Cafe
Esplanade
Fiddleheads
Hall St. Grill
Harborside Rest.
Higgins Rest.
Hudson's B&G
Jo Bar & Rotisserie
Joel Palmer Hse.
Laslow's Broadway
London Grill
Paley's Place
Papa Haydn
Paragon Rest.
Red Hills Provincial
Three Sq. Grill
Tina's
Trio Restaurant
Waterzoies
Wildwood
Winterborne

American (Traditional)
Anne Hughes Kit.
Beaches Rest.
Beaterville Cafe
Cadillac Cafe
Cindy's Helvetia
Couch St. Seafood
Cup & Saucer Cafe
Dan & Louis'
Foothill Broiler
Fuller's Coffee Shop
Good Dog/Bad Dog
Huber's Cafe
Jake's Famous
Jake's Grill
John St. Cafe
Morton's
Paragon Rest.
Red Electric Cafe
Red Star Tavern
Ruth's Chris
Sammy's
Sayler's Old Country
Stanich's
Tabor Hill Cafe
Zell's

Asian
Avalon
Celadon
Fusion
Saigon Kitchen
Saucebox Cafe
Stickers
Tao of Tea

Bakeries
Grand Central Bakery
Il Fornaio
Marsee Baking
Pazzoria
Pearl Bakery

Bar-B-Q
Buster's Barbecue
Campbell's Bar-B-Q
Doris' Cafe
Tennessee Red's

Cajun/Creole
Bernie's Southern
Delta Cafe
Jake's Crawfish
Le Bistro Montage

Caribbean
Salvador Molly's
Sweetwater's Jam Hse.

Chinese
Bamboos
Fong Chong

Portland Indexes

FuJin
Good Day
Hunan
Legin
Stickers
Thien Hong

Coffee Shops/Diners
Beaterville Cafe
Cadillac Cafe
Cindy's Helvetia
Fat City Cafe
Fuller's Coffee Shop
John St. Cafe
Original Pancake Hse.

Continental
London Grill
Trianon

Delis/Sandwich Shops
Dog House
Ken's Home Plate
Kornblatt's Deli
Little Wing Cafe
Marsee Baking
New York Richie's
Produce Row Cafe

Dim Sum
Fong Chong
Legin

Eclectic/International
Bijou Cafe
Brazen Bean
Bread & Ink Cafe
Caswell
Compass Cafe
Cup & Saucer Cafe
Dot's Cafe
Fiddleheads
Fusion
Hands on Café
Higgins Rest.
Indigine
Ken's Home Plate
Lucy's Table
Marco's Cafe
Old Wives' Tales
Papa Haydn
Salvador Molly's
Sammy's
Veritable Quandry
Wild Abandon
Zefiro

Ethiopian
Jarra's Ethiopian

Filipino
Manila's Best

French
Avalon
Winterborne

French Bistro
Brasserie Montmartre
Cafe des Amis
Laslow's Broadway
Le Bistro Montage
Le Bouchon
Paley's Place
Red Hills Provincial

French (New)
Couvron
Heathman
L'Auberge

German
Berlin Inn
Gustav's Bier Stube
Widmer Gasthaus

Greek
Alexis
Berbati

Hamburgers
Besaw's Cafe
Bread & Ink Cafe
Fat City Cafe
Foothill Broiler
John St. Cafe
Red Coach
Stanich's

Health Food
Marco's Cafe
Old Wives' Tales

Indian
Bombay Cricket Club
India House
Indigine
Plainfields' Mayur
Swagat Indian

Indonesian
Satay House

Portland Indexes

Italian
(N=Northern; S=Southern; N&S=Includes both)
Assaggio (N&S)
Bastas Trattoria (N&S)
Bugatti's Ristorante (N&S)
Caffe Mingo (N&S)
Cozze (N&S)
Fratelli (N&S)
Genoa (N)
Gino's (N&S)
Il Fornaio (N&S)
Il Piatto (N)
La Buca (N&S)
Nick's Italian Cafe (N)
Paparazzi Pastaficio (N)
Pasta Veloce (N&S)
Pazzo Ristorante (N&S)
Piatti on Broadway (N&S)
Portofino (S)
Riccardo's (N&S)
Rustica (N&S)
3 Doors Down (N&S)
Tuscany Grill (N&S)

Japanese
Big Dan's
Bush Garden
Celadon
Kento Bento
Koji Osakaya
Obi Japanese
Restaurant Murata
Saburo's Sushi Hse.
Takahashi
Umenoki
Uogashi
Yoko's
Zen

Jewish
Bread & Ink Cafe
Kornblatt's Deli

Mediterranean
Alexis
Berbati
Fernando's Hideaway
Fusion
La Catalana
Lucy's Table
Southpark Seafood
Tapeo
Zefiro

Mexican/Tex-Mex
Bima
Cafe Azul
Chevy's
Chez Grill
Chez Jose
El Burrito Loco
Esparza's Tex Mex
Hungry Dog Burrito
La Cruda
Macheezmo Mouse
Maya's Taqueria
Santa Fe Taqueria
Taco del Mar
Taqueria Chavez

Middle Eastern
Abou Karim
Al-Amir
Garbonzos
Nicholas' Rest.

Moroccan
Casablanca
Marrakesh

Nuevo Latino
¡Oba! Restaurante

Pacific Rim
Noho's Hawaiian

Pizza
Accuardi's Pizza
BridgePort Brewpub
Escape From NY
Hot Lips Pizza
Pazzoria
Pizzicato
Vista Spring Cafe

Seafood
Couch St. Seafood
Dan & Louis'
Jake's Crawfish
McCormick & Schmick's
McCormick's Fish Hse.
Opus Too
Restaurant Murata
Ringside
Sayler's Old Country
Southpark Seafood
Waterzooies
Winterborne
Zefiro

Portland Indexes

Southern/Soul
Bernie's Southern
Delta Cafe
Doris' Cafe
Le Bistro Montage
Tennessee Red's

Southwestern
Bima
Chez Grill

Spanish
Fernando's Hideaway
La Catalana
Tapeo

Steakhouses
Dan & Louis'
Jake's Grill
McCormick & Schmick's
Morton's
Opus Too
Portland Steak
Ringside
Ruth's Chris
Sayler's Old Country

Tearooms
Tao of Tea

Thai
Bangkok Kitchen
Khun Pic's
Lamthong
Lemongrass Thai
Misohapi
Saigon Kitchen
Tara Thai Hse.
Thai Kitchen
Thai Orchid
Thai Touch
Thai Villa
Thanh Thao
Typhoon!

Vegetarian
(Most Chinese, Indian and Thai restaurants)
Alameda Brewhse.
Cup & Saucer Cafe
Old Wives' Tales
Uogashi

Vietnamese
Misohapi
Pho Van
Saigon Kitchen
Thanh Thao
Thien Hong
Yen Ha

LOCATIONS

Beaumont
Alameda Brewhse.
Stanich's

Beaverton
Chevy's
Hall St. Grill
Lamthong
Macheezmo Mouse
McCormick's Fish Hse.
Sayler's Old Country
Swagat Indian
Thai Kitchen
Trianon

Chinatown/Old Town
Accuardi's Pizza
Alexis
Couch St. Seafood
Dan & Louis'
Fong Chong
Good Day
Obi Japanese
Opus Too
Uogashi

Clackamas
Chevy's
Gustav's Bier Stube
Macheezmo Mouse

Clinton Street
Dot's Cafe
La Cruda
Noho's Hawaiian

Downtown
Abou Karim
Al-Amir
Alexander's
Atwater's
Berbati
Bijou Cafe
Bistro 921
Brasserie Montmartre
Bush Garden
Cassidy's
Escape From NY
Esplanade
Fernando's Hideaway
Good Dog/Bad Dog
Harborside Rest.
Heathman
Higgins Rest.
Huber's Cafe
Hunan
India House
Jake's Crawfish
Jake's Grill
Koji Osakaya
Lamthong
London Grill
Macheezmo Mouse
Marsee Baking
Maya's Taqueria
McCormick & Schmick's
Morton's
Pasta Veloce
Pazzoria
Pazzo Ristorante
Piatti on Broadway
Pizzicato
Portland Steak
Red Coach
Red Star Tavern
Restaurant Murata
Ruth's Chris
Saucebox Cafe
Southpark Seafood
Taco del Mar
Typhoon! On Broadway
Veritable Quandry

Hawthorne
Bread & Ink Cafe
BridgePort Ale Hse.
Casablanca
Chez Grill
Compass Cafe
Cup & Saucer Cafe
FuJin
Garbonzos
Jarra's Ethiopian
Ken's Home Plate
Tabor Hill Cafe
Taco del Mar
Thanh Thao
3 Doors Down

Hillsdale
Garbonzos
Koji Osakaya
Lamthong
Pizzicato

Portland Indexes

Red Electric Cafe
Salvador Molly's
Three Sq. Grill

Lake Oswego
Marsee Baking
Riccardo's
Thai Villa

Lloyd Center/NE Broadway
Cadillac Cafe
Chez Jose East
Grand Central Bakery
Laslow's Broadway
Macheezmo Mouse
Marsee Baking
Rustica
Saigon Kitchen

Metro Area
Bugatti's Ristorante
Bush Garden
Buster's Barbecue
Chevy's
Hands on Café
Hot Lips Pizza
Macheezmo Mouse
Marsee Baking
Pizzicato
Thai Orchid

Multnomah Village
Fat City Cafe
Marco's Cafe

Northeast Portland
Bernie's Southern
Dog House
Doris' Cafe
El Burrito Loco
Gustav's Bier Stube
Horn of Africa
Koji Osakaya
Lemongrass Thai
Paparazzi Pastaficio
Pizzicato
Thien Hong
Trio Restaurant
Widmer Gasthaus
Winterborne
Yen Ha

North Portland
Beaterville Cafe
El Burrito Loco

Northwest Portland
Bamboos
Bastas Trattoria
Besaw's Cafe
Big Dan's
Brazen Bean
BridgePort Brewpub
Cafe des Amis
Caffe Mingo
Celadon
Foothill Broiler
Garbonzos
Hungry Dog Burrito
Il Fornaio
Jo Bar & Rotisserie
Kornblatt's Deli
La Buca
L'Auberge
Lucy's Table
Macheezmo Mouse
Marrakesh
Marsee Baking
Misohapi
Paley's Place
Papa Haydn West
Pizzicato
Ringside
Sammy's
Santa Fe Taqueria
Swagat Indian
Takahashi
Tapeo
Tara Thai Hse.
Thai Orchid
Tuscany Grill
Typhoon!
Umenoki
Waterzoies
Wildwood
Zefiro

Pearl District
Bima
Cafe Azul
Cindy's Helvetia
Fratelli
Fuller's Coffee Shop
Le Bouchon
Little Wing Cafe
¡Oba! Restaurante
Paragon Rest.
Pearl Bakery

Portland Indexes

Southeast Portland
Anne Hughes Kit.
Bangkok Kitchen
Berlin Inn
Bombay Cricket Club
Campbell's Bar-B-Q
Caswell
Cozze
Delta Cafe
El Burrito Loco
Esparza's Tex Mex
Fusion
Genoa
Il Piatto
Indigine
Khun Pic's
La Catalana
Le Bistro Montage
Legin
Manila's Best
Nicholas' Rest.
Old Wives' Tales
Pho Van
Produce Row Cafe
Ringside
Saigon Kitchen
Sayler's Old Country
Sweetwater's Jam Hse.
Taco del Mar
Takahashi
Tao of Tea
Taqueria Chavez
Tennessee Red's
Thai Touch
Wild Abandon
Yoko's
Zell's

Southwest Portland
Avalon
Chez Jose
Couvron
Hot Lips Pizza
Koji Osakaya
Macheezmo Mouse
Marsee Baking
Noho's Hawaiian
Original Pancake Hse.
Plainfields' Mayur
Satay House
Stanich's
Thai Orchid
Vista Spring Cafe
Zen

St. John's
John St. Cafe

Troutdale/Gresham
Black Rabbit
Buster's Barbecue

Vancouver, WA
Beaches Rest.
Buster's Barbecue
Chevy's
Hudson's B&G
Kento Bento
New York Richie's
Thai Orchid

Westmoreland/Sellwood
Assaggio
Caprial's Bistro
Fiddleheads
Gino's
Marsee Baking
Papa Haydn East
Pizzicato
Portofino
Saburo's Sushi Hse.
Stickers

Wine Country
Joel Palmer Hse.
Nick's Italian Cafe
Red Hills Provincial
Tina's

Portland Indexes

SPECIAL FEATURES AND APPEALS

Brunch
(Best of many)
Besaw's Cafe
Bijou Cafe
Bread & Ink Cafe
Compass Cafe
Fiddleheads
Fratelli
Hands on Café
Heathman
Indigine
London Grill
Old Wives' Tales
Original Pancake Hse.
Papa Haydn
Red Star Tavern
Sammy's
Three Sq. Grill
Wildwood
Zell's

Buffet Served
(Check prices, days and times)
Bistro 921
India House
London Grill
Swagat Indian
Tennessee Red's

Business Dining
Alexander's
Atwater's
Avalon
Bistro 921
Couch St. Seafood
Couvron
Esplanade
Hall St. Grill
Heathman
Higgins Rest.
Huber's Cafe
Hudson's B&G
Hunan
Il Fornaio
India House
Jake's Crawfish
Jake's Grill
Laslow's Broadway
L'Auberge
London Grill
McCormick & Schmick's
McCormick's Fish Hse.
Morton's
Nick's Italian Cafe
¡Oba! Restaurante
Paley's Place
Pazzo Ristorante
Piatti on Broadway
Plainfields' Mayur
Portland Steak
Red Star Tavern
Restaurant Murata
Ringside
Ruth's Chris
Southpark Seafood
Typhoon!
Veritable Quandry
Wildwood
Zefiro

Caters
(Best of many)
Abou Karim
Al-Amir
Berlin Inn
Bernie's Southern
Big Dan's
Bijou Cafe
Black Rabbit
Bush Garden
Buster's Barbecue
Cadillac Cafe
Campbell's Bar-B-Q
Caprial's Bistro
Casablanca
Cassidy's
Chez Grill
Compass Cafe
Cozze
Doris' Cafe
Esplanade
Fernando's Hideaway
Fiddleheads
Good Dog/Bad Dog
Gustav's Bier Stube
Hands on Café
Higgins Rest.
Hot Lips Pizza
Huber's Cafe
Hudson's B&G
India House

185

Portland Indexes

Indigine
Jo Bar & Rotisserie
Ken's Home Plate
Koji Osakaya
La Buca
Laslow's Broadway
Little Wing Cafe
Macheezmo Mouse
Manila's Best
Marco's Cafe
Marrakesh
Marsee Baking
Maya's Taqueria
New York Richie's
Nicholas' Rest.
Noho's Hawaiian
Opus Too
Papa Haydn
Paragon Rest.
Pazzo Ristorante
Pizzicato
Red Hills Provincial
Santa Fe Taqueria
Sayler's Old Country
Stanich's
Swagat Indian
Sweetwater's Jam Hse.
Taco del Mar
Tao of Tea
Tara Thai Hse.
Tennessee Red's
Thai Kitchen
Thai Orchid
Thanh Thao
Typhoon!
Uogashi
Vista Spring Cafe
Yoko's
Zen

Cigar Friendly

Alexis
Avalon
Berbati
Bistro 921
Brazen Bean
Bush Garden
Fernando's Hideaway
Gino's
Hall St. Grill
Harborside Rest.
Higgins Rest.
London Grill
McCormick & Schmick's
Morton's
¡Oba! Restaurante
Paragon Rest.
Ringside
Ruth's Chris
Sammy's
Sayler's Old Country

Dancing/Entertainment

(Check days, times and performers for entertainment; D=dancing; best of many)
Al-Amir (varies)
Alexander's (D/piano)
Alexis (belly dancer)
Atwater's (jazz)
Berbati (varies)
Brass. Montmartre (jazz/magic)
Bush Garden (karaoke)
Esplanade (jazz)
Heathman (jazz)
Hudson's B&G (piano)
Legin (D/karaoke)
London Grill (varies)
Marrakesh (belly dancer)
McCormick & Schmick's (piano)
Opus Too (jazz)
Paragon Rest. (blues/jazz)
Produce Row Cafe (varies)
Restaurant Murata (piano)
Saucebox Cafe (DJ)
Trianon (piano)
Veritable Quandry (jazz)
Yen Ha (karaoke)

Delivers*/Takeout

(Nearly all Asians, coffee shops, delis, diners and pasta/pizzerias deliver or do takeout; here are some interesting possibilities; D=delivery, T=takeout; *call to check range and charges, if any)
Abou Karim (D,T)
Alameda Brewhse. (T)
Al-Amir (T)
Alexis (T)
Anne Hughes Kit. (T)
Bastas Trattoria (T)
Beaches Rest. (T)
Berbati (T)
Berlin Inn (T)
Besaw's Cafe (D,T)

Portland Indexes

Bima (T)
Bistro 921 (T)
Black Rabbit (T)
Bombay Cricket Club (T)
Bread & Ink Cafe (T)
BridgePort Ale Hse. (T)
Bugatti's Ristorante (T)
Caffe Mingo (T)
Campbell's Bar-B-Q (D,T)
Casablanca (T)
Cassidy's (T)
Caswell (T)
Chevy's (T)
Chez Grill (T)
Chez Jose (T)
Compass Cafe (T)
Delta Cafe (T)
Doris' Cafe (T)
El Burrito Loco (T)
Esparza's Tex Mex (T)
Esplanade (T)
Fiddleheads (T)
Foothill Broiler (T)
Garbonzos (T)
Gino's (T)
Good Dog/Bad Dog (T)
Grand Central Bakery (T)
Gustav's Bier Stube (T)
Hall St. Grill (T)
Hands on Café (D,T)
Harborside Rest. (T)
Heathman (T)
Horn of Africa (T)
Huber's Cafe (D,T)
Hungry Dog Burrito (T)
Il Fornaio (T)
Il Piatto (T)
India House (T)
Jake's Grill (T)
Jarra's Ethiopian (T)
Jo Bar & Rotisserie (T)
La Buca (T)
Le Bistro Montage (T)
Macheezmo Mouse (D,T)
Manila's Best (T)
Marco's Cafe (T)
Marrakesh (T)
Maya's Taqueria (T)
McCormick & Schmick's (T)
McCormick's Fish Hse. (T)
¡Oba! Restaurante (T)
Old Wives' Tales (T)
Opus Too (T)
Paparazzi Pastaficio (T)
Paragon Rest. (T)
Pasta Veloce (T)
Piatti on Broadway (D,T)
Plainfields' Mayur (T)
Portland Steak (T)
Red Coach (T)
Red Electric Cafe (T)
Red Star Tavern (T)
Riccardo's (T)
Ringside (T)
Rustica (T)
Salvador Molly's (T)
Sammy's (T)
Santa Fe Taqueria (T)
Satay House (T)
Sayler's Old Country (D,T)
Stanich's (T)
Swagat Indian (T)
Sweetwater's Jam Hse. (T)
Tabor Hill Cafe (T)
Taco del Mar (T)
Taqueria Chavez (T)
Tennessee Red's (T)
3 Doors Down (T)
Three Sq. Grill (T)
Trianon (T)
Tuscany Grill (T)
Veritable Quandry (T)
Waterzoies (T)
Widmer Gasthaus (T)
Wild Abandon (T)
Zell's (T)

Dessert/Ice Cream
Brazen Bean
Bread & Ink Cafe
Paley's Place
Papa Haydn
Zefiro

Dining Alone
(Other than hotels, coffee shops, sushi bars and places with counter service)
Bread & Ink Cafe
Caswell
Good Dog/Bad Dog
Grand Central Bakery
Higgins Rest.
Hungry Dog Burrito
Jo Bar & Rotisserie
Misohapi
Pearl Bakery
Pizzicato

Portland Indexes

Red Coach
Red Electric Cafe
Ringside
Thai Touch
Zefiro

Fireplaces
Bamboos
Beaches Rest.
Buster's Barbecue
Esplanade
Heathman
Hudson's B&G
Hunan
Il Fornaio
Jake's Crawfish
Joel Palmer Hse.
L'Auberge
McCormick's Fish Hse.
¡Oba! Restaurante
Paragon Rest.
Piatti on Broadway
Plainfields' Mayur
Red Hills Provincial
Ringside
Sayler's Old Country
Tina's
Trianon

Game in Season
Bastas Trattoria
Bernie's Southern
Fiddleheads
Il Fornaio
Joel Palmer Hse.
La Catalana
Le Bouchon
Legin
London Grill
Paley's Place
Tuscany Grill
Waterzoies
Wildwood

Historic Interest
(Year opened; *building)
1857 Joel Palmer Hse.*
1879 Huber's Cafe
1892 Jake's Crawfish
1903 Besaw's Cafe
1912 London Grill*
1941 Fuller's Coffee Shop
1944 Ringside*
1946 Sayler's Old Country
1949 Stanich's

Hotel Dining
Benson Hotel
  London Grill
  Piatti on Broadway
Embassy Suites Hotel
  Portland Steak
Fifth Avenue Suites
  Red Star Tavern
Governor Hotel
  Jake's Grill
Heathman Hotel
  Heathman
Hotel Vintage Plaza
  Pazzo Ristorante
Imperial Hotel
  Typhoon! on Broadway
Portland Hilton
  Alexander's
  Bistro 921
River Place Hotel
  Esplanade

"In" Places
Assaggio
Brazen Bean
BridgePort Brewpub
Cafe Azul
Higgins Rest.
¡Oba! Restaurante
Paley's Place
Paragon Rest.
Pearl Bakery
Red Star Tavern
Ringside
Saucebox Cafe
Southpark Seafood
Tapeo
3 Doors Down
Veritable Quandry
Wildwood
Zefiro

Late Late – After 12:30
(All hours are AM)
Brasserie Montmartre (2)
Cassidy's (2)
Dot's Cafe (2)
Garbonzos (1)
La Cruda (2)
Le Bistro Montage (2)
Sweetwater's Jam Hse. (1)

Portland Indexes

Meet for a Drink
(Most top hotels and the following standouts)
Assaggio
Atwater's
Bima
Brasserie Montmartre
Brazen Bean
BridgePort Ale Hse.
BridgePort Brewpub
Cafe Azul
Cassidy's
Caswell
Chez Grill
Fiddleheads
Gino's
Hall St. Grill
Harborside Rest.
Higgins Rest.
Huber's Cafe
Jake's Crawfish
L'Auberge
Lucy's Table
McCormick & Schmick's
McCormick's Fish Hse.
¡Oba! Restaurante
Paley's Place
Paragon Rest.
Ringside
Saucebox Cafe
Southpark Seafood
Sweetwater's Jam Hse.
Trio Restaurant
Veritable Quandry
Wildwood
Zefiro

Noteworthy Newcomers (13)
Bernie's Southern
Cafe Azul
Fratelli
Fusion
John St. Cafe
Laslow's Broadway
Le Bouchon
Lucy's Table
Morton's
Portland Steak
Saburo's Sushi
Southpark Seafood
Tao of Tea

Noteworthy Closings (7)
Alligator Pear
Cafe Sol
Ron Paul Charcuterie
Ron Paul Express
Shakers
Square Peg
Toulouse

Offbeat
Bastas Trattoria
Beaterville Cafe
Brazen Bean
Caswell
Compass Cafe
Dog House
Dot's Cafe
Esparza's Tex Mex
Fiddleheads
Fuller's Coffee Shop
Fusion
Good Dog/Bad Dog
Indigine
Jarra's Ethiopian
La Catalana
Le Bistro Montage
Manila's Best
Marrakesh
Obi Japanese
Salvador Molly's
Saucebox Cafe
Sweetwater's Jam Hse.
Tao of Tea
Wild Abandon

Outdoor Dining
(G=garden; P=patio; S=sidewalk; T=terrace; best of many)
Assaggio (S)
Bastas Trattoria (P,S)
Beaches Rest. (P)
Berlin Inn (T)
Besaw's Cafe (P)
Big Dan's (P)
Bima (S)
Bombay Cricket Club (P)
Brazen Bean (P)
Bugatti's Ristorante (P)
Bush Garden (P)
Caffe Mingo (S)
Campbell's Bar-B-Q (P)
Caswell (S)
Celadon (P)

189

Portland Indexes

Chevy's (P)
Chez Jose (P,S)
Compass Cafe (G)
Dog House (T)
Doris' Cafe (P)
Escape From NY (S)
Esparza's Tex Mex (S)
Esplanade (P)
Fiddleheads (S)
Fuller's Coffee Shop (S)
Garbonzos (P)
Gino's (S)
Gustav's Bier Stube (P)
Hall St. Grill (P)
Hands on Café (P)
Harborside Rest. (P,W)
Hot Lips Pizza (P,S)
Huber's Cafe (S)
Il Fornaio (P)
Il Piatto (S)
Indigine (G)
Jake's Crawfish (P)
Joel Palmer Hse. (P)
Khun Pic's (P)
Koji Osakaya (P)
Kornblatt's Deli (S)
La Buca (P)
Laslow's Broadway (G)
L'Auberge (P)
Little Wing Cafe (P)
Lucy's Table (S)
Macheezmo Mouse (P)
Marrakesh (S)
Misohapi (S)
¡Oba! Restaurante (S)
Opus Too (S)
Paley's Place (P)
Papa Haydn
Paragon Rest. (P)
Pasta Veloce (S)
Pazzo Ristorante (P)
Pearl Bakery (S)
Piatti on Broadway (S)
Pizzicato (P,S)
Plainfields' Mayur (P)
Produce Row Cafe (P)
Red Electric Cafe (P)
Red Hills Provincial (P)
Riccardo's (T)
Ringside (P)
Rustica (S)
Saigon Kitchen (P)
Salvador Molly's (P)
Sammy's (S)
Santa Fe Taqueria (S)
Satay House (T)
Saucebox Cafe (S)
Sayler's Old Country (P)
Southpark Seafood (P,S)
Swagat Indian (P)
Sweetwater's Jam Hse. (P,S)
Tapeo (S)
Tara Thai Hse. (P)
Tennessee Red's (P)
Thai Villa (P)
Trio Restaurant (G)
Tuscany Grill (S)
Typhoon! (P,T)
Veritable Quandry (P)
Waterzoies (G,P,T)
Widmer Gasthaus (P)
Wildwood (P)
Zefiro (S)
Zell's (S)

Parking/Valet
(L=parking lot;
V=valet parking;
*=validated parking)
Abou Karim (V)*
Alameda Brewhse. (L)
Alexander's (L,V)*
Atwater's (L)*
Avalon (V)
Bamboos (L)
Bangkok Kitchen (L)
Bastas Trattoria (L)
Beaches Rest. (L)
Beaterville Cafe (L)
Besaw's Cafe (L)
Bistro 921 (L)
Black Rabbit (L)
Bugatti's Ristorante (L)
Bush Garden (L,V)*
Buster's Barbecue (L)*
Cadillac Cafe (L)
Cafe des Amis (L)
Caffe Mingo (L,V)*
Campbell's Bar-B-Q (L)
Celadon (L)
Chevy's (L)
Chez Jose (L)
Couch St. Seafood (L,V)*
Couvron (L)
Cozze (L)
Dan & Louis' (L)
Delta Cafe (L)
Dog House (L)

Portland Indexes

Doris' Cafe (L)
Esparza's Tex Mex (L)
Esplanade (V)*
Fiddleheads (L)
Foothill Broiler (L)
Fusion (L)
Garbonzos (L)
Gustav's Bier Stube (L)
Hall St. Grill (L)
Hands on Café (L)
Harborside Rest.*
Heathman (V)
Horn of Africa (L)
Hot Lips Pizza (L)
Hudson's B&G (L)
Hunan (V)
Hungry Dog Burrito (L)
Il Fornaio (L,V)
Jake's Crawfish (L)
Jake's Grill (V)
Jarra's Ethiopian (L)
Jo Bar & Rotisserie (L)*
Joel Palmer Hse. (L)
Kento Bento (L)
Khun Pic's (L)
Koji Osakaya (L)
La Buca (L)
L'Auberge (L)
Legin (L)
London Grill (V)*
Lucy's Table (V)
Manila's Best (L)
Marco's Cafe (L)
McCormick & Schmick's (L)
McCormick's Fish Hse. (L)
New York Richie's (L)
Old Wives' Tales (L)
Opus Too (V)
Original Pancake Hse. (L)
Paley's Place (L)
Paparazzi Pastaficio (L)
Paragon Rest. (V)
Pearl Bakery (L)
Pho Van (L)
Piatti on Broadway (V)*
Pizzicato (L)*
Plainfields' Mayur (L)
Portland Steak*
Portofino (L)
Produce Row Cafe (L)
Red Electric Cafe (L)
Red Hills Provincial (L)
Red Star Tavern*
Restaurant Murata*

Riccardo's (L)
Ringside (L,V)
Ruth's Chris (V)
Saigon Kitchen (L)
Salvador Molly's (L)
Sammy's (L)
Satay House (L)
Sayler's Old Country (L)
Southpark Seafood*
Stanich's (L)
Stickers (L)
Swagat Indian (L)
Taco del Mar (L)
Takahashi (L)
Taqueria Chavez (L)
Thai Orchid (L)
Thai Touch (L)
Thai Villa (L)
Thien Hong (L)
Three Sq. Grill (L)
Tina's (L)
Trianon (L)
Tuscany Grill (L,V)*
Umenoki (L)
Widmer Gasthaus (L)
Wild Abandon (L)
Wildwood (L)
Winterborne (L)
Yen Ha (L)
Zefiro (V)
Zen (L)

Parties & Private Rooms
(Any nightclub or restaurant charges less at off-times; * indicates private rooms available; best of many)

Abou Karim
Accuardi's Pizza
Alameda Brewhse.
Al-Amir
Alexander's*
Alexis
Atwater's*
Bamboos
Berlin Inn
Black Rabbit*
Brasserie Montmartre
BridgePort Brewpub
Bush Garden*
Cadillac Cafe*
Campbell's Bar-B-Q
Caprial's Bistro*
Casablanca*

Portland Indexes

Cassidy's*
Chevy's*
Chez Grill
Couch St. Seafood*
Couvron*
Dan & Louis'
Doris' Cafe
Dot's Cafe
Esparza's Tex Mex*
Esplanade*
Fernando's Hideaway*
Fiddleheads*
Fong Chong
Fusion
Genoa
Good Day
Hall St. Grill*
Hands on Café
Harborside Rest.
Heathman*
Hot Lips Pizza
Huber's Cafe
Hudson's B&G*
Hunan
Il Fornaio*
Il Piatto
Jake's Crawfish
Jake's Grill
Joel Palmer Hse.
Koji Osakaya
La Catalana
La Cruda
Lamthong
Laslow's Broadway*
Legin*
London Grill*
Lucy's Table
Marrakesh*
Maya's Taqueria
McCormick & Schmick's
McCormick's Fish Hse.
Misohapi*
Morton's*
Nick's Italian Cafe*
¡Oba! Restaurante*
Old Wives' Tales*
Opus Too*
Paley's Place
Papa Haydn
Paparazzi Pastaficio
Paragon Rest.*
Pazzo Ristorante*
Piatti on Broadway*
Pizzicato*
Plainfields' Mayur*
Red Electric Cafe
Red Hills Provincial*
Red Star Tavern
Restaurant Murata*
Riccardo's
Ringside*
Rustica
Ruth's Chris*
Saigon Kitchen
Salvador Molly's
Sammy's*
Santa Fe Taqueria
Saucebox Cafe*
Sayler's Old Country*
Stanich's*
Takahashi
Thai Orchid*
Thai Touch*
Thien Hong
Tina's*
Trianon*
Trio Restaurant*
Tuscany Grill
Typhoon!*
Umenoki
Uogashi*
Veritable Quandry
Waterzoies*
Widmer Gasthaus*
Winterborne
Yen Ha
Zen

People-Watching
Alexis
Assaggio
Atwater's
Berbati
Bijou Cafe
Bima
Brazen Bean
BridgePort Ale Hse.
Cafe Azul
Delta Cafe
Esparza's Tex Mex
Heathman
Higgins Rest.
Il Fornaio
Jake's Crawfish
Jo Bar & Rotisserie
Le Bistro Montage
Legin
McCormick & Schmick's

Portland Indexes

¡Oba! Restaurante
Paragon Rest.
Pazzo Ristorante
Red Star Tavern
Ringside
Santa Fe Taqueria
Saucebox Cafe
Southpark Seafood
Wildwood
Zefiro

Power Scenes
Atwater's
Avalon
Heathman
Jake's Crawfish
McCormick & Schmick's
McCormick's Fish Hse.
Morton's
Pazzo Ristorante
Portland Steak
Red Star Tavern
Ringside
Ruth's Chris
Southpark Seafood
Zefiro

Pubs/Bars/Microbreweries
Alameda Brewhse.
Black Rabbit
BridgePort Ale Hse.
BridgePort Brewpub
Gustav's Bier Stube
Produce Row Cafe
Stanich's
Widmer Gasthaus

Quiet Conversation
Atwater's
Bush Garden
Cafe des Amis
Casablanca
Genoa
L'Auberge
Marrakesh
Nick's Italian Cafe
Opus Too
Ringside
Tina's
Uogashi
Winterborne

Romantic Spots
Al-Amir
Assaggio

Atwater's
Brasserie Montmartre
Brazen Bean
Cafe des Amis
Caffe Mingo
Casablanca
Couvron
Esplanade
Genoa
Heathman
Higgins Rest.
Huber's Cafe
Il Piatto
Joel Palmer Hse.
La Catalana
L'Auberge
Lemongrass Thai
Lucy's Table
Marrakesh
Nick's Italian Cafe
Paley's Place
Plainfields' Mayur
Red Hills Provincial
Ringside
Tao of Tea
Tapeo
3 Doors Down
Tina's
Trio Restaurant
Tuscany Grill
Winterborne

Saturday – Best Bets
(B=brunch; L=lunch; best of many)
Abou Karim (L)
Accuardi's Pizza (L)
Alameda Brewhse. (L)
Bamboos (L)
Beaches Rest. (L)
Berlin Inn (L)
Besaw's Cafe (B,L)
Bijou Cafe (L)
Bima (L)
Bistro 921 (L)
Black Rabbit (L)
Brasserie Montmartre (B)
Bread & Ink Cafe (L)
BridgePort Ale Hse. (L)
BridgePort Brewpub (L)
Caprial's Bistro (L)
Chevy's (L)
Chez Grill (L)
Chez Jose (L)

Portland Indexes

Compass Cafe (B)
Delta Cafe (L)
Doris' Cafe (L)
El Burrito Loco (L)
Escape From NY (L)
Esparza's Tex Mex (L)
Fat City Cafe (L)
Fiddleheads (B,L)
Fong Chong (L)
Foothill Broiler (L)
FuJin (L)
Fuller's Coffee Shop (L)
Garbonzos (L)
Gino's (L)
Good Day (L)
Good Dog/Bad Dog (L)
Grand Central Bakery (L)
Gustav's Bier Stube (L)
Harborside Rest. (L)
Heathman (B,L)
Hot Lips Pizza (L)
Huber's Cafe (L)
Hudson's B&G (B,L)
Hunan (L)
Hungry Dog Burrito (L)
Il Fornaio (B,L)
Il Piatto (L)
India House (L)
Jake's Grill (L)
Jo Bar & Rotisserie (L)
Joel Palmer Hse. (L)
Ken's Home Plate (L)
Koji Osakaya (L)
Kornblatt's Deli (B,L)
La Buca (L)
Lamthong (L)
Legin (L)
Little Wing Cafe (L)
London Grill (B,L)
Macheezmo Mouse (L)
Manila's Best (L)
Marco's Cafe (L)
Maya's Taqueria (L)
McCormick's Fish Hse. (L)
Misohapi (L)
New York Richie's (L)
Old Wives' Tales (B,L)
Paparazzi Pastaficio (L)
Pasta Veloce (L)
Pazzoria (L)
Pazzo Ristorante (L)
Pearl Bakery (L)
Pho Van (L)
Pizzicato (L)
Produce Row Cafe (L)
Red Electric Cafe (B)
Red Star Tavern (B)
Salvador Molly's (L)
Sammy's (L)
Santa Fe Taqueria (L)
Southpark Seafood (B,L)
Stanich's (L)
Swagat Indian (L)
Tabor Hill Cafe (L)
Taco del Mar (L)
Tao of Tea (L)
Taqueria Chavez (L)
Tara Thai Hse. (L)
Tennessee Red's (L)
Thai Orchid (L)
Thai Touch (L)
Thien Hong (L)
Three Sq. Grill (B)
Trianon (B)
Typhoon! (L)
Uogashi (L)
Veritable Quandry (B)
Vista Spring Cafe (L)
Widmer Gasthaus (L)
Wildwood (L)
Zell's (B,L)

Sunday – Best Bets
(B=brunch; L=lunch; D=dinner; plus all hotels and most Asians)
Alameda Brewhse. (L,D)
Beaches Rest. (L,D)
Berlin Inn (L,D)
Besaw's Cafe (B,L)
Bijou Cafe (L)
Black Rabbit (B,D)
Brasserie Montmartre (B,D)
Bread & Ink Cafe (B,D)
BridgePort Ale Hse. (L,D)
BridgePort Brewpub (L,D)
Chevy's (L,D)
Compass Cafe (B)
Delta Cafe (L,D)
Doris' Cafe (L,D)
El Burrito Loco (L,D)
Escape From NY (L,D)
Fiddleheads (B,L,D)
Garbonzos (L,D)
Good Dog/Bad Dog (L,D)
Grand Central Bakery (L,D)
Gustav's Bier Stube (L,D)
Hands on Café (B)

Portland Indexes

Harborside Rest. (L,D)
Hot Lips Pizza (L,D)
Hudson's B&G (B,L,D)
Hungry Dog Burrito (L,D)
Il Fornaio (B,L,D)
Indigine (B)
Jo Bar & Rotisserie (B,L,D)
Kornblatt's Deli (B,L,D)
Macheezmo Mouse (L,D)
Manila's Best (L,D)
Marco's Cafe (L)
Maya's Taqueria (L,D)
Old Wives' Tales (B,L,D)
Paparazzi Pastaficio (L)
Pizzicato (L,D)
Produce Row Cafe (L,D)
Red Electric Cafe (B)
Sammy's (L,D)
Santa Fe Taqueria (L,D)
Southpark Seafood (B,L,D)
Swagat Indian (L,D)
Tabor Hill Cafe (L,D)
Taco del Mar (L,D)
Taqueria Chavez (L,D)
Tennessee Red's (L,D)
Three Sq. Grill (B)
Veritable Quandry (B,D)
Vista Spring Cafe (L,D)
Widmer Gasthaus (L,D)
Wildwood (B,D)
Zell's (B,L)

Senior Appeal

Alexander's
Bistro 921
Black Rabbit
Bread & Ink Cafe
Couch St. Seafood
Couvron
Esplanade
Gustav's Bier Stube
Hall St. Grill
Heathman
Jake's Crawfish
London Grill
McCormick & Schmick's
Original Pancake Hse.
Red Star Tavern
Ringside
Ruth's Chris
Sayler's Old Country
Widmer Gasthaus

Singles Scenes

Accuardi's Pizza
Atwater's
Berbati
Bima
Black Rabbit
Brasserie Montmartre
Brazen Bean
BridgePort Ale Hse.
Cassidy's
Chez Grill
Delta Cafe
Escape From NY
Esparza's Tex Mex
Garbonzos
Harborside Rest.
Hot Lips Pizza
Jake's Grill
Kornblatt's Deli
Le Bistro Montage
Macheezmo Mouse
¡Oba! Restaurante
Produce Row Cafe
Rustica
Santa Fe Taqueria
Saucebox Cafe
Taco del Mar
Veritable Quandry
Wildwood
Zefiro

Sleepers

(Good to excellent food, but little known)
Bamboos
Berlin Inn
Celadon
Gino's
Horn of Africa
Hudson's B&G
Joel Palmer Hse.
Ken's Home Plate
Lamthong
Little Wing Cafe
Obi Japanese
Pazzoria
Red Hills Provincial
Restaurant Murata
Taqueria Chavez
Thai Villa
Thien Hong
Trio Restaurant
Uogashi

Portland Indexes

Teflons
(Get lots of business, despite so-so food, i.e. they have other attractions that prevent criticism from sticking)
Alameda Brewhse.
BridgePort Ale Hse.
BridgePort Brewpub
Chevy's
Chez Grill
Foothill Broiler
Garbonzos
Macheezmo Mouse
Maya's Taqueria
Produce Row Cafe
Santa Fe Taqueria
Sweetwater's Jam Hse.
Taco del Mar

Teenagers & Other Youthful Spirits
Accuardi's Pizza
Bangkok Kitchen
Big Dan's
Brasserie Montmartre
Delta Cafe
Escape From NY
Esparza's Tex Mex
Garbonzos
Le Bistro Montage
Maya's Taqueria
Misohapi
Original Pancake Hse.
Ringside
Santa Fe Taqueria

Theme Restaurants
Casablanca
Cozze
Joel Palmer Hse.
Original Pancake Hse.
Ringside

Visitors on Expense Accounts
Atwater's
Couch St. Seafood
Couvron
Esplanade
Heathman
Higgins Rest.
Jake's Crawfish
L'Auberge
Morton's
Plainfields' Mayur
Portland Steak
Restaurant Murata
Ringside
Ruth's Chris
Wildwood
Zefiro

Wheelchair Access
(Most places now have wheelchair access; call in advance to check)

Wine/Beer Only
Accuardi's Pizza
Anne Hughes Kit.
Assaggio
Bamboos
Bangkok Kitchen
Berlin Inn
Bernie's Southern
Bijou Cafe
Bread & Ink Cafe
BridgePort Ale Hse.
BridgePort Brewpub
Bugatti's Ristorante
Bush Garden
Buster's Barbecue
Cadillac Cafe
Caffe Mingo
Casablanca
Compass Cafe
Couvron
Cozze
Dan & Louis'
Dot's Cafe
Fratelli
FuJin
Fusion
Garbonzos
Good Day
Good Dog/Bad Dog
Hot Lips Pizza
Hunan
Hungry Dog Burrito
Il Piatto
India House
Indigine
Ken's Home Plate
Khun Pic's
La Buca
La Catalana
Lamthong
Laslow's Broadway

Portland Indexes

Lemongrass Thai
Little Wing Cafe
Macheezmo Mouse
Marco's Cafe
Marrakesh
Misohapi
New York Richie's
Nick's Italian Cafe
Noho's Hawaiian
Old Wives' Tales
Papa Haydn
Paparazzi Pastaficio
Pasta Veloce
Pazzoria
Pho Van
Pizzicato
Produce Row Cafe
Red Electric Cafe
Red Hills Provincial
Restaurant Murata
Saburo's Sushi Hse.
Saigon Kitchen
Stanich's
Swagat Indian
Tabor Hill Cafe
Takahashi
Tapeo
Tara Thai Hse.
Tennessee Red's
Thai Orchid
Thai Villa
Thanh Thao
Thien Hong
3 Doors Down
Three Sq. Grill
Typhoon!
Umenoki
Vista Spring Cafe
Widmer Gasthaus
Winterborne
Yoko's

Winning Wine Lists

Assaggio
Atwater's
Caprial's Bistro
Couvron
Genoa
Gino's
Heathman
Higgins Rest.
Joel Palmer Hse.
Nick's Italian Cafe
Paley's Place

Red Hills Provincial
Ringside
Tapeo
Tina's
Tuscany Grill
Wildwood

Worth a Trip

Dayton
   Joel Palmer Hse.
Dundee
   Red Hills Provincial
   Tina's
McMinnville
   Nick's Italian Cafe
Troutdale
   Black Rabbit
West Linn
   Bugatti's

Young Children

(Besides the normal fast-food places; * indicates children's menu available)
Accuardi's Pizza
Alameda Brewhse.*
Beaches Rest.
Bijou Cafe
Bistro 921*
Black Rabbit*
Bread & Ink Cafe
BridgePort Ale Hse.
Campbell's Bar-B-Q*
Caswell
Chevy's*
Chez Grill*
Chez Jose*
Dog House
Doris' Cafe*
Fong Chong
Foothill Broiler
Gino's*
Grand Central Bakery
Gustav's Bier Stube*
Hudson's B&G*
Il Fornaio*
Il Piatto*
Jake's Crawfish*
Jo Bar & Rotisserie*
Kornblatt's Deli
Legin
Little Wing Cafe*
Manila's Best*
Marco's Cafe*

Portland Indexes

Marrakesh*
Marsee Baking
Maya's Taqueria*
McCormick's Fish Hse.*
Misohapi
Old Wives' Tales*
Original Pancake Hse.
Pasta Veloce*
Pho Van
Pizzicato*
Portland Steak*
Red Electric Cafe*
Red Star Tavern*
Rustica*
Ruth's Chris*
Saigon Kitchen
Salvador Molly's*
Sayler's Old Country*
Taco del Mar*
Takahashi
Tennessee Red's*
Three Sq. Grill*
Uogashi
Vista Spring Cafe
Widmer Gasthaus*

NOTES

NOTES

NOTES

NOTES

NOTES

Wine Vintage Chart 1985-1997

This chart is designed to help you select wine to go with your meal. It is based on the same 0 to 30 scale used throughout this *Survey*. The ratings (prepared by our friend **Howard Stravitz**, a law professor at the University of South Carolina) reflect both the quality of the vintage and the wine's readiness for present consumption. Thus, if a wine is not fully mature or is over the hill, its rating has been reduced. We do not include 1987 or 1991 vintages because, with the exception of cabernets and '91 Northern Rhônes, those vintages are not especially recommended.

	'85	'86	'88	'89	'90	'92	'93	'94	'95	'96	'97
WHITES											
French:											
Burgundy	24	25	20	29	24	24	–	23	28	27	26
Loire Valley	–	–	–	26	25	19	22	23	24	25	23
Champagne	28	25	24	26	28	–	24	–	25	26	–
Sauternes	22	28	29	25	26	–	–	18	22	24	23
California:											
Chardonnay	–	–	–	–	–	25	24	23	26	23	22
REDS											
French:											
Bordeaux	26	27	25	28	29	19	22	24	25	24	22
Burgundy	25	–	24	27	29	23	25	22	24	25	24
Rhône	26	20	26	28	27	16	23*	23	24	22	–
Beaujolais	–	–	–	–	–	–	20	21	24	22	23
California:											
Cab./Merlot	26	26	–	21	28	26	25	27	23	24	22
Zinfandel	–	–	–	–	–	21	21	23	20	21	23
Italian:											
Tuscany	27	16	24	–	26	–	21	20	25	19	–
Piedmont	26	–	25	27	27	–	19	–	24	25	–

*Rating is only for Southern Rhône wine.

Bargain sippers take note: Some wines are reliable year in, year out, and are reasonably priced as well. These wines are best bought in the most recent vintages. They include: Alsatian Pinot Blancs, Côtes du Rhône, Muscadet, Bardolino, Valpolicella and inexpensive Spanish Rioja and California Zinfandel.